THE Cofounder's HANDBOOK

THE Cofounder's

HANDBOOK

The Ultimate Guide to Starting, Building, and Exiting a Successful Business Partnership

TANIS JORGE
The Cofounder's Hub

This book is for informational purposes only. It is not intended to serve as a substitute for professional advice. The author and publisher specifically disclaim any and all liability arising directly or indirectly from the use of any information contained in this book. A professional should be consulted regarding your specific situation. Any product mentioned in this book does not imply endorsement of that product by the author or publisher.

The conversations in the book are based on the author's recollections, though they are not intended to represent word-for-word transcripts. Rather, the author has retold them in a way that communicates the meaning of what was said. In the author's humble opinion, the essence of the dialogue is accurate in all instances.

The Cofounder's Handbook copyright © 2022 by Tanis Jorge

Tanis Jorge
The Cofounder's Publishing House
5515 60st
Surrey, BC V3Z1G2

Send feedback to tanis@thecofoundershub.com

Publisher's Cataloging-In-Publication Data
    Names: Jorge, Tanis, author.
    Title: The cofounder's handbook : the ultimate guide to starting, building, and exiting a successful business partnership / Tanis Jorge.
    Description: Surrey, BC : The Cofounder's Publishing House, [2023]
    Identifiers: ISBN 9781777477913 (hardcover) | ISBN 9781777477929 (softcover) | ISBN 9781777477905 (ebook)
    Subjects: LCSH: Partnership--Handbooks, manuals, etc. | New business enterprises--Handbooks, manuals, etc. | Industrial relations--Handbooks, manuals, etc. | Success in business--Handbooks, manuals, etc. | LCGFT: Handbooks and manuals.
    Classification: LCC HD69.S8 J67 2022 (print) | LCC HD69.S8 (ebook) | DDC 658.042--dc23

Special discounts for bulk sales are available.
Please contact tanis@thecofoundershub.com.

To my dear friend Stephen Ufford, who has been my friend and cofounder throughout the last twenty-five years.

Thank you for being the example of tenacity, perseverance, belief, and loyalty; I'm sure it's not possible to build a company with a better business partner.

I am so grateful for the adventures we have been able to go on together, and I truly appreciate your friendship and the gift of who you are in my life.

I will forever cherish all the memories, all the laughter, and the stories that will be told for years to come.

Contents

Tell Me What You Think

Let other readers know what you thought of *The Cofounder's Handbook*. Please write an honest review for this book on your favorite online bookshop.

Foreword by David J. Blumberg

I am David J. Blumberg, founder and managing partner of Blumberg Capital. If you don't know us, we're an early-stage venture capital firm that partners with visionary entrepreneurs to build successful technology companies that empower individuals, businesses, and society through the innovative use of AI, big data, and other transformative technologies. We are passionate about nurturing B2B technology companies from the seed stage through their growth journey as active board members and hands-on advisers. And we've invested in 150+ companies with $760 million in assets under management.

But enough about me. I want to share with you how I met Tanis Jorge.

It was 2011, and I was a regular visitor at the well-known incubator Plug&Play in Silicon Valley to meet some of the latest in promising start-ups and hear their pitches to raise venture capital. On one particular day, I sat down with two serial entrepreneurs who were pitching an ambitious venture. By the end of their presentation, I was convinced this was a solid founding team with the vision to build an exciting company that could grow very large.

That was how I met Tanis Jorge and Stephen Ufford, cofounders of Trulioo.

There were many factors that led us to invest. Our team was impressed that the pair had already founded three previous companies together and had managed serial successful exits with each one. This factor alone, for us as early investors, demonstrated that they understood how to build successful businesses as a team. It also demonstrated they had the dedication, persistence, grit, and alignment to build the large company they had set out to create.

And I liked the two founders as people. They were smart, articulate, and persistent but humble rather than arrogant in their determination to reach a big exit as a shared goal. As partners, they were determined, bonded, and showed they could balance and support one another through both good times and bad. They had experience building companies and also had a track record of surviving the roller-coaster ride of entrepreneurship without driving one another crazy. They learned together how to do the necessary blocking and tackling to succeed in business.

Best of all, they were not newbies but a vetted pair of serial entrepreneurs. We could tell those two founders had been tested through fire. Over the years, they had enjoyed successes but also worked together to navigate the many challenges they encountered along the way.

The positive impression they left with me that day led Blumberg Capital to invest in them at Trulioo. And our firm and our limited partners are very glad we did. Apart from the excellent financial returns we have made together, working with them has confirmed to me they are highly ethical human beings. That includes with each other and with their staff. I've seen Tanis and Stephen face issues and make tough decisions where others might have failed. They're a true complementary team.

In nearly four decades as a venture capitalist, I've never seen perfect cooperation with zero arguments between founders; it's not possible. I've also seen every possible issue within business partnerships: fraud, divorce, fights, greed, death, and even suicide. Why? Because we are all human. Over the years at Blumberg Capital, we have met many founders with an excellent education but who were not aligned in their values, so their companies fell apart as a result. If issues arise between the founders, problems start to develop, especially if they don't tell anyone. So we've learned to watch for the warning signs. We see the founders start to get stressed and distracted trying to solve their relationship issues. Those of us looking from the outside then begin asking, "What's going on? There's something going wrong there. Why are they making those decisions? They are not acting normally, let alone optimally."

Entrepreneurs are often under a lot of pressure. Pressure to please customers, investors, strategic partners, and employees. And it's crucial for you as cofounders to build and maintain the right relationship to handle and adjust to that pressure together. For the founders of a start-up, selecting the right partner(s) is one of the most important decisions of your life. It ranks up there along with finding your spouse, choosing to have children, moving to a new community, and all the big consequential decisions in life. Selecting the right cofounder is crucial, and, done well, it leads to some peace of mind—because you have one another's back.

One needs to go in with open eyes and positive expectations or at least be an "optimistic skeptic" tuned in to reality. Optimistic about the potential for the future, for change, growth, and development, while being a skeptic knowing that what you set out to do may need to change and pivot. You have to agree to trust each other but also trust each other to tell the truth. Trusting does not mean unconditional love; it means I am going to trust you, and I'm going to tell you about my honest conclusions from analysis of the data. You want objective, honest sharing among yourselves and with investors. Start-ups are so potentially tension filled that additional founder-related stress is not helpful, and it breaks down trust. The distrust cycle is so painful and destructive because then you have to spend many hours questioning everything. "Are they telling the whole truth?"

Partnerships are important, but it's difficult and time consuming to fashion the right one. The choice of the right partner is a challenge. Once you find the right cofounder relationship, sustaining it is like caring for a plant: you have to nurture it and fertilize it so that it can grow. When a branch grows in a way that you don't want, you will need to trim it. You need to invest ongoing effort to keep the relationship alive, dynamic, vibrant and not let it wither away.

That's why I was so pleased and gratified when Tanis told me she was writing a cofounder's handbook. It's mind boggling that this book hasn't already been written! There is such a huge, latent need for this. Every VC is going to tell you the same thing; this is much needed, so overdue.

The Cofounder's Handbook is for cofounders, but it's very useful for investors too. Tanis's book will save us time, hassle, brain damage, and money. We will be better investors if we learn from the guidelines Tanis writes about in this book. We can utilize the questions she has framed in interviews and during diligence sessions. For founders, this handbook will give them the support and tools to help counsel them and keep the dynamic vibrant and adaptive along the way.

If you're looking to start a company and want to know how to pick the right partner, Tanis's guide contains crucial guidelines and insights from experience for you. You need not figure it all out on your own. Why reinvent the wheel? There is so much wisdom here that Tanis has distilled from hundreds of interviews and thousands of hours of research, all condensed into this guidebook.

Do yourself a favor. Do your investors a favor. Read this book. Then apply it in your business, in your life. Do that, and you can build prosperity into your company from the start and live a more successful, happier, healthier, relaxed, and fulfilling life.

—David J. Blumberg

www.blumbergcapital.com

WHO, WHAT, HOW, AND WHY: An Explanatory Note

Most people can pinpoint a single moment that put them on the path they took in life.

My moment came on the first day of junior high—set in motion by the first letter of my last name. Trivial at the time, but these two factors together were ultimately responsible for the next two-and-a-half decades of my life.

Lockers at my school were assigned in alphabetical order, so on the first day of grade eight, I, Tanis Wingenbach, was placed beside Stephen Ufford. This insignificant act began a neighboring locker relationship that lasted beyond high school. Morning greetings, gossip at lunch, quick shout-outs between classes, and after-school recaps forged our friendship.

Because we attended many classes together, we often teamed up for school assignments, and through these projects and the routine monotony and teenage drama of high school, we found a way to navigate the ups and downs of our friendship. We also discovered each other's strengths, celebrated our commonalities, learned to make up for each other's imperfections, and came out on the other side with a deep understanding of one another. We had no way of knowing that these times of collaboration were laying the groundwork and foundation for our future business partnership.

Despite our best intentions, Stephen and I drifted apart after high school. Without the luxury of eight hours a day of school to keep us together, we both started down our own individual paths. However, not long after graduation, Stephen reached out to me with a business idea. The proposal was interesting enough, but it was the prospect of working together and reconnecting that really excited me. Little did I know that this decision would define the next two decades of our lives.

From 2001 to 2011, Stephen and I founded three tech companies. That's one company every three years. Each of these businesses began from an idea and, after following the classic startup story, all ended in a successful acquisition. They were roller-coaster rides, each consisting of the quintessential highs and lows, all with epic stories of lessons learned that we readily pass on to inquiring entrepreneurs. Each company was lit by our passion and drive to see an idea come to fruition. Stephen and I conceived, strategized, and implemented the beginning steps of each start-up until the company was equipped to be acquired by an organization with the people and capital needed to take it from the early stages to the next level.

When our third company sold, Stephen and I shook hands, believing that was the end of the line for us. But entrepreneurship is much like that famous movie quote by Michael Corleone in *The Godfather*: "Just when you think you're out, it sucks you back in."

With a decade as experts in our industry, Stephen and I decided to move forward with our most ambitious endeavor yet: Trulioo. I had two kids under the age of two when we started the company, but we found ways to make it work. Stephen moved to Silicon Valley to focus on raising money and development while I managed our small team in Vancouver. We raised our Seed round and never looked back.

Trulioo was unlike any company we'd built before. It tested our resolve, tenacity, and perseverance, but it was also an incredibly exciting and growing experience. We started with the intention to see it past our three-year average but once we arrived there, I came to realize two things: My passions and strengths were best realized in a startup and early stages of a business, and building a company with family obligations was a challenge I felt I wasn't able to successfully navigate in parallel.

These two factors put me in the position of looking honestly at where my heart was for both me and our company. Stephen proved to have the aptitude, skills, and desire to take the company further, so after serious deliberation, we decided to hunt for someone who could take over my COO position. When that person was found and brought up to speed, I exited, staying involved exclusively on the Board for many years after. By the time I stepped away, Trulioo had achieved "Unicorn" status becoming a multi-billion-dollar global leader in its industry; a feat I am very proud to have played a part in.

The Next Phase

When the dust settled, I looked at all the knowledge, skills, and experience I collected over the years and thought about how I could apply them in the next chapter of my life. One area stood out more than any other. For many years, I had been mentoring and advising people who were embarking on their entrepreneurial journeys. And I realized that a particular theme kept popping up. I was consistently being asked for advice on how to find the right cofounder and how to keep the cofounder partnership strong. In addition, I was asked how one could extinguish the fires in a crashing-and-burning founding relationship. I discovered that many businesses were built on fragile, incendiary partnerships, capable of sending the entire businesses up in smoke.

Because I had built four businesses with the same person, I was in the unique position to share what worked and what didn't. I explored this topic and realized the available tools and resources for helping business partners navigate this unique yet vital relationship were sorely lacking. I came to the conclusion that someone needed to step up to fill in that gap. And at that moment, my journey to assist those building a cofounder partnership began.

I interviewed multiple cofounders in all stages of business, from all kinds of industries and walks of life. I learned that many were silently struggling with concerns and issues that couldn't be brought to light for fear of the backlash from spooked investors, unpredictable employees, disinterested friends and family, and fickle customers. I spoke to retired entrepreneurs, whose past experiences yielded a treasure trove of wisdom in the form of, "I wish I had . . . " "If only I had . . . " and, "Thank God I . . . " With each conversation, I discovered other tidbits, unique to each situation, that could be a warning or a guide to ensuring a partnership can withstand the heat of the entrepreneurial journey.

I also reached out to lawyers, accountants, mediators, and advisors to hear both the horror stories and triumphant reconciliations that occurred inside their office walls. I spoke to investors whose business models hinge on the ability of founders to work together, to find out what they saw within their portfolio companies, especially the warning signs. Every one of these professionals stated that there was a direct correlation between strong partnerships and strong businesses. When they saw cracks begin to form, they knew a storm was on its way.

So when all my research was completed, I came away with this: Your co-founder partnership is the most important factor in the success of your business. More important than a great product or tons of capital? Yes! More important than both of those and more. The reason is that when a cofounder partnership goes awry, no matter how amazing the business model or product/service is, the business can easily erode from the inside. Arguments, stealing, lying, absenteeism, failed expectations, poor communication, and lack of trust, are just a few factors that can create a rift within the founding partnership and destroy even the greatest of companies.

This realization motivated me to design and prescribe multiple tests, conversations, and due diligence exercises that can detect cracks within the partnership, allowing those involved time to fix them or walk away before too much time and money gets invested. I ran these tools past the cofounders I advised, saw success in their implementation, and wrote my findings in what is now The Cofounder's Handbook.

This book is the fruition of twenty years of building successful businesses with one cofounder. It's my credibility, experiences, musings, advice, counsel, and instruction all rolled up in one. It's also the hindsight, wisdom, and recommendations of countless other entrepreneurs who shared with me their reflections on the triumph and demise of their partnerships. The information within these pages makes The Cofounder's Handbook the most comprehensive guide for avoiding the pitfalls that befall many business partners before you start the business, then teaches you to nurture the relationship into maturity, whatever that looks like for your situation.

This book is the first step to building a successful company, through building a cofounder partnership that lasts.

A Few Questions You May Have
Who Is This For?

The information found in this book is for people looking for a cofounder. It's also for people who are navigating a partnership and understand the importance it plays in their business success. Finally, it's for people having trouble with their cofounder, or at least don't feel like you are "gelling" together and are googling for help because you're struggling. "My cofounder is lazy / getting divorced / on drugs" etc. In short, this book is for anyone who needs direction in managing the cofounder relationship. Not just how to avoid the pitfalls but how to set yourself up for lifelong success.

The suggestions, tips, and tricks put forward in The Cofounder's Handbook will be exhaustive, and I do not expect you to take each of them on right away. Many of the recommendations can be looked at as mini insurance policies, each one protecting your business or you individually. You can go through them and decide whether the recommendation is applicable or even worth it for your circumstance.

Keep in mind that many of the ideas presented come from someone's experience in the trenches and are a product of some event that could have been averted or undertaken to increase the likelihood of success. They are recommendations that would have made an entrepreneur's life easier, and so may do the same for you should you find yourself in a similar position. These recommendations include the documents that failed business partners wish they had in place at the time of solvency. They are the conversations that an entrepreneur wished they'd had before they ever signed on the dotted line. They're also the actions that one wished they had taken if they had known their partner would be tragically killed in a car accident. You never know what the future holds. Again, I am not proposing you take on everything that is recommended. But know that the more you tackle, the more prepared you will be for whatever comes your way.

Another thing to note is that some of the suggestions will be uncomfortable. But business is uncomfortable! You have to get used to doing duties you either don't want or are ill-equipped to do. You have to accept that there will be times when you will need to have conversations that border on intrusive, aggressive, and pessimistic. Completing these difficult tasks early is like digging your well before you're thirsty. It enables you to stand on more stable ground and build a level of trust that will assist you in making better decisions. You'll be able to bask in the comfort of knowing that you and your cofounder are headed in the same direction and that's a luxury you will quickly learn is envied by many.

Remember, it's not just you and your cofounder who will be affected by the stability of your partnership. Your employees, customers, investors, and your family are relying on you to have done your homework on the one person or group of people who will be the foundation for the legacy you are building. Choose and build wisely.

How Is This Book Structured?

From start to finish you will follow the evolution of a business partnership. Part I is about finding and building a new partnership. Part II is about managing, thriving, and troubleshooting the partnership. Part III covers how to exit the partnership.

Does this mean if you already have a cofounder or partner you should skip Part I? No. Because it's how to set things up from the very beginning, you might find steps you missed and need to address. If the foundation of your relationship is not as strong as it could be, this section will help you strengthen it. Part I also covers contracts you need to have between each other, as well as other factors you may not have considered that are essential for cofounders at every level of the journey.

To say it simply, whatever stage you are in your partnership, there will be valuable information that you can implement throughout the entire book. Those starting out could benefit from having an eye toward their partnership's potential conclusion, and a partnership already on the go can find ways to fill in gaps they missed when starting out.

What Does The Cofounder's Handbook Do for You?

After finishing this book and implementing the teachings you will find:

You're becoming intentional about working on the strength of your partnership, and not leaving your relationship to the fates.

You are in sync with your partner as you go through the challenges of your business with your partner.

You are able to view things from your partner's perspective.

You are able to see past minor issues and focus on the big picture that a strong partnership brings to the table.

You are a united front.

Your communication is on point.

You're able to have difficult conversations and remedy issues within your partnership.

You're thinking about things you otherwise would not have thought as you read through the stories of other cofounder partnerships.

You see your partnership as the asset it is to the company, but you also grasp its weight— understanding that it can become a liability if you let it.

You've built a relationship with someone or a group of people who you can rely on and reference for the course of your lifetime. A friendship unlike any other.

What if You Need Help Beyond the Book?

I've made tools available in The Cofounder's Hub. There, you can get access to the contracts you need, conversation starters and questions to ask prospective cofounders, and self-analysis tools. You'll be able to take the data about yourself and find people looking for a cofounder. It's all about cofounder connections!

You'll also gain access to experts like lawyers, mediators, coaches, and advisors, all with experience working with cofounders. You will be able to learn from their clients through more inside stories about partnerships—how they found each other and worked out their partnerships. I've also created an online community where you can engage and network with other entrepreneurs navigating their partnerships. I provide additional insights and evaluation tools on a regular basis to stay intentional and keep your partnership strong, and communication tips and tools for growing business. All of these tools will help you plan out your business while simultaneously strengthening the partnership.

Finally, you'll gain access to unique offerings you won't find anywhere else. Cofounder retreats and team building events which focus on the partnership and 2345 help you tackle any issues when they arise.

Check it out at www.thecofoundershub.com

On a side note: If you are just getting started in your business, this is the point where you are least likely to take precautions and truly analyze your partnership. Due to the flood of optimism in your new venture, you will likely be seeing the future and your cofounder through rose-colored glasses, a perspective that could blind you to the pitfalls your partnership could be heading towards. Because of that, The Cofounder's Handbook will walk you through the reality checks that are necessary to ensure that you are looking at all the angles objectively and seeing the pros and cons of your partnership going forward.

Also, note that I'm assuming your success. I'm assuming your business will flourish for years to come and that you are embarking on a business relationship that will carry on for decades. Laying a positive framework in the beginning will be the ultimate insurance policy that future conflict (which will happen, I assure you) will be mitigated, handled professionally and fairly, and resolved to the best advantage for you and your company.

This book is only the beginning. You've got a whole journey ahead of you, and I'll give you the tools to succeed.

—Tanis Jorge

PART I

How to Find
and Secure the
Right Partner

CHAPTER 1

The Cofounder Debate

my business partner is| 🎤

🔍   my business partner is - Search

🔍   my business partner is lazy

🔍   my business partner is stealing

🔍   my business partner is making decisions without me

🔍   my business partner is getting a divorce

🔍   my business partner is suing me

🔍   my business partner is toxic

🔍   my business partner is wanting out

(The stories you will read at the beginning of every chapter are true. I have changed the names of the people and companies for the sake of anonymity and privacy.)

B rian and Chris worked the line together at a local restaurant. Both were in their early twenties and had honed their skills in the kitchen. Over the course of a couple of years, they grew to be friends. Great friends. "When we were not working together we were often hanging out with one another," Brian told me. When Brian bought a modest duplex house as an investment, Chris moved into the second suite as a tenant. "Even our girlfriends were friends, so we were very interconnected."

One day, Brian got word that a restaurant had become available in the outskirts of their city. The lease was manageable and the family restaurant concept was right up his alley. "The first thing I did was tell Chris," Brian remembered. "I knew that I didn't want to start a business on my own, and I wanted to have someone who could come along beside me to carry the weight and to help me figure it all out." Brian had a few years of experience in restaurants with Chris. They worked well together and complemented each other's skill sets. So when he broached the idea to partner with Chris, it didn't take much convincing.

"It was a fifty-fifty venture," Brian explained. "We did that because we both needed money. Neither of us could afford to go without a paycheck, so it went without saying that we would split profits down the middle." The two knew they had to make money quickly in order to afford the basic cost of living, so it was imperative they were both ready and willing to roll up their sleeves and get to work.

The first obstacle they hit was the startup costs. Brian laughed as he recalled the earliest days. "We had no money. I mean zero. I borrowed $10,000 from my parents to get started and that went to cover inventory, a few minor repairs and touch-ups, and our first food and beverage order." That money was gone by the time they opened their doors. Chris, like Brian, didn't have any savings to contribute, and he didn't have anyone who could help him out either. Because of this, Brian was the one who took the financial risk. "I will say that Chris was on board to repay my parents for their loan as soon as possible. He understood the relationship risk I was taking borrowing from them and was just as eager to square things up."

The other thing that Brian and Chris discussed early on was that no family members would work in the business. "I guess upon reflection I had concerns that Chris was going to want his then-fiancee to work with us." Brian believed that having her work on the team could create an "Us vs. You" atmosphere and he felt that the two cofounders needed to rely upon each other, no one else. "I wish we had stuck to our guns on this one, as it would have saved us a lot of trouble down the road."

The restaurant was an instant success. That proved both a blessing and a curse. Unlike most businesses which ramp up slowly, Brian and Chris had little time to find their groove before they were overwhelmed. Brian recalls that it helped to be young and full of energy. "The thing about the restaurant business is that it's all-encompassing. We started our day at six am and went till ten pm, every night, seven days a week." But even with the strength of youth, the workload got heavy. "We were ok for a year or so but then the cracks started to show."

Eventually, Brian learned that Chris was carrying secret debts. "One day he came to me and said he needed to make more money because he had significant debts that needed to be paid down." Brian had no idea about these expenses, and their existence put the two friends in a pre-dicament. Because of their fifty-fifty relationship and the state of their business, the only way they could pay Chris more would be to increase hours of operation and add on more working hours for both of them. "I became resentful of Chris for the added pressure I had to take on because of his financial issues," Brian admitted. The added workload made their already exhausting day-to-day working relationship even more stressful.

Then, not long after shuffling the business around to accommodate more revenue, Chris informed Brian that he and his fiancé were having a baby. His new request was now to work less in order to spend more time with his new family addition, yet he still needed the extra money to cover his ongoing debts. This request meant Brian would have to work close to double Chris' working hours but still split the profits down the middle. When Brian informed him that wasn't possible, Chris walked out.

Chris came back a couple of days later with a list of demands, which included a redesign of the schedule which ensured they'd almost never work together. "Basically Chris would work the morning shift and I the night. We would see each other briefly as we transitioned shifts but oth-erwise we were passing ships. That hurt. I became very angry, and we basically stopped talking. What we should've done was hash things out. But in the back of my mind, I was afraid of a major fight and him walking out permanently." So Brian kept his mouth shut and they started following opposite schedules in order to avoid working together.

To make matters worse, Chris' fiancé started working part-time during the day shift. Supposedly this was to help out, but also so that the couple could spend more time together. Brian recollected: "As expected, the two of them began to make decisions about the business without my input. And the environment within the restaurant became fractured." Even the staff began to take sides, with "Team Chris" and "Team Brian" attitudes. It started to get unbearable. Finally, the two partners decided to sell the business.

Brian's shoulders slumped when he recalled the fighting. "I thought I knew Chris well, but when you get into business it changes the relationship. The way I see it is, I don't think you can ever know how the situation is going to change someone. You can't always know what that person will become in a stressful environment or when they're up against significant obstacles. It would be nice to have a crystal ball. In the end, you need to make a calculated guess and then be proactive in making it work."

I asked Brian what he would advise people to do differently. "If you are seeking a partner you need to be prepared, should things go sideways, to run the business yourself. I wanted someone to come alongside me, to work together, so I was never prepared for the idea that I could have to run it myself. A backup plan would have been valuable."

Brian figures that a few key conversations could have helped him to figure out their problems. "We should have discussed our financial situation prior to getting into the business." In particular, Brian felt that a few major decisions they had to make were based on Chris' financial predicament. "We may have been able to sketch out a better payment situation, or we could have determined that the scale of work to make the revenue we needed would be too much and we may not have even gotten started."

The all-too-common idea that you can sweep things under the rug seldom pans out in a cofounder partnership. Eventually, there's an explosion, and you cross the threshold of the possibility of repair.

Ironically, Brian felt that the fifty-fifty nature of their equity split, while an issue when it came to salaries, kept Chris tied to the business when things were difficult. "I believe that if our equity split recognized the additional work and early financial investment I contributed, it's possible that it wouldn't have given Chris enough incentive for him to stick it through. If we were seventy-thirty or even sixty-forty, I think I would have been left holding the bag." The larger, equal paychecks ensured that everything felt fairer and the equity upside made it worth the stress and pain.

I asked Brian about his relationship with Chris after they left the restaurant. "We only saw each other one more time after we sold the business. It was a week later to hand over a set of keys to the new owner. And we never saw each other again. It's funny, talking about it after all these years, how it brings up such emotion. It still makes me feel sad."

Still, Brian had hope. "I bet that if you had a good partnership, if you were more honest with each other and handled problems when they were small like we should have, you could build your dream together. That would be something pretty special."

Something Special, Done Right

I would argue that the cofounder partnership is one of the most significant human relationships one can enter into, next to that with a spouse and children. The reason for this is that cofounding a business together has a substantial effect on every facet of one's life experience: personal life, professional life, financial life, political life, and even spiritual life. It requires a depth of honesty, vulnerability, compromise, expression, and respect between people that is necessary for few other relationships.

The people in the partnership can become so intertwined that often one partner cannot make a significant move in any area of their own life without it affecting the others involved. That is why entering into a partnership requires the same amount of caution, due diligence, discussion, and care that one undertakes when entering into a marriage and family planning. The consequences of a mismatch could make or break the financial success, emotional well-being, and professional status of those involved, potentially limiting the growth and experiences they have throughout their lifetime.

So, after reading the horror story above, you might ask yourself, "Why would anyone want to partner up with someone on a business venture?" That's a valid question. The answer lies in people's desire to take their destiny and future into their own hands. Owning a business gives you the opportunity to embark on an adventure that, despite the risks, has the potential to provide a better life for yourself, your loved ones, and your community. Many feel compelled to take an idea and bring it to reality and try their hand at improving on a product or service they believe in. So once that decision is made, the question becomes how to proceed and where to begin.

Entrepreneurship tests even the smartest, hardest-working, and most tenacious person. Its 80 percent failure rate isn't lost on a new business owner, and it will take everything a person has to make their dreams a reality. So many turn to the idea of finding one or even two people to support them in the battle. To stand with them through thick and thin. People who have equal passion and belief in the same vision. As partners, they will be able to retreat from the battlefield, tend to their wounds, and prepare and strategize for the next attack. They will be able to collaborate on the execution of their plan and draw from the wisdom, knowledge, skills, and strengths of others besides themselves.

This is the picture that I believe compels entrepreneurs to find a partner. Just like a two-string rope is stronger than a single thread, when starting a company, having two or more sets of hands, minds, and bank accounts lets you get things done sooner, better, and cheaper.

All this being said, it's imperative for you to recognize that going into business with someone does have its own set of pitfalls. Bringing together different personalities, habits, perspectives, and goals can make a working relationship difficult. Pile on top of that the challenges of starting a business, and it could be a recipe for disaster.

The objective, then, is to find the person or persons who can provide the greatest assistance in reaching your goals and invite them to undertake the journey with you. You need to find someone who compliments your personality, has skills that fill your gaps, and has the same passion to fulfill the shared vision. It's among the most important tasks you will undertake in the early stages of your business as it will lay the foundation going forward. It cannot be taken lightly.

A Risky Proposition

Remember the image of the predictive results of a Google search for the term "My business partner is" at the beginning of the chapter? Did you try the search for yourself? The Internet makes cofounding sound like a horror show waiting to happen.

What interests me is that the entrepreneurs doing these searches probably started their partnership devoid of misgivings and doubts. They were likely flush with excitement, hope, and anticipation, relishing that they had found each other and that their business was going to flourish. They probably worked well in the early stages, unaware that their relationship would deteriorate with time.

Sadly, the searches above represent common turns for many business partnerships. The breakdown of a partnership is among the top three reasons for a company's demise. Few founders intentionally take the time and effort to avoid that danger. Often they put the majority of their focus on raising capital, gaining substantial market penetration, or sourcing a quality product. Unfortunately, they do not pay enough attention to the growth and maintenance of their business's foundation: the founding partnership.

I have discovered that cofounders who fail to acknowledge their partnership's impact also don't prioritize communication, disclose expectations, give proper respect, or commit to a shared vision. As such, the foundation crumbles.

Keep this picture of the cofounder partnership in mind as you consider whether you are ready to jump into business with someone. It can go either way. I've compiled a long list of people who regret having brought on a partner and an equally long list of those grateful they did.

Having spoken to many cofounders and solopreneurs, I've realized there is no simple way to determine if you should have a cofounder. However, for the rest of this chapter, I will provide insights into ways that can help you make that decision. Should you decide you do, the following section will help you determine what to look for.

It's Not Enough to Be Friends

Statistically, 64 percent of businesses fail because of issues between the founding partners. Additionally, of those that fail, 65 percent end with one partner buying out the other. A shared business can be amazing, but the cofounder relationship must be built on more than friendship. Transparency, a willingness to compromise, and self-sacrifice are all traits that need to be demonstrated out of the gate to ensure that a relationship built on trust is created.

All parties must keep in mind that the cofounder relationship is a business asset, and you need to treat it that way. You aren't just friends. You're two or more people with a massive vested interest in the success of your shared business. You cannot think of your relationship equation as $1 + 1 = 2$. Instead, you need to look at it more like $1 + 1 = 10$. Your combined effort multiplies each other's strengths. You can do together what you could never have accomplished alone. When you look at it this way, you realize that you would be foolish to leave your partnership's success to the fates and not milk it for its full potential.

That's why seeing founding teams tear each other apart breaks my heart. Cofounders usually start as friends, and they presume their friendship will be enough to see them through. They fail to see the value of building the strength of their partnership, so when something happens in the relationship, they aren't prepared for the impact it makes. Feelings of betrayal, disappointment, resentment, and mistrust are powerful, and they have the capacity to do great damage and can be very difficult to recover from.

So what can these cofounders do? The first thing I noticed when I began researching this topic was that there were very few resources available. Many books that have been written are by business coaches, academics, and mediators, not real-life cofounders who've been there in the trenches. Their advice was valuable, but it missed that key component of having lived in the shoes of someone going through the experience. They lacked that intimate understanding of the emotional complexity that comes with striving to be the best version of a cofounder. It made their advice feel a little "easy for you to say."

This lack of resources, plus the struggles and successes of my own cofounder relationship, paired with the silent suffering many cofounders have shared with me, made me realize I needed to step up. I felt compelled to provide one comprehensive resource that would be applicable to those seeking and starting a cofounder relationship, in the middle of navigating one, and those struggling with challenges. To help partners start off on the right foot and then learn the tools to achieve decades of peace and harmony.

So this is what I'm going to do. I'm going to teach you everything you need to know about cofounder relationships based on what I've learned and experienced. By the end of this book, you'll be ready to duplicate what Stephen and I accomplished together.

But first, we need an answer to an important question.

Do You Even Need a Cofounder?

Maybe, maybe not. We'll explore this question together. For now, consider some data points.

Only 4% Of Y Combinators top 100 startups don't have a cofounder.

According to Crunchbase, a data source on tech companies, 45.9% of companies successful in raising over $10 million did so with a solo founder.

Octopus Ventures, a British VC, discovered that almost two in five entrepreneurs (39%) said that the relationship with their co-founder was more stressful than with their life partner. YIKES!

Yet, the same VC determined that among their portfolio, almost 9 in 10 (87%) entrepreneurs with co-founded businesses said that having one has made their business more successful.

There's so much to unpack here but all in all, when it's done right, a business partnership puts you further ahead than you would be going solo. It all comes down to the setup and maintenance.

The website Foundr shares a great amount of data on cofounder success. The Startup Genome Report states that solo founders take up to 3.6 times as long to scale their business compared to teams of two or more founders. And teams with multiple founders are more likely to attract investors. According to Foundr, that's because a team makes it look like more than just one person believes in your idea. And they suggest the perfect number of cofounders is 2.09.

All these statistics show that when it comes to the cofounder partnership there's benefits and risks to consider. One way to determine what they are is to start by weighing the pros and cons.

The Pros of a Cofounder Partnership

Don't Wanna Be All By Myself

When I ask solopreneurs about the downside of not having a business partner, bar none, the number one answer is "Loneliness."

As any entrepreneur will tell you, business creation is a solitary endeavor, made more so without a partner. The long hours and need for laser focus can turn a solopreneur into a borderline recluse. Even one's closest family members and friends can feel distant. This absence of someone who shares and fully understands what you are going through can make these challenges increasingly daunting. Wins may feel empty if you have no one to share them with.

This loneliness is why many choose to go the path of a partnership and forgo the potential benefits of sole ownership. You may be extremely confident in your abilities to launch and scale a business, but the prospect of talking through an idea or challenge with someone who intimately knows and understands all the angles, as well as supports you through the ups and downs, is undeniably an asset to anyone.

Factors To Consider

That said, maybe you work better alone, and handling tasks in solitude is preferred over collaboration. Understanding your natural tendencies in these environments will help you assess whether you gravitate towards others or would rather work alone. There are multiple ways to determine this.

1. Reflect on the times you worked within a team or partnership setting. Taking notice of whether there was an increase in productivity and a boost to your emotional state while working with others can be helpful in determining whether you actually need a cofounder.

2. Recall your past experiences in school. Did you enjoy working on team projects? Or did you find group interactions daunting and limiting?

3. How about the times you had to work by yourself? Did you enjoy the solitude or did you struggle with the silence and the sole weight of responsibility?

4. Consider your hobbies. Do they involve group fellowship or do you prefer to retreat solo?

5. Look at your relationships. Are you outgoing or more reserved? Do you love to share the good and the bad with others or do you prefer to keep your life private?

6. How do you spend your spare time? Do you like to do life on your terms or are you open to the suggestions and plans of others?

Your answers to these questions will help you discern if a partnership suits your personality type and working style. The main thing to note is that if it goes against your natural tendency to work with someone, putting processes and boundaries in place can very easily create a cohesive working environment.

The Value of Ownership

Nobody cares more about a business than the owner or founder. This care manifests in time spent on the business, cash invested, and willingness to persevere in times of trial. As a business owner, you are often the first one to arrive and the last one to leave. You're the one bearing the responsibility for making money but often the last to get paid.

If you see value in having a strong person to lean on, then the best option may be to find someone as devoted to the business as you. Two or more people dedicated to a mission will trump a loner every time.

Factors to Consider

1. Will your business require a long ramp-up to revenue? Many people expect the money to roll in quickly, but revenue, let alone profitability, typically takes longer to attain than expected.

    Some business models take longer to turn a profit than others. My partner and I knew our last company was not going to make money for a couple of years due to its disruptive and innovative nature. Blazing the company's uncharted path alone, with all its uncertainty and ups and downs, would have greatly complicated the journey to launch.

2. If you choose to be a solopreneur, even if a key employee shares your vision, do you have the capital to incentivize them through the long journey ahead? If you are flush with cash, financial motivation may suffice. However, finding a partner may alleviate that financial burden and give you enough time to launch your company. Equity and pride in ownership have the ability to carry people through hard times.

3. Employees can take undue liberties in leadership's absence. When launching a business, every minute of effectiveness lost can exponentially affect your time to market. If your business will require you to take long periods of travel or absence from

the office, you may want to consider a partner with a vested interest to cover the home front.

Divide and Conquer

Starting a business involves a nonnegotiable laundry list of tasks. Delegating portions of that list to others can shorten the road to success. The less time it takes to get into the black, the better off you'll be monetarily. In addition, the ability to tap others' complementary skill sets makes accomplishing business tasks easier, quicker, and more enjoyable.

Factors to Consider

If you need to hire for the myriad of jobs necessary to start or scale your company, you will see a large portion of your capital taken up in salaries. While some tasks may require someone specific who has skills you lack, a partner will be more willing to try their hand at something new despite the awkwardness and inexperience.

Take the time to create your business plan for reaching the next stage of your business. Be honest about whether you have the skills and desire to go it alone. If your business plan is simple, you may not need a partner. However, if your plan has many moving parts and multiple growth stages, a cofounder may be the smart move.

Insurance Policy

Many people become entrepreneurs because they know business ownership can support their loved ones long-term. Assume that over the course of your company's lifetime, you will get sick, retire, or die. A business is more likely to outlive you if two or more people start it. A strong partnership can help you plan an exit that benefits all parties involved.

Additionally, investors love companies with multiple collaborating founders. Partnerships enable more stability since both founders rarely face personal crises at the same time. One can always be the rock. Some investors will refuse to invest in a single-owner company, thus limiting the pool of capital.

Early-stage investment is as much about the team as the idea. Having a variety of skills and capabilities in the founding team can give your venture a higher chance of raising funds and achieving success.

Factors to Consider

1. No one plans for a major setback or starts a business anticipating its early demise. But if you want businesses that will last decades, consider having a partner. Life throws many curveballs, and taking them on with someone at your side can bring peace of mind.

2. Note that more and more people are starting businesses after retirement. The energy and grit necessary to build a company can daunt even the most vigorous entrepreneur. If you lack the stamina to go it alone, don't be afraid to find a partner. It could be the best retirement decision you ever make.

Reality Check

It takes a degree of eccentricity to come up with a new idea and a lot of faith to bring it to life. These unique traits are some of the most powerful tools in an entrepreneur's arsenal, but they can also be the most destructive.

Many of you have watched Dragon's Den or Shark Tank and seen someone who has spent huge sums of money developing a product that clearly won't get off the ground. One's business can easily become an extension of oneself, and that attachment can cloud a person's judgment.

The need for a pivot or a complete shutdown of one's initial idea is more common in business than people think. It requires an honest evaluation, a willingness to let go of ego, and the strength to pull the trigger. Especially if it means forfeiting the return on one's investment to date.

A partner could mitigate undue attachment, catch bad ideas sooner, and let you make changes or close shop before your investment becomes too substantial. It's easier to fool one person than two.

Factors to Consider

1. Are you overly optimistic? Or overly pessimistic? Some people are blinded by their dreams or crushed by their fears before they even start. Finding someone to keep you grounded and who takes a practical approach to business may be an asset you cannot do without.

2. Has your business plateaued? Bringing on a cofounder isn't just for budding businesses. Sometimes a company falls into a rut that the founder cannot push through. That may be the time to seek out a partner whose fresh perspective can help take it to the next level.

Two Heads Are Better Than One

Strategizing, brainstorming, analyzing, and creating are substantial parts of business ownership. Your ability to excel in and manage all of these tasks is limited. Two or more people with a firm understanding of all the moving parts will be more effective.

Imagine you think of a way to improve your product or service. Now imagine not having a partner to run your idea by. What are your options? Without knowing the ins and outs of your business, outsiders won't be able to give sound advice.

Entrepreneurship is an emotional roller coaster. When one person is upset and ready to quit, the other can provide encouragement. Countless entrepreneurs have told me that they motivated their partners when the going got tough; their cofounders ended up reciprocating later.

Factors to Consider

1. Are you a good multitasker? Or do you excel at only one facet of the business? If the latter, you may need a partner to fill in the gaps.
2. How's your focus? Are you tenacious when bringing ideas to light? Or are you easily distracted? A partner can help you stay on course.
3. Are you emotionally stable? Do life's minor setbacks shake you? If so, you'll need tougher skin or a partner who can keep you focused.

The Cons of a Cofounder Partnership

A partnership is not all sunshine and unicorns. In some cases, having a cofounder can be the wrong decision.

The majority of cons arise from personality conflicts. All involved need to accept the compromises required in a partnership. Without total commitment, doubt, mistrust, and resentment can erode collaboration.

You'll find the main reasons solopreneurs choose to go it alone below.

Multiple Decision Makers

A solopreneur is free to make decisions without asking someone else's opinion or permission. In a cofounder partnership, most issues require consensus. Significant challenges can emerge if partners lack the maturity, trust, or shared vision to compromise.

Factors to Consider

1. Your business may have a clear path to success you don't want to deviate from, but a partner will want a say in the company's direction. If conflict would result, you may not want to bring in a cofounder.

2. Is your potential partner someone with whom you can have a constructive decision-making conversation? Or do you have to fully explain each choice you make? A cofounder who requires proof for every thought process may be a stumbling block.

Division of Equity and Profits

Money is the leading reason why many entrepreneurs hesitate to bring on a partner. Forgoing a partnership allows them to maintain more equity and receive more of the profits. But the point may be moot if failing to bring on the right support means you never get your business off the ground.

That said, if you can do what it takes to make the company succeed on your own, giving away a substantial piece of the business might be a mistake.

Factors to Consider

1. Greed can destroy a business before it even starts. If wanting to keep all the money for yourself is your only reason for not bringing in a partner, you won't be ready for the give and take necessary to have a cofoundership, let alone run a company.

2. It's true, you must spend money to make money. Whether dealing with customers, investors, employees, or potential cofounders, money is often the best tool for getting what you want. Adopt a win-win mentality, and you'll see the division of profits as the necessary price of achieving your goals.

3. If you are sure you don't want to share your business' equity and profits, consider creative forms of compensation. Employees who join early may find attractive stock options based on time commitment or milestones.

Partnering With a Dud

One of every entrepreneur's greatest fears is that a partner will become more of a liability than an asset. When a partnership goes awry, the resulting tension can weaken your business. Partnering with the wrong person can place even a successful company in jeopardy.

Only time will tell if you chose the right cofounder. That said, conducting a thorough vetting process, creating a tight partnership agreement, and having hard conversations in advance will likely reveal any warning signs early on.

Factors to Consider

1. Initial enthusiasm can obscure potential business obstacles. That goes double for two founders with equal excitement for their shared vision. Be sure to look at your partnership AND your business model from a reality-based perspective.
2. This early stage may not feel like a good time to pump the brakes, but when choosing a cofounder and planning a partnership agreement, it's essential that you take the necessary time. Your company's structure, your working partnership, and your mutual vision are all put in place at this juncture. If you don't take time to discuss the worst-case scenarios, you may not plan appropriately.
3. Every entrepreneur I know who ended up in a terrible partnership regrets not taking an honest look at the relationship early on. Don't wait for hindsight to reveal your missteps. Identify potential issues in advance.

Relationship Management

Maintaining a strong cofounder partnership takes work. The easy part is finding a cofounder, the hard part is keeping the partnership strong.

The following list contains many of the necessary tasks for maintaining a healthy partnership:

- Frequent and honest communication
- Fostering an environment of earning and imparting trust
- Mitigating the consequences of big ego
- Learning how and when to compromise
- Focusing on enabling and retaining autonomy
- Identifying when and where to hand over control
- Working towards sharing the spotlight
- Discovering and implementing methods to show your partner you value the partnership
- Choosing your battles

Keep these items at the top of your business' to-do list, even as it keeps growing.

Factors to Consider

1. If you or your cofounder don't take relationship management seriously, resentment, frustration, and mistrust may creep into your business. If these risks are not caught early, your ability to mitigate them may become limited and your partnership could disintegrate. Taking the time to plan out intentional methods of strengthening the relationship is a must.

2. Are you prepared to make the personal changes that will foster a mature, professional partnership? If not, save yourself the trouble and build your empire solo.

Three Insufficient Reasons to Bring on a Cofounder

There are three seemingly legitimate but ultimately poor reasons to bring on partners.

#1 They contributed in the early stages

We've all come up with a great idea and no matter what, our first inclination is to tell everyone what it is. Sometimes one or two people in particular, see its potential and, like a gig session, start riffing on ways to improve on it and make it a reality. Then sometimes, the conversation continues over a longer period of time until the idea and execution plan becomes as much a creation of theirs as the initial idea creator. But does this mean that they would make a great business partner?

According to Concentric, a VC firm based out of London, a third of entrepreneurs that they surveyed started a partnership because they felt obliged to include the partner in the business after coming up with the idea together. I'm here to say that dream building and talking out a plan is completely different from execution and not yet enough evidence that a partnership will work.

Don't get me wrong, that person may check off many of the boxes just because of their early participation: intimate involvement in the creation of the product/service, a strong understanding of the vision, a passion for what it offers, and a grasp of the possibilities. However, a deeper dive into what will be required by all the parties is essential for ensuring everyone is aware of how the dynamics and expectations will change.

So what do you do when the person who helped you conceive a business plan isn't the right person to execute it? The only way to head this issue off is to recognize their contribution and clearly define why you believe that the partnership will not work. This shouldn't be an off-the-cuff conversation. They deserve an honest and factual explanation. Without this, you may be at risk of someone claiming ownership, especially if the idea takes off. The conversation may be difficult, but having it early could be significantly easier and potentially less expensive in the long run.

Consider acknowledging early contribution with advisor-sized equity which typically falls in the range of 0.25 to 2 percent. You could offer the higher range if they vest the equity over a period of time in exchange for further support, ideas, and time.

This may also be a great opportunity to get your first investor. Already they understand the potential upside and instead of providing capital AND elbow grease they can just write a cheque. Be sure to consider the equity percentage with what is competitive but it may be the perfect trade-off for what you need to get the business up and running.

You may also structure considerations like a Kickstarter campaign. Provide mini perks that contributors can choose from such as special mention on the site, first run of the product, a value of X amount for the goods or service you are going to provide down the road, or an option to buy in post-X milestone.

Just remember to put your offer on paper. Doing so makes the consideration more concrete and protects you from "he said, she said" arguments down the road. Be sure to offer only what you're willing and able to provide, as you will be held to it.

#2 They want in

Nothing is more of a compliment to an entrepreneur than someone who gets excited about what they are trying to accomplish. Oftentimes, the validation and belief can blind a founder into mistaking excitement for the willingness to do what it takes. Do they really want in, or are they just caught up in the business' potential? Are they looking for all the rewards with no risk?

Sometimes your idea is so great that people forget the hard work you did to grow the business, and they want to jump in after the fact. I remember a story from a founder who brought on their bookkeeper as a partner only to discover that she had no willingness or desire to broaden her role or responsibility from the one she held previously. Often, people overlook that ownership is a responsibility that sometimes requires self-sacrifice. If the business, market, or economy falters, these people start looking for an exit.

Zeal doesn't equal work ethic. A lot of activity goes into building and maintaining a successful company. While it might look easy from the outside, there's a lot of hard work happening behind the curtain. Be sure that anyone you bring on board demonstrates firm commitment in both word and deed.

#3 We are Really Good Friends

A shared business can be amazing but the cofounder relationship must be built on more than friendship. Transparency, a willingness to compromise, and self-sacrifice are all traits that need to be demonstrated out of the gate to ensure that a relationship built on trust is created.

Cofounders usually start as friends, and they presume their friendship will be enough to see them through. They fail to see the value of building the strength of their partnership so when something happens within the relationship, they aren't prepared for the impact it makes. Feelings of betrayal, disappointment, resentment, and mistrust are powerful and they have the capacity of doing great damage and can be very difficult to recover from.

Just because you are great friends, and never argue or disagree, doesn't mean your friendship alone will stave off the pressures and demands that a cofounding partnership will have on you. Consider the story at the beginning of the chapter. Even as colleagues Brian and Chris were able to work well. It was when the responsibility and weight of the business fell on their shoulders that their friendship was found insufficient for carrying them through.

Alternatives to a Cofounder

A cofounder might not be for you. But if you still want someone to help get your business off the ground, what are your options?

Co-contributor

I came up with the title "Co-contributor" specifically for founders who feel a sense of obligation to those who assisted in a key component of their business growth. Whether it be in the ideation stage, through a pivotal product/

service recommendation, or a specific task completed, these key contributions are recognized for their influence but not for long-term involvement. The title of co-contributor can provide recognition that has value on a resume or business profile. It highlights the contribution they brought to the table and could act as a recommendation to others who may need similar assistance. Oftentimes people merely want acknowledgment of their role in a successful business and the title of Co-contributor, preferably with a written letter as to why the title was given, is sufficient.

Along with the title and letter, advisor-level equity could also be in order. How much that would be is up to you. Just be aware that generosity is always a good idea. For example, if their contribution meant a whole new successful division or product line was created, then be sure to reward them in a way that reflects the level of success achieved.

Finally, the number of co-contributor titles you bestow does not need to be limited. Potentially, throughout the stages of your business, outside influencers, employees, customers, and even investors, could be recognized for the key value or timely contribution that impacted your company. I wouldn't suggest you hand them out for every positive contribution but maybe, if not hopefully, along your entrepreneurial journey, a small handful will deserve to be credited. It costs nothing but could mean so much.

(For an example of a Co-contributor letter visit The Cofounder's Hub.)

Mentor/Business Coach

Taking on a mentor solves the loneliness factor and can provide you with vital feedback, advice, and support. Here are a few points to keep in mind when choosing and working with a mentor or business coach:

1. To get the necessary vantage point, a mentor or coach should be given unprecedented access to your business.
2. A background understanding of your industry eliminates the need to teach a mentor the basics of your business. That said, past experience is not essential, and an outsider's viewpoint may help you think of solutions you otherwise wouldn't have.

3. Ensure a mentor is in it for the long run. The process of bringing your idea to life is long and arduous. Explain that you want a two-year commitment to start.

4. Communication is the cornerstone of a mentor-protégé relationship. Create a communication plan, and follow it. Establish whether emergency calls are acceptable. Book time for in-depth reviews of financials, sales plans, and marketing ideas. Keep everyone in the loop via email, and schedule major meetings at least twice a year.

5. A coach or mentor should have a track record of success. Don't choose your aunt or best friend unless your choice is supported by measurable, consistent results. Make sure the person who helps you make major business decisions is capable of offering the best course of action.

How will you reward coaching/mentorship? Time is money and typically anyone with any success should not be expected to trade their time for a pat on the back. I know for myself that if I went "for coffee" with every person who "just wanted to pick my brain", I'd spend most of my day at Starbucks.

Also, don't put anyone in the position of having to ask for compensation. Believe me, they know they are offering value, and they won't be insulted or perplexed if you offer to compensate them for their time. Much better that they offer to do the service pro-bono than you to ask it of them.

There are a couple of factors to consider when determining compensation for a mentor. The first, is the time commitment. I've already explained above what their involvement would look like at a basic level so anything above or below this should be taken into consideration. Second, look at the mentor's level or ability to act. If you have access to a mentor who can network you into the world of key potential clients or provide extremely specific guidance that could catapult your business forward, don't be stingy. Calculate the time and cost to get to that level on your own and offer fair compensation for the fast track they can initiate.

Some business coaches charge $1500 per hour or more. If that's not an option for you, consider a non-cash arrangement. Find other means of compensation for a mentor's time whether it be stock options, exchanges of services or goods, or future bonuses. All could be excellent possibilities.

What are the options if you cannot find someone who fits the bill of mentor or coach? You could attempt to join an organized business group in your area. Examples such as TEC or Young Presidents' Organization are business owner groups that encourage you to share your wins and challenges on a monthly basis. The members of the group, under NDA, get deep access into your business and your future plans and are able to offer advice on how to move forward. The fee to join can be expensive but the rich sources of insights, tips, and encouragement could make the experience priceless.

I want to reiterate. Don't be stingy or ungrateful toward mentors. These people will be taking time out of their busy schedules to help you achieve your dreams. If you do not show a mentor due respect, you could lose a powerful ally. Speaking of which, mentors and business coaches make excellent references for investors, banks, and potential employees. At the very least, cherish these relationships for their future value.

Hire

If you are confident in your ability to lead your business without a cofounder but still have a major role to be filled, consider hiring someone. Keep in mind that interviewing candidates can be a time-consuming chore and in today's market, finding someone willing to fill the role could be even more difficult. That said, hiring within your budget and delegating crucial tasks lets you focus on what you do best while retaining precious equity in your company.

Keep the following points in mind when hiring.

1. A hired employee does not have the same vested interest as you. This reality will become glaringly obvious in times of struggle. If your company is in a nosedive, your hire will probably start searching for another job. Communication will be vital in

keeping employees engaged through hard times. Be sure to stay open about setbacks and thorough in explaining your action plan.

2. Structure employee rewards carefully. Make sure to keep wages and bonuses at pace with the growth and success of your business. You want your employees to look back and feel that their efforts were worthwhile. Their trust in your ability to provide a secure and fulfilling job is a major compliment and a significant responsibility. Reward your employees' trust in you.

Delay

If you are seeking a cofounder but haven't been able to find the right person, just get moving, start the company, and search for a partner as you go. Searching for the right person could take time and waiting could bring your business' growth to a standstill or even worse affect the excitement that you feel for the venture. Don't become stagnant or paralyzed, keep timing at the forefront of your mind.

There may be other advantages too from moving full steam ahead. The road to revenue could be shorter than you expect. You may discover that you won't need a partner after all! Alternatively, you may find your requirements in a partner changing as you progress. You'll be able to hone the list of skills and traits necessary for your needs. Waiting also gives you time to meet people within your industry. It broadens the net for finding potential candidates.

One should also keep in mind that the number of people willing and able to work for equity, or at most minimum wage supplemented by equity, is much smaller than most entrepreneurs often expect. Even in Silicon Valley, where more people understand the value of stock ownership than anywhere else, few will put in long hours for the years it takes to start a business, for free. Therefore, the fact that a partner may not need to be paid means that more capital can be assigned to building the business.

Finally, building up value solo can help you negotiate a higher equity split for yourself since more groundwork will have been completed and the signals of success made clear. Being able to offer a higher level of security in someone's investment and time commitment to the business will also broaden the number of the candidates willing and able to join forces.

Next Steps

So what will it be? Will you seek a cofounder or not?

By now you should have a better idea of whether a cofounder is right for you. For now, my main advice is don't waste precious time looking for "the One." Instead, start/continue building your first iteration of a product, networking with people about your service, or even making money!

It may be impossible to find the perfect partner who checks every box you are looking for, but this book will teach you to assess and manage risks to help you find someone who is close. Apply the information in this book now, so that you won't have to Google, "my business partner is…" in the future.

Here's to your epic origin story!

CHAPTER 2

Do an Honest
Self-Evaluation

Hannah had an idea for an app that kept her up for weeks on end. "I came up with the concept while I was in the shower. How utterly cliche!" She utilized what she'd learned in the few coding classes she took in college to create a prototype. This allowed her to envision a finished product. "Once I was able to see it in action, I showed friends, family, and business associates. Through them, I got the feedback that I wanted: they loved it!"

She saw that her app would fill a need in the marketplace, but she didn't want to build it alone. So she began her search for a business partner. "I shared the idea with a couple of my friends in the hopes that one of them would want to work with me on it." When no one showed interest, she decided to extend her search to her wider network. "I had a lot of friends from college, so I knew someone would have to be interested."

While she searched for a cofounder, Hannah stumbled across an online personality assessment. Remembering that she had taken a similar one in the past and enjoyed the insights that came from the results, she decided she needed a refresher and retook the assessment. "I didn't expect much to come from it, but in the back of my mind, I wondered if knowing more about myself could give me an advantage. Being in the process of starting a new venture, I wanted to identify where I had strengths and weaknesses." The test itself only took twenty minutes, but Hannah spent days poring over the results. "I decided to take each trait and reflect on how it had served me or held me back in my life."

The insights were a revelation. Three of the personality traits in particular stuck out to Hannah, and she realized they would be important criteria to consider when she sought out a business partner: perfectionism, adaptability, and easygoingness.

"Honestly, my first set of criteria for a business partner was only one thing: Are they excited about the idea?" Hannah had mostly been looking for someone who saw the potential in the app and who wanted to find a way to bring it to market. "While coding skills or marketing experience was a hopeful possibility, I didn't have a specific list of skills or experience I wanted the candidate to have." However, once she took the test, she determined a cofounder with the perfectionism, adaptability, and easygoingness traits would enhance their chances of success in the venture.

Results to Real Life

Hannah scored low on perfectionism. "I knew I would score low on this because my sister was the textbook example of what it looked like to be a perfectionist, and I definitely did not fit that mold." Hannah remembers teachers in both high school and college taking her to task for not fully completing assignments to the level they were looking for or for not double-checking her work for errors or omissions. "I was more focused on getting the job done. To what extent wasn't a priority." Hannah figured if she could find someone who was high on perfectionism, they could mitigate any cut corners and raise standards on deliverables.

The second trait that jumped out to Hannah was adaptability. "Again, I saw my score in adaptability reflected in the success and challenges of my life to date." Being adaptable translates into the ability to be flexible and malleable. But it also means structure and routine can take away from the craving for novelty and spontaneity. "I realized that, for what we were doing, we needed to be able to change course quickly and adapt to the needs of our early adopters." She wanted someone who wouldn't struggle with the twists and turns that the entrepreneurial journey would bring.

Finally, her significantly low result in easygoingness was one she wanted to match with a business partner. "There were a couple of reasons that I felt would be valuable in having a business partner on the lower end of easygoingness." Hannah believed that time to market was essential for her app. "I know the tides change quickly in tech, and I wanted our product out into the world as quickly as possible." She wanted to find someone who didn't want to waste any time putting the app together. Additionally, she knew that this time in her life, while she was single and had no children, would be a time to plow through her career goals and achieve some of her professional aspirations. Hannah wanted someone who also felt a sense of urgency and wanted to make the most of their time untethered by responsibility.

Armed with these traits, Hannah began her search. And that search would lead her to a great surprise.

The Power of Self-Evaluation

Before we discover what type of cofounder you need, I want you to do a little exercise. Please take out a pen and paper and answer the following two questions:

- Make a list of qualities that you are looking for in a potential partner?
- What are the three most important factors on this list?

Even if you have already found a potential partner, this exercise is still valuable to you. Start by taking them out of the picture and imagine that you have to start again in finding someone. This allows you to be objective in assessing whether your current candidate meets your actual needs.

Got your answers? Good. But I can almost guarantee that by the end of this chapter, your list will have changed. Why? Because most people do not undertake the due diligence necessary to dig deep and compile an extensive assessment of the skills, talents, and temperament they need to find in a partner. They often have what I call the "obvious list," but they do not drill down to look at the peripherals and prioritize their findings.

For example, a restaurateur may decide to open a restaurant. But because they do not know how to cook, they decide, "OK, I need a chef." That's their "obvious list." Then they proceed to make this their primary criteria. A technical founder may have a great idea and prototype but lack business skills and decide to look for a front-facing partner with a business degree. These might be important factors, but there are a multitude of other points to consider when creating a partnership.

The first step in figuring out what kind of cofounder you need is to take the time to better understand yourself.

Looking in the Mirror

Knowing yourself better and understanding your strengths and limitations sheds light on where you may need to fill in your gaps in order to find a complementary cofounder for your business. Until you have a clear picture of where you stand, you cannot know what to look for in someone else. By taking a closer look at where you excel and fall short, you can unveil strengths that you offer to accelerate growth, as well as weaknesses that could hinder your efforts.

Taking stock to achieve this complete picture isn't easy. It takes introspection and a willingness to be honest about yourself, warts and all. Lucky for you, the marketplace is filled with self-evaluation tools that can streamline your efforts and give you new insights and perspectives about yourself.

These evaluations come in many shapes and sizes. There are some for discovering your strengths and weaknesses, knowing your personality type, determining your EQ, establishing your mission statement, defining your value system, identifying your passions, pinpointing your learning style, and a plethora more.

Do you need to do all of these? *Yes!* Think about it this way: you are likely going to invest tens, if not hundreds of thousands of dollars in your venture. You will also be investing the vast majority of your waking life for the next X years as you build, scale, and run this company. What is it to take a few assessments, sit and ponder the results, and make adjustments to your execution plan to ensure that the money spent and time given isn't wasted? It's barely a blip or a struggle in the scheme of things. Imagine if what you discover is the difference between minor success, a major success, and even failure. You will be glad you put in the effort. Remember, the more you learn about yourself, the better equipped you will be to identify the missing components you need to find in your partner(s).

(At the Cofounder's Hub, we have an extensive list of products and online quizzes that will assist you in doing this deep dive into yourself. Head over to www.thecofoundershub.com for more info.)

Your business will ultimately be an extension of you. It will not only stand as a record of your decisions and how they were executed but also bear the fingerprint of your personality, your work ethic, your character, your preferences, your values, and all the things that make up who you are, good and bad. Ensuring that you bring your best to the table requires you to investigate all the ways you will impact the company.

To make this easier, I'm going to break down your self-exploration into three key areas: strengths and weaknesses, assets and liabilities, and dreams and reality. As you assess where you stand in each of these categories, know that the more honest you are, the better. Everyone has strengths in some areas and weaknesses in others, so do not get discouraged when you find faults as it only means you may need to find someone stronger in those areas. This is the great advantage of a cofounder partnership. Think of it as people coming together to create a super version of themselves. Your combined strengths, coupled with the counterbalances to each other's limits, will make you an unbeatable machine.

There is also a practical level to taking stock on the following categories. When you sit down with your potential partner, you will be able to list what it is that you bring to the table and demonstrate your value. This could translate into additional equity or pay. It also allows you to warn them about potential pitfalls, which highlights the thought you put into your plan and shows your willingness and preparedness to adapt to challenges.

Strengths and Weaknesses

Your strengths and weaknesses can be found through that which comes to you inherently as well as through your upbringing, environment, training, and culture.

Research suggests that no matter where your strengths and weaknesses land on a scale of one to ten, your ability to improve upon them by more than a couple of points is limited and probably not worth the effort. That's why it's better to identify where you are strong and then find someone who excels where you fall short. This plan can take considerably less time than overhauling your entire personality to become someone you weren't born to be.

Identifying your strengths and weaknesses, in the context of your business, can both help to propel you forward and avoid costly mistakes. It will also help you better relate to and communicate with others therefore allowing you to live out your business and personal life in a more authentic and contented way.

Personality

Personality has a huge impact on business. The restaurant industry is a prime example. Chefs are notoriously shy and introverted when it comes to public relations, which doesn't cut it in the restaurant industry, where you need to make your guests feel welcomed and wanted. For this reason, you will often see the introverted chef paired with a social extrovert who is most comfortable in the front of the house, mingling and socializing with the guests. Both need each other. A restaurant needs someone who can cook and who can create a great experience for diners. By knowing your personality style, you can identify what type of personality will complement or clash with yours and even assist you with doling out roles and responsibilities.

There are many evaluations to determine your personality. At the Cofounder's Hub, we have our own assessment, which is offered alongside a guide that explains how a low or high score in each trait affects those specifically in the context of a cofounding partnership. That said, no matter which kind of test you choose, be sure to spend extra time studying your own style and those that complement and conflict with it. I also recommend you have potential or current cofounders, as well as any key people you are going to hire, take the test. These tests bring to light tendencies that are often difficult to detect without spending significant time with someone. That's helpful if you don't know each other well at the start.

Outlook

Are you a pessimist or an optimist? This may not be as scientific as a personality test or as easy to categorize. But we all know those who slant toward a defeatist ideal or who are eternally positive about what lies around the corner. A healthy dose of both is needed as an entrepreneur, but too much of one or the other can be disastrous.

In the context of self-evaluation, a simple way to know where you fall is to ask someone who knows you where they think you sit. Those who find themselves on the far spectrum of either side are often unaware because they think it's normal and rational to believe as they do. An objective outside opinion could give you the insights you need. Another option is to practice intentional listening to what you say on a daily basis and what goes on with your internal dialogue. Often, we speak off the cuff without much thought about what we are communicating, so taking the time to reflect on the words we use will help us identify what our outlook is on life and then make adjustments if necessary.

This distinction is important. If, for example, you score high on the optimism chart, you may need to find someone who is willing to throw a dose of realism into the ring. Too much faith in a positive outcome could find you failing to seek out and identify dangers that could derail your efforts. On the opposite side of the spectrum, if you doubt the success of everything, then you may need someone who can help you weigh the risks or consider the potential upside with more clarity. The majority of people sit in the middle, but being aware if you are at the extreme level of either side will help you find a valuable counterbalance.

Your Learning Style

I'm a visual learner. If you have a concept to run by me, you'd better have a diagram to help explain it, or else you'll be facing glazed eyes and a loss of attention. Knowing your learning style is important not only for understanding yourself better but also to make communication (the single most important factor in having a strong partnership) more effective. When you figure out how you and your partners learn, you will be better equipped to communicate ideas and make decisions.

There are four recognized learning styles:

- Visual: through images, graphs, and graphic organizers
- Auditory: through listening and speaking
- Read & Write: through the written word
- Kinesthetic: through hands-on learning

Your Multiple Intelligences

Another way to better understand yourself and more effectively communicate with your cofounder is to learn your "Intelligence" or "Smarts". Think of these as the ways that information can best be presented to you in order to maximize your understanding.

There are nine recognized intelligences:

- Visual (spatial): You prefer using pictures, images, and spatial understanding.
- Aural (auditory-musical): You prefer using sound and music.
- Verbal (linguistic): You prefer using words, both in speech and writing.

- Physical (kinesthetic): You prefer using your body, hands, and sense of touch.
- Logical (mathematical): You prefer using logic, reasoning, and systems.
- Social (interpersonal): You prefer to learn in groups or with other people.
- Solitary (intrapersonal): You prefer to work alone and use self-study.
- Nature (naturalistic): ability to recognize and categorize plants, animals and other objects in nature.
- Existential (philosophical): sensitivity and capacity to tackle deep questions about human existence.

Many people have top-three intelligences, meaning they tend to lean towards three areas in particular. In business, most are necessary or valuable. Depending on your industry, certain intelligences will have more value than others. That means you can cover three by yourself and may need someone to fill the gaps elsewhere. The more you can cover, the better.

Conflict Style

How do you handle issues that arise in your life? Taking the time to know your knee-jerk response during times of conflict will help you step back and see where you contribute to the issue. Additionally, knowing how your cofounder handles conflict will assist you both in navigating each other's styles and move more quickly towards resolution.

The are five recognized conflict styles:

- Competing: "I win, you lose"
- Avoiding: "I lose, you lose"
- Accommodating: "I lose, you win"
- Compromising: "I half win, you half win"
- Collaborating: "I win, you win"

Your conflict style will become an invaluable point of understanding down the road when disputes and disagreements occur in your partnership.

Values and Character

Values and character are the substances that make life enjoyable. Character strengths are the moral and ethical qualities of your personality that impact how you think, feel, and behave and are the keys to you being your best self. Your values are the things you believe are important in the way you live and work. By understanding your character, you will identify and determine the overarching rules and standards that you use to make decisions. In knowing your values, you will be able to build and keep your business in a direction that will make the journey feel satisfying and successful. Examples of character strengths include: courage, future mindedness, optimism, work ethic, hope, honesty. Examples of values include: integrity, dependability, flexibility, self-respect, frugality, support.

Emotional Intelligence

How are your stress levels? Entrepreneurship is guaranteed to send them through the roof. How do you deal with it? Emotional intelligence, otherwise known as emotional quotient or EQ, is the ability to understand, use, and manage your own emotions in positive ways. This allows you to relieve stress, communicate effectively, empathize with others, overcome challenges, and defuse conflict.

EQ affects your performance, physical and mental health, relationships, and social intelligence. It should be clear why knowing, understanding, and managing your EQ is important in a cofounder partnership.

Assets and Liabilities

Your assets and liabilities are things that you have acquired along your life's journey. They are the tangibles that you bring to the table, the qualities that will assist you in making your business a success. They're also the drawbacks to working with you and the risks you need to keep in mind. Taking account of each of these will enable you to see yourself in the big picture and illuminate the gaps where you may fall short.

Skills

A skill is defined as "the ability, coming from one's knowledge, practice, aptitude, etc., to do something well." Being able to identify your skills will allow you to determine the assets you bring to the table.

A great way to discover your skills is to look at factors like education, work experience, volunteer activity, and hobbies. These are things you've learned to do, and the behaviors you use in those pursuits become individual skills. Of course, many skills are industry specific, so being able to identify those that are applicable to your business and those that are universally valuable will allow you to think both narrowly and broadly. It all adds up to your unique offer.

Many people think their skills are limited to the education they received. Not so! There are many traits that cannot be honed in a classroom yet are extremely valuable in a business. Skills such as negotiation, strategy, communication, discernment, networking, time management, organization, budgeting, fundraising, and many more can be learned outside scholarly institutions and the marketplace. You can even learn them growing up in your family.

Keep in mind that in order to be able to say you are skilled at something, there needs to be recordable proof, which means you need some way to show that you have, in fact, acquired the ability. This might mean a business school diploma, but it can also be a verifiable demonstration of the skill on the spot or a reference from a trusted source. Do not allow yourself or your potential partner to get away with a "trust me on this" approach to skills. Quantifying the effectiveness of your skill is necessary in order to use it as leverage. Where possible, seek tangible proof that the skill has led to success in previous ventures or situations. This will allow you to stand strong in your abilities and trust that decisions that stem from your experience are backed by knowledge.

Also, be sure to dig deep into your hobbies, which are another place skills can be fostered. A great golf swing, martial arts, home cooking, coaching, and any other pursuit may have applications, depending on the venture you are undertaking. Take model aircraft building, for example. To be a success at that, many skills are needed: patience, attention to detail, aerial physics, and engineering knowledge all are a by-product of a hobby that seems purely recreational. Being able to identify the skills necessary to excel in your chosen hobbies will give you further insight into your personal arsenal.

Volunteer work is yet another source for determining your skill set, as your volunteer experience can identify where your confidence lies. For example, few people volunteer to help differently abled children if they know they lack patience and empathy. You should also be able to catch a glimpse of what others value in you. Many nonprofits have great systems to determine the skill set of someone and how to best put it to use within the organization. Some people are even headhunted by organizations for particular skills and talents.

Education

This would be the time to list out the education you have gained throughout your life. Don't forget side courses, online courses, additional classes, and conferences. While education is a clear method of showing dedication to a particular skill set, it's also a way to demonstrate where you have a passion and have flourished within that subject.

Experience

Experience often takes center stage on a résumé. It's the section in your CV where you list all the work experience you have had in your career to date.

We all leave certain ones out and for good reason. Some bits of experience are not applicable or were not positive or productive. But in this case, be sure to write them all down. Every working experience you have should give you a deeper understanding of yourself. What did you excel at during your time there? What did you hate doing or lack the confidence and skill in? How were your interpersonal relationships? How did you grow within the organization? What issues do you think kept you from achieving your goals? Why did you leave, or were you asked to leave? Take the time to list the job description and what you undertook and accomplished in each role. This will create an even clearer picture of how you have grown and developed as a person.

They say, "Experience is the best teacher," so a thoughtful, expansive assessment at this level is essential.

Accolades

Awards, honors, or any laudatory notice is an asset to a business. Acknowledgment of achievement by an outside source gives credibility to your work and demonstrates expertise in an industry or a role. Look at awards, trophies, titles, certifications, mentions, articles, and endorsements while taking the time to reflect on what made you excel at this endeavor.

Notoriety

Celebrities will often become partners by offering their names in connection with the business. When a successful marketing effort plays a dominant role in the success of a business, attaching a name that creates buzz and has mass appeal provides a significant leg up. That said, a name doesn't always bring experience, so you want to be very clear upfront about how involved someone with notoriety will be.

I interviewed one celebrity cofounder who brought their name to a fashion company with the expectation that they would play a small role in the day-to-day work but would bring much-needed buzz to the brand. What they never anticipated was the level of personal attachment that would come to the success of the business to whose name they were tied. As the company took off, the celebrity ended up spending more time in the day-to-day work, ensuring that their name was not tainted by a lack of proper execution, quality, or service. This micromanaging created its own problems in the business.

Let this be a warning for those on both sides of the table: for the business owner who expects minimal involvement in the business but gets someone who becomes adamant about ensuring that the business, on the whole, is the proper reflection of them and for the celebrity who may have expected minimal involvement but underestimated the personal damage that could come from a poorly executed business tied to their name. Always be clear about the roles to be played, expectations to be achieved, and boundaries to be observed.

Influence

Do you have 100,000+ followers on social media? This type of reach is often more powerful than any traditional marketing campaign, so be sure to take the time to assess where you stand on that front.

There are many authentic ways to boost your influence list. It may make sense to build your brand up on the side, as influence is the new currency. Additionally, there are some companies that put a monetary value on the reach and interaction level of influencers. It may be worth running your followers and interaction rate through these calculators to find a number that represents the value you bring.

References

My cofounder and I were surprised by the amount of weight put on references throughout our careers. As founders raising money, investors were as interested in us as a team as they were in our business idea. As we got closer to closing a term sheet, we were asked to provide references who could vouch for our expertise, our experience, and our ability to run a business.

You will need references. Take the time to identify people who can speak to your talent, character, leadership qualities, business capabilities, and any other relevant information that may be applicable to your business. When the time comes, you will be ready with names of those who can effectively vouch for you.

Additionally, you will want to request references from your cofounder candidates. Be specific about what counts. Do not let them tell you who to talk to, like their mom or their favorite coworker. Consider their past experiences and request specific people whose opinions you think will come untouched and objective. Speaking to a reference is powerful. Look for what isn't said, and take liberties when reading between the lines. An unwillingness to answer a question can tell you as much as a long-winded response.

Network and Connections

Any successful business owner will agree with the following statement: "It's not what you know; it's who you know." The network you have built is touted as the most valuable tool you can have in your arsenal. Silicon Valley is the epitome of understanding this value and has created a culture of cooperation and collaboration, where helping someone without the expectation of reward is standard behaviour and will be paid forward down the road.

In some industries, your network has a direct monetary value. I have a good friend who worked for an investment banker for many years. During this time, she got to be quite connected within the community where the business was located. We couldn't walk into a store anywhere in our city without her being stopped by someone she knew. When she left to start a fundraising company to assist local schools with their funding efforts, her network was a valuable asset to the new start-up. When she sat down with her potential cofounder, she was able to explain that her connections to the people in the community were going to make it easier to find potential big-ticket donors. This meant that marketing efforts would be more effective, and access to funds would be expedited, keeping more money in their pockets and increasing their chances for success.

If you see that your network will play an important role in your business (and it will), take the time to make sure you have a list of the people you are connected to. Your LinkedIn profile can be a great asset here. Use it effectively, and it can assist you in gathering even more connections.

Time

There is no better time in the history of mankind to be an entrepreneur. Technology has made it possible for anyone, no matter their age, sex, economic standing, education, or race, to step up and try their hand at business ownership.

What comes with this opportunity, however, is a new myriad of challenges that need to be addressed. You have high school entrepreneurs still dealing with exams in the midst of speaking with investors, women redefining the logistics between motherhood and career, and even retired folks who find themselves full of vigor and excitement long past their retirement age. By bringing the "everyman" into the entrepreneurial arena, time commitments become a more glaring elephant in the room that needs to be addressed.

We all have twenty-four hours in a day. It's what we do with those hours that determines our success in life. Some are at stages in their lives when they do not have anything tying them down, enabling them to commit 100 percent of their time to their venture. And starting a business does require an all-in work ethic. But for many, commitments of some sort or another mitigate their ability to be all in at all times. Knowing if your access to time is an asset or a liability should be a big determining factor in who you look for. If you are a single parent with a couple of kids under the age of ten, you will have less time available for the needs of the business than, say, a university graduate still living with their parents.

I do not buy into the idea that having other commitments is a liability. I believe that it can be a moot point. But only if, and it's a big if, you can find a way to mutually work around the commitments in a way that is clearly defined and understood by all parties. There will need to be significant give and take on both sides, and having a high level of trust and belief in the mission of the company will be imperative. Without these clear understandings, resentment will begin to bubble up to the surface, and the breakdown of the partnership will be a looming possibility.

Financial

Two things are guaranteed when starting a business:

- It always takes longer and costs more money than you expect.
- Because capital is one of the most important tools for building your business, your financial status will quickly show itself to be an asset or a liability.

Unfortunately, nowhere in their lives are people more ignorant than in their finances. Few take the time to assess where they truly stand until they need a loan or mortgage. A smart move would be to take the time to determine how much money you can invest now and in the future, before bringing on a partner. Once you have that information, you can determine how much you need your potential partner to bring to the table or, at a minimum, have access to should the need arise.

Additionally, financial and time equity are big bargaining chips when discussing ownership equity. Having a clear understanding on where you stand and what you need will help you charter those challenging waters.

Dreams and Reality

Once you have that clear picture of <u>who</u> you are, you need to determine <u>how</u> you want the journey to look as you go forward and solidify the goals that you are looking to attain.

Your end goal will determine the path you take and the decisions you make. Without a clear picture of your "end game", you are liable to roam aimlessly and waste valuable resources and time. Because this path will take many years, you want to take the time to decide what will make it bearable and enjoyable. Many people don't realize the impact identifying goals have on living a life they love and consequently, they experience unnecessary discontentment and frustration as they build their businesses.

So how do you get this clarity? I break it down into three components: goals, needs, and wants. Knowing these three will allow you to plan for the road ahead and find that special someone who wants to head in the same direction with a synchronous idea on how you are going to get there. These goals, needs, and wants do not need to be written in concrete. But they will set the stage and the tone for what the path will look like going forward. If you don't know these three things for yourself, you may find a partner with a completely different idea of what the future is going to hold. That invites conflict and risks the success of your business.

Goals

Most people's goal is to make money, but that isn't specific enough. You want to take the time to pin down what exactly that looks like because it can have many faces.

In my case, we built our first company to make an exit. It was never our desire to run the company forever. After following the same format for two other companies, we decided that our fourth venture would be one that we would take on for the long haul. By deciding this together, we didn't take the first offer that came to us and were content with the decision (and the risk) because we had discussed and agreed on the plan early on.

Know that goals are not written in stone. A business doesn't always have the luxury of "deciding" its prospects. You may set off to build a family-legacy business only to realize that it will not be possible to maintain. You still need to discuss and plan your endgame; just be open to the fact that the goal posts could potentially change. The key is for you and your cofounder to always be in good communication and let each other know if and when this happens. Believe it or not, the vision one has for the future, even if in the back of their mind, will strongly determine almost every decision made. A cohesive and smooth-running business relies on the founders always striving for the same goal.

This has played out for many cofounding pairs. Michale, the cofounder of a manufacturing company, told me his story: "We wanted to sell right away. Our goal was to build a prototype and sell that off to a predetermined set of potential buyers. When no one bit, we had to decide whether to keep going or cut our losses. Neither of us was in the position to take on the financial and time requirements it would take to turn the business into a working model, so we closed our doors."

Michale and his partner, Pete, talked about their goals ahead of time, so the value of deciding the desired outcome early on is obvious. Because they both knew that they were in this for a short-term stint, with the understanding of the risk that there could be no buyers, they were both on the same page for the next step of closing the doors. No surprises and no hard feelings. Both men were financially and mentally prepared for the outcome. Serious issues arise only if the founders are not on the same page.

Here are some examples of what to think about when planning your goals:

- Do I want a long-term company or short-term exit?
- Do I want a business where my family can join me, either now or down the road?
- Do I want to be a local business or am I thinking global?
- Do I want $100,000 a year, or am I looking to become part of the world's top 1 percent?
- Do I want to give back to society/community?
- Do I want to be able to work thirty hours a week with X income?
- Am I looking for notoriety to build my name?

Hopefully, you have taken the time to determine whether or not your business is the vehicle that can get you to your goals. If not, you may want to cross-reference these new insights with your business plan to ensure that the venture is worthy.

Needs

Your needs are those things that you must make concessions for. They may be permanent issues you have to work around, or they could be temporary and able to be downgraded in the future if you hit a certain milestone. It could be a particular threshold of income, the need to work flexible hours for childcare, or anything else that you just can't negotiate around.

This isn't going to be a big list. The list should consist of needs, not wants. Because these are absolute nonnegotiables, it's likely that someone would have only one or two needs, if any.

These needs will affect how you proceed in building your business, but I firmly believe that any situation can find a work-around. Don't be discouraged; life throws us many curve balls, and it's not worth dwelling on what cannot be helped. You can't help it if you are a single parent and have to pick up your kids at school at two thirty p.m. You can't help it that you came up with a brilliant idea at the age of seventeen, and you haven't had a job yet, let alone savings to draw from. You may be deaf, going through bankruptcy or divorce, scheduled for jury duty, or any other potential challenges. They are all needs that must be addressed and handled in some way or another.

Needs have to be defined and laid out clearly early on as they will affect how you make business decisions. By not being clear with your future partner about your needs, you may surprise them and cause them to say, "I didn't sign up for this," or "I wish I had known this before." These abrupt surprises can tear apart a partnership.

So if you are dealing with a particular issue, you just need to be creative. For example, if you need a certain starting salary, then you may need to be prepared to take less equity. If you need more time to balance family or some other extenuating circumstance, then you may need to be prepared to work after the kids go to bed or before the rooster crows.

Whatever the case may be, be prepared to offer a remedy or two to your partner. It enables the conversation to continue and shows that you are not trying to be difficult.

One caveat: make sure the need is really a need. You may think you need more money, but you may not. Be honest with yourself. A need is something that absolutely must take place in order to move to the next stage. It may change in the near or late future but should be focused on only the immediate next step. Save your wants for the wish list.

Examples of needs may include:

- I need to be home with my family from three to eight p.m. as I cannot find or afford childcare during that time.
- I need a guaranteed income of $X or to keep my job until I can replace the income.
- I need to be able to attend to an aging parent should they require my assistance.
- I have health issues that need to be prioritized.
- I need to deal with X issue over the next few months/years.

All these issues requiring special attention are reasonable and, with the right mindset, can be accommodated in a way that suits all parties.

Now that you've got your needs, let's talk about your wish list of wants.

Wants

Here's where you decide what you prefer. These requests are not necessary to build the business, but you value them enough that they are almost a need for you. This is not the time to compile a diva list, though. It's a time to determine what's important enough to get you excited and interested in building your company.

For example, Mary's parents were aging and living in a senior home in Portugal. "I knew that their days were numbered and that I wanted to make time on an annual basis to visit them." A three-week trip to Portugal doesn't really fly when you're trying to build a company, but for Mary, the trip was really important. "By stating this at the get-go, my cofounder and I worked out that I would work during the Christmas season so that she could have some time with her family. It wasn't exactly three weeks for three weeks, but for her, it was worth the exchange."

Thinking of wants is a way to put how you spend your days into perspective. Starting a company is challenging as it is. Finding ways to make it more bearable is a smart decision. Like Tom did with his cofounder, Ed. "Ed and I lived an hour commute from each other: Ed downtown and me in the 'burbs. Access to public transit was limited for me, but Ed had a plethora of transit alternatives to choose from. Because of this, we chose an office location that was closer to my home but near a subway station so that he could easily get to the office." By doing this, both Tom and Ed could get to work within fifteen minutes, even though the office was closer to Tom. "Having to spend two hours a day in traffic would have been hard to swallow. By having the office closer, I could spend more time at the office and feel like hours weren't being wasted on the road."

Examples of some wants could be:

- I want my own private office or a say in the decor.
- I want to have my name as part of the company name.
- I want to exit when we can personally get $1 million or more.
- I want the last word on the menu.
- I want to be the lead singer.
- I want an X role or title.
- I want a car, to travel, to speak to the media, to hire employees.
- I want my relative to have this role in the company.
- I want to pass the company on to my children.
- I want to be able to pursue other things on the side.

Will you always get what you want? Of course not. But when you vocalize what is important to you, you may be able to find a working solution.

Putting It All Together

Now that you have completed your self-assessment, it is time to look at the big picture. I suggest doing the following five steps:

1. Jot down the top three insights that you discovered yourself within each section, taking the time to tweeze out the best and worst that you have to offer.

2. Decide within each section what the optimum contribution a cofounder could provide to compensate for your weaknesses and to complement your capabilities.

3. Consider your cofounder list, and prioritize those contributions that must be found in your cofounder and those that would be a close second.

4. Identify any contributions that could be found in a key employee or hire instead of a cofounder: for example, a good bookkeeper. By doing this, you can streamline your search and minimize the checklist needed for finding the perfect match.

5. Create a simple report for quick reference going forward.

Now you've got the perfect list to take into your meetings with your cofounder candidates and decide if you're a good match. This is a great start!

Learn from Hannah

With her key personality traits in mind, Hannah went out into the world with a new set of criteria. She attended a few cofounder speed-dating events in her area and ran the candidates she was considering through the assessment process. "I weighed everything that they brought to the table. But I was specifically looking for someone who complimented those three traits."

Four months into Hannah's search, she found a match. "Vivian was a self-taught software engineer with a passion for the industry we were in."

Her personality profile matched up to Hannah's, and while Vivian wasn't able to go all-in without a salary, they were able to work out a payment and equity structure that facilitated her becoming a partner.

Hannah feels lucky to have found Vivian, and she recognizes the role of assessments in creating that luck. "I feel like I dodged a bullet. If I hadn't taken the personality test and hadn't taken the time to analyze what I brought to the table and what I needed someone else to bring, I think I would have missed out on three incredible assets that bolstered our rate of success."

Do the assessments I've detailed above, and you can find your ideal match too. It's all in the process.

Visit www.thecofoundershub.com for everything you need to do a deep dive into what makes you, you.

CHAPTER 3

Time for the Pitch

Before I start this chapter I want to ask you something: Did you take the time to do the assessments mentioned in the previous chapter and ponder the results? If not, please don't read ahead. Why? Because the insights you will glean from the assessments will change the lens through which you read the words of the following chapters.

If you are like me, maybe you love to gobble up information and have been known to fail to actually put it into action. If you are serious about being an entrepreneur and a cofounder you need to put this information into practice. Take the minutes you are giving yourself to read this chapter now and use them instead to take the assessments (you can find them at www.thecofoundershub.com), ponder the results, and/or make an actionable list that will solidify your execution plan going forward.

You have everything to gain and nothing to lose, so I give you permission to put the book down/turn the audiobook off and start getting to know yourself. I promise you will be glad you did it.

I now return you to the regularly scheduled program.

"He was actually a pie-in-the-sky business partner," Rodrick explains to me when I ask him about how he started his cofounder relationship. His surveying business had grown to the point that new opportunities were sprouting up on a regular basis. "Not only were the possibilities enticing, but, as a company, we finally had the cash flow and the capital to be able to take advantage of them."

The only thing missing? A partner who could help him bring the opportunities to fruition. And finding the perfect candidate was going to take a miracle.

But Rodrick had been considering the prospect of bringing on a partner for quite a while. "While we were in the trenches growing and expanding the company, there wasn't time to make that idea a reality." Eventually, the business began to stabilize, and routine and structure became more the norm. Rodrick took this moment of calm to revisit the idea of finding someone to help him take the business to the next level.

His first thought was to turn to the leaders who worked within the company. "I had a handful of incredible leaders in our business who would all be great candidates for joining as partners." Aware of the risks associated with proposing a partnership and then having it fall through, Rodrick decided to put together a covert plan to assess who would be effective, interested, and willing to step up to the challenge.

"The first thing I did was determine who might be irreplaceable in their current role within the company." Rodrick didn't want to risk upturning a key division by leaving the role vacant and in need of a replacement. "Once my assessment was completed, I determined that one of my key executives who I was considering was too integrated into his position. Moving him out of his role would definitely have been very detrimental to the company." That left four more possible candidates.

"The second exercise I did was to take a look in the mirror." Rodrick sat down and took some time to determine where he fell short as a leader and where he needed a counterbalance when considering a partner. He also looked at many of the pain points in his business and examined whether he himself had played a role in their occurrences. "I saw that I am big on control and struggle with delegation. I have a tendency to micromanage, and looking back, it may have limited the growth of my business; it definitely added additional stress."

Rodrick determined that his partner needed to be strong enough to hold him to task when he was squeezing too tight on control and who also instilled in him confidence that they were capable of taking on tasks effectively. When he looked at his leadership team, he felt that would exclude two more of the total five he was considering.

Finally, Rodrick looked to the future. By examining the company's opportunities, he tried to determine what skills, knowledge, and expertise would be needed to bring them to fruition. "I determined a few factors. The opportunities were innovative and therefore needed someone comfortable in the unknown. Two, they needed to be executed quickly and efficiently, requiring someone committed both mentally and physically to doing whatever it takes. Three, the ideas were uncharted but had potentially big upsides." Rodrick wanted someone who would be open to a lower pay-to-responsibilities ratio in exchange for equity and a bigger chunk of the upside. With these three factors in mind, Rodrick determined that no one in his organization was partnership material.

"It was a bit disheartening, I have to admit. I realized I would either need to search outside the organization or drop the idea of a partner altogether." While the idea of heading out into the world to find that perfect business partner wasn't appealing, one person in particular came to mind: Fernand. He was a young executive at another firm who led a major project that was awarded to him by Rodrick's company. "He impressed me from the first day we met and continued to do so throughout the life of the project." Rodrick felt that Fernand had the skills, makeup, and hunger he was looking for in a partner.

But he didn't think Fernand would be interested because, from what Rodrick could see, Fernand had been with his current company since its early stages and seemed happy there. "He actually already had experience taking a division and building it from the ground up."

Additionally, the company Fernand worked for was notorious for paying their executives exorbitant salaries and bonuses. "I knew I wouldn't be able to compete with that. I was going to be asking him to take a pay cut and a risk." To make matters even more challenging, Rodrick knew Fernand's wife was pregnant with their first child. The deck was stacked against him. Rodrick believed the likelihood that Fernand would want to take on more responsibility was little to none.

Even so, Rodrick couldn't get Fernand out of his head. He decided the worst-case scenario was Fernand would just tell him no. "I knew that because I was going to be asking him to leave a well-paying, secure job with what I was sure would have a lot of growth potential, I'd better have a strong argument for him to leave it all behind."

So Rodrick set out to design the perfect campaign to entice Fernand to join him.

Arming Yourself

If you have completed the homework from the previous chapter, you have a strong understanding about yourself and a good idea of what you need to look for in your potential partner or partners. That was key to Rodrick's journey, and it will be the key to yours too. You must know what you're working with and what you're seeking before you post your HELP WANTED sign. Avoiding that work is how star-crossed partnerships form, break, and destroy the lives of everyone involved.

Now it's time to create a package that outlines the opportunity you're proposing. And you've got to do it in a way that is informative enough to build interest and clear enough to create excitement in the right person.

Sound like a tall order? Let me show you how to do it. You'll need the following five pieces.

Research

Before you open your mouth to talk to anyone about your idea, do some research. It doesn't have to be extensive, but you need to know your market, your competitors, and any potential pitfalls in the industry.

Your first real meeting about the opportunity should be no different than what you would demonstrate to a potential investor or funder. Have you seen *The Dragon's Den* or *The Shark Tank* on television? These are TV shows where people with great ideas pitch to investors in the hope of accessing capital. While much more due diligence occurs after the show has ended, they need to enter the pitch with enough information to be able to answer basic questions. Having to say "I don't know" to simple questions related to your idea makes investing in you look like a serious risk.

Use those shows as a template for how to prepare for your first discussion with your potential cofounder. Be prepared to answer questions about possible revenue streams, statistics about market size, and any information that demonstrates you know the industry. Be compelling with your pitch, but also stay direct and to the point with your info. Know your stuff so you can inspire confidence in your potential partner. You can both tackle the heavy research together after they indicate interest.

NDA or Confidentiality Agreement

For all intents and purposes, nondisclosure agreements are more of a symbolic agreement than an enforceable contract. Enforcing a NDA is notoriously difficult. But using one creates mental weight in the conversation and communicates that the discussion is meant to be private. It also sets the tone that the discussion needs to be taken seriously. Signing an NDA makes potential cofounders say, "Wow, you mean business, and this idea is valuable enough to protect."

Are you really concerned that people will steal your idea? I wouldn't be. On the whole, we creative types overestimate other people's ambition. If your idea is really good, it's going to take work, and putting in work is hard for most people to do. The risk and sacrifice to start a business scares off a majority of the population; adding on top of that the unique requirements to successfully execute your idea makes the pool even smaller. So, with that in mind, don't let your fear stop you from reaching out. You won't be unveiling too much about the opportunity during initial contact anyway, so overexposure is not likely going to be an issue.

That said, the few instances that a NDA could be applicable is when you are approaching someone currently working in competition with your idea, or if they're in a position to immediately implement it. This contract could provide enough of a deterrent to potential competitors seeking an edge in their business. Additionally, put an NDA in place if someone is a social media influencer or in the media in any way. You want to make sure they do not report or unveil your venture before you are ready.

The Dream

Now you're ready to share your idea, and I suggest you start by sharing the dream. When you reach out to a potential partner, the first goal should be to help someone feel the potential. Don't overwhelm them and bombard them with every detail of your world domination plan. Leave behind the graphs and spreadsheets you've been toiling over for months, and avoid overloading them with data.

Start with a story. Grab their attention. Walk them through how you discovered the pain point and your journey coming up with a solution. Let them have insight into all your concerns and misgivings, but also allow them to see the scope of the possibilities. Pepper your conversation with facts and figures, but don't be afraid to dabble in the "pie in the sky." Your goal in the initial interaction is to communicate your excitement and see if they pick it up.

Elevator Pitch

Sometimes, while on the search for a partner, you come across a potential candidate when you least expect it. You need to be ready to capture the moment whether it's on a long commute home on transit or in the short amount of time it takes to ride in an elevator. Anyone can share their idea without time constraints; it's in a time crunch that you need to be ready. If you're out to woo potential business partners, you need to be able to grab their attention quickly and boil the whole idea down to a few sentences.

That means you need to develop a quick thirty- to sixty-second explanation about your business concept. Memorize this elevator pitch so you're always ready to go. Use it as an intro to gauge initial interest. Think of it as throwing your line into a full pond: if there are no quick bites, your bait isn't interesting to that fish. It's also a great tool for prospecting strangers or acquaintances in short order . If they show interest, you can ask for their contact info to discuss the details at a later date. The best news is that the pitch can also be used to open doors of opportunity wherever you are: for example, to gauge the interest of a would-be customer, investor, or employee.

Keep in mind that a good elevator pitch is more difficult to create than you might think. It needs to clearly communicate the opportunity in a way that grabs the attention of the listener and entices them to seek out more information. Take your time in writing it. And run each iteration by trusted folks who can give you honest feedback.

Self/Cofounder Assessment Summary

In the last chapter, you completed the work to determine what kind of partner you need. Now it's time to get a summary of all the factors on that list you must have and would like to have. This will help you weed through people as you carry out your search.

Do not compromise on this list. You spent a lot of time looking inward at what you do or do not bring to the table and what your partner needs to contribute. It isn't helpful if you push it all aside in a moment of hurriedness or overt optimism. You won't be doing yourself or your potential cofounder any favors if you ignore what's best for the business and build a relationship that's doomed from the start. The best of intentions can lead you both to disaster.

That said, be willing to hear every person out even if they don't fit what you are initially looking for. It might be that you didn't even think of the key elements that someone you speak to is able to offer. That might lead you to revise your list on the spot and build an even better picture of what's needed. And no one says you can only have a single cofounder. You might find a dream candidate who opens up the potential for enough growth that you can split the profits multiple ways and still corner your market.

What Not to Write

Because some people can err on the side of being over prepared, I'll tell you two documents that you do not need to write or construct. At least, not yet.

Partnership Agreement

We will discuss this contract in Chapter 10, but for now, consider it the final piece for solidifying the partnership. You will not have all the details necessary to draft it early on, so it can wait. If you try to wave a partnership agreement in front of someone in the first couple of meetings, you'll likely add undue pressure and potentially scare them off. Plus, the type of reckless person who would sign a partnership agreement at the first meeting isn't the sort of cofounder you want to do business with.

Equity Split, Compensation, Titles, Roles, et Cetera

There is a mountain of work to do before these things get hashed out. And your initial ideas probably aren't worth writing down until you know what your cofounder will bring to the table. You never know what will change when new people get involved.

In the early conversations, hold off on handing out corner offices and drafting bonus structures. Too much information at this stage would be the same as a first date where one of the people hops in the car and immediately starts discussing wedding plans, home decor ideas, and who will stay home with the kids. Keep the conversation light so you don't come off as reckless or micromanaging.

Learn from Rodrick

Rodrick needed a solid pitch to convince his dream candidate, Fernand, to leave his cushy job to become partners.

To start, Rodrick decided to flesh out the top five opportunities available to his company. Then he put together a business plan for each of them. Two opportunities stood out. In his eyes, both were worth his company's focus and risk. "I put together the numbers that I saw for revenue growth and opportunity, and that determined how I would incentivize Fernand should he choose to partner." Rodrick chose a sixty-forty split, with him taking the lesser share. He even determined that a portion of his own salary would be up for negotiation should the salary he offered Fernand not meet his needed threshold.

Rodrick called Fernand at the end of the day. "I told him that my company was growing at a strong pace and that some opportunities had arisen that I felt he may be interested in exploring." Rodrick also let Fernand know that he did not want him to take on these opportunities in his current role with his current employer. "I didn't want him thinking I was asking his firm to work for us again. I made it clear that this was something totally separate."

To Rodrick's surprise, Fernand agreed to a meeting over brunch that Saturday. He even admitted he was impressed with Rodrick's company and was excited to hear what he had to say.

At their brunch, Rodrick started off sharing about the history of the company, some of the key exciting points about its journey to date, and a brief overview of what his company was looking to achieve. As he did so, he searched Fernand's body language to try and gauge his interest. "He understood the potential upside right away and had a bunch of questions. That put me at ease as it signaled his understanding of what we were trying to do." When Rodrick felt that Fernand was more than just curious, he pulled out the business plan he'd prepared, and they skimmed it together.

By the time brunch was over, it was obvious to Rodrick that there would be a second meeting. "He was already asking where he would fit in within the plan. I knew we needed to set up another time to go even deeper into detail."

To his surprise, Rodrick discovered Fernand was growing tired of his role in his current company. He was spending more and more time managing operations instead of building and creating new opportunities. "For him, the idea of getting back into the creative process, the start-up phase, if you will, was very appealing." It also turned out that the salaries at his company were high, but the bonuses were tied to growth. Since Fernand's division wasn't at that stage any longer, his income wasn't as high as it had been years before. "He understood the risks my opportunities presented, but he was confident in his ability to make them succeed."

After weeks of discussion, Fernand decided to partner with Rodrick. Rodrick smiles at the memory. "I was so happy. And I was so glad I didn't analyze my way out of reaching out to him. I would have missed the perfect candidate to partner with me in the next stage of my business."

Taking the time to put all this info together is a great investment in your future. Using it will not only demonstrate your commitment to and knowledge about your idea; it will also make a great tool for pitching to potential clients, suppliers, investors, and employees.

If you feel like the perfect candidate is out of reach for you right now, think again. I'd bet with the right presentation and clear communication of why someone would be great in the role, you can attract talent you never would have dreamed. Follow the above steps and design your opening presentation so it displays exactly what, together, you can accomplish. That will get your potential cofounder just as excited as you are about bringing the idea to life.

CHAPTER 4

Where to Find Your Cofounder

David met his first partner in university. "Josh was in the same program as me, working toward becoming a CGA." Both men were also taking a business course on the side for additional credits and, because of their similar schedules, often found themselves hanging out during their downtime. "Josh was a lot of fun. Not your typical accountant personality. We got along really well and found we had similar plans for our lives after achieving our degrees."

Both men wanted to start their own businesses and saw how their different specialties could complement one another should they choose to partner up. For David, whose family owned a large multinational company, it was exciting to see the potential each brought to the table. "We came up with a business model that allowed me to utilize my family's connections and network to acquire customers, and Josh was able to contribute the capital requirements necessary to get the business up and running." With a plan hatched, they agreed to open up shop as soon as they completed their degrees.

Their business boomed. Within twelve months, their team grew to fifteen members. "They were exciting times. Josh and I were doing eighteen-hour days sometimes, trying to manage the growth and tackle the challenges that went alongside it." While they had their own specialties within the business, there was a point when David started to take on the tasks that would become the president's role. "Because the connections were more mine and because I had the relationships and a proximity to the customers, I just fell into the role."

It took David some time and adjustment to get comfortable telling Josh what he needed him to do. "It no longer became a sharing of responsibilities, but more of a delegation of roles, with my role being more of a leadership position." It was awkward at first, but David credits Josh's maturity and professionalism for helping them navigate the transition. "Josh was actually the one who called it out." He asked David one afternoon if he was comfortable with the responsibility he had slipped into and whether now was the time for them to formalize it with titles. It was this move that solidified how their working relationship would continue over the next ten years together.

When the market began to demonstrate a possible disruption, both Josh and David sat down to decide how they wanted to proceed. "We had a strong business with good growth potential, but neither of us wanted to undertake the work to bring the business to the next level." The pair approached a firm to shop their company to potential buyers. Within months, two other companies brought acceptable offers. "We took the one that required the least amount of management post-sale, and we closed that chapter of our lives."

For David, the sale was bittersweet because he enjoyed working with Josh on a daily basis. "We never got tired of our work or each other. We both came to work every day excited for what could unfold and ready for challenges."

David wasn't sure he would ever work with another partner again. But three years later, he got an unexpected answer.

No, Seriously . . . Where to Actually Find Your Cofounder

You've decided partnership is for you. Great! Now it's time to seek out the person you want to take the journey with you. If you have already found someone, even better! But for those who haven't, it's time to start looking. This chapter will guide you through all the places you can find a cofounder. And even if you have someone in mind, it doesn't hurt to run through the list just in case your current option doesn't pan out.

The Great Pool of Candidates

The following list isn't exhaustive by any means, but it should give you plenty of ideas for where to find potential cofounders. I suggest you make a list of potential candidates from each category as a starting point. That will give you a long list of people to consider.

Friends and Family

Not knowing where to find a business partner is a significant barrier to starting a business for many entrepreneurs. According to research from Octopus Group in the UK, one in three entrepreneurs (34 percent) wouldn't know where to look for a cofounder while 29 percent would start by looking through family and friends.

Many people say you should never do business with your close inner circle. They also say you should never mix business and pleasure. Obviously, few heed this warning because statistically, the vast majority of people start a business with someone from a preexisting relationship. There are many reasons for this.

First, if you know the person, you probably have a long-standing, positive relationship (hopefully). The elements of likability and tolerability cannot be underestimated.

Second, it's the devil-you-know phenomenon. Besides knowing the positive traits of a person you've been friends or family with for years, you are also likely aware of at least some of their quirks and idiosyncrasies. You may know that they are controlling or have a lack of attention to detail, but you still manage to make the relationship work. Oftentimes, knowing the problems in advance is half the battle and can make working together more manageable.

And third, we often hang around people and circles who are like minded and similar to ourselves. Therefore, you and your friend were probably brought together by a common interest or ideology that would enable a good working relationship.

My advice when it comes to friends and family: look at the situation with an understanding that the business may not work out, and the chances of you maintaining a positive relationship after dissolving a business are slim. Sixty-five percent of business partnerships end in failure, and 95 percent of those failures end the relationship completely. Take a look at the fallout of such a circumstance and determine if the reward is worth the risk of losing the relationship with your loved one.

Business Colleagues

We often spend more time with our coworkers than we do our family and friends. This gives us an excellent opportunity to get to know these people and to see them in both working and personal environments. On a professional level, we have a front row seat to determine their work ethic, investigate how they think, and see their skills in action. On a personal level, the water cooler, lunchroom, and office chit chat enable us to establish the likability factor, saving time and de-risking our selection process.

One word of caution: do not disrespect the company you or they are working for by discussing your opportunity during business hours or while at the place you do business. Not only is it unfair to the employer paying for you to be focused on your tasks, but it is also not professional. Since you cannot know the outcome of your conversation, you do not want to risk your or their employment by misusing company time.

Social Media

I probably don't need to go into detail why today's social media outlets are great places to find a cofounder. But for those who need a refresher, here are a few options.

LinkedIn is the professional social media. It allows individuals to showcase their careers, education, skills, hobbies, accolades—anything related to their business lives. Check out groups in industries like the one you are venturing into, join, and get involved. Some groups will let you post that you are seeking a business partner, making it a great way to advertise and connect. "Connections" allows you to find people within six degrees of separation, and, should it be a first or second connection, you can seek out a personal reference, creating an even greater chance that you will get a response or even a meeting. Use your LinkedIn newsfeed to post information about what you are doing and to share that you are seeking a partner.

Facebook, TikTok, Twitter, Instagram, and Snapchat are also options. Depending on your business, all of these are great ways to search for a cofounder. Opening a restaurant? Search out people who cook or eat the kind of food you are looking to offer. Look at fan pages of those who are in your space and privately message them that you have an opportunity they may be interested in. Facebook allows you to search by occupation, location, and a plethora of other factors that could help you nail down a particular requirement you are seeking. Hashtags on all platforms can expose your opportunity quickly to others who may be searching for a partner.

Clarity and Quora

Need an expert? These sites both allow people to answer questions on any topic. You will find access to extremely knowledgeable people on any given subject. Use this platform as a place to message those who seem to understand your space and who have the expertise you are looking for. Additionally, you may want to contribute to the site in order to showcase your own knowledge for reference later on.

Meetups

There is a great saying: "Your network is your net worth." Attending meetups and events within your industry is an excellent way to meet people and seek out potential cofounders or individuals who may know potential cofounders. In this day and age, there is no excuse not to build a network.

One great website to check out for this form of networking is Meetup. com. You can find people gathering to discuss just about any topic in homes, bars, offices, or conference rooms around the globe. These meetups are often attended by like-minded individuals meeting up informally to discuss ideas or debate topics. It's a great way to get to know people and tap into a network.

The one thing you need to be intentional about is being proactively engaging and communicating your message. Make sure you have a goal of telling X number of people about what you are looking for and taking the contact information for any intros. Events and meetups are great, but they can be big time wasters if you are not proactive and focused on achieving your outcome.

Conferences and Events

Conferences open you up to a world of people seeking training, connections, and opportunities within an industry that matches your business. Sign up for the meet and greets, information seminars, and extra events where you can pre screen candidates based on the information found conveniently on their name tags or conference passes.

However, like meetups, you need to be extremely proactive and not afraid to start conversations. People are unlikely to come up to you and ask to be your cofounder, so you will need to put your timidity aside and boldly engage with the other attendees. Otherwise, you will waste time and money, two resources that are precious at this stage of the game.

In the world of social distancing and the new normal of videoconferencing, engaging in online conferences makes meeting others even simpler as the net you can cast is even broader.

Cofounder Groups

With the growth of tech and the ease with which everyone can get into business, more and more people are looking to become entrepreneurs. Many realize they are only a portion of a whole and want to find one or more people to complete the team. That has given rise to many organizations that focus on introducing people based on skill and ideas.

These organizations often function similarly to dating sites, apps, and events, where people seeking a business partner get matched with those seeking their individual talents and capital. A Google search for "cofounder finder" will provide a great starting point. Check out www.thecofoundershub.com for access to a pool of candidates seeking partnerships.

VCs/Lawyers/Accountants

The firms in these industries are often connected to entrepreneurs and businesspeople. They likely have an ear to the ground on where the entrepreneurs are, or, at the very least, they will likely know people who know someone. Cold calls may not yield the best results as these people will not want to risk their relationship with their clients on a request from a stranger. Reach out to your own lawyers, accountants, and VCs; leverage your existing relationship; and then reach out to friends and family who can do the same while vouching for your character and legitimacy.

Start-up Advisers

These are people who provide advice to entrepreneurs in the early start-up stage. Whether through an incubator or business assistance organization, these folks meet entrepreneurs regularly and could likely provide an introduction to a potential partner or keep an ear to the ground should one show up. Additionally, if the adviser themselves seem excited about the opportunity, you may want to see if they would be open to exploring a greater involvement. Oftentimes, these folks are seasoned entrepreneurs themselves, and the pull of taking a great business idea into reality could be a magnet they cannot resist.

Job Sites

Look over the résumés of people seeking employment in your field or industry. You may find someone with the chops to take the plunge as a business owner. What better way to get a snapshot of people's skills, experience, interests, and goals in a few short clicks? Just be clear when you speak to them that you are looking for a business partner, not an employee. This will allow you to weed out those not interested in entrepreneurship or who are not in the financial position to get involved. That said, it might also serve you to save the résumés of stellar candidates for future employee openings in your business.

Current or Previous Employees

You may be lucky enough to have an employee who works in a way that would make an outsider think they're already a co-owner. These people take their roles within the organization very seriously and often go above and beyond what most others do in the same role. They are dedicated, dependable, and a trusted team member day in and day out. These people could very well step into an ownership position as they will bring with them intimate knowledge of your business.

For example, if the employee works in your dental office and your new venture is the creation of an alternative to dentures, their background and experience may be the perfect fit. But beware: moving the wrong employee from team member to owner could be a disaster. Not only will you have to deal with the bad fit as a partner, but you may also lose a great employee. Weigh the decision with care.

Referrals

When it comes to asking for referrals, be bold. Let everyone know you are looking for a business partner. You never know who someone knows. I find people on the whole are more than happy to at least give the idea a quick thought. A referral is also a great method of weeding out duds as many are hesitant to volunteer someone if their own reputation is on the line.

School/University/Classes

Pull out that yearbook, that email list, that sign-up sheet, whatever you've got with contacts you used to know. Reach out to those with whom you shared a class or another connection. Even if you haven't kept in touch, you have a warm intro and a common interest with which to start a conversation.

Competitors (And Their Employees)

There are a couple of reasons you may want to reach out to your potential competitors and their team.

Are your competitors struggling? Could you bring them value with your fresh ideas, skills, and capital in exchange for a foundation that they have already built? Maybe an acquisition is the best kick-start to your business. Imagine joining forces with your rival to form the ultimate company.

Even if they're not struggling, they may be seeking a partner to grow. Many entrepreneurs get their businesses off the ground, then realize they need help. Your call may be just what that founder was waiting for.

Your competitors' employees know your space and can jump into action in ways someone outside it cannot. They will likely have their own valuable insights into what your business should offer. Just know this is risky ground that will likely not be met with enthusiasm from your competitor. You may make an angry enemy this way, someone who may cut their prices and lose profits just to see you suffer.

It goes without saying that when speaking with competitors, you should keep the details of your business under your hat. There's a chance, if your competitor is smart, that they will meet with you just to see what the new kid on the block is planning. They may try and find out what unique angle you want to bring to market and then beat you to it. That means stealing your ideas for themselves. Don't be paranoid, but just keep this possibility in the back of your mind. If you choose to meet with them and go ahead with joining, this is the time to require a signed non-disclosure agreement on both sides.

Potential Customers

Connecting with potential customers is always smart. Not only is it a great way to feel out the market, but your idea may also resonate with someone who understands the value your business could bring. At the very least, you will garner great market knowledge or even a future purchase order.

Professionals Who Know the Field

Pretend you are going to start an online fashion store. It may be worth talking to all those who know the fashion industry. For example, suppliers. These folks would know what kind of product you need and what suppliers would look for in a distributor. If they see you with a great idea, there may be a reason to form a strategic partnership.

Bloggers, marketers, and influencers who write about your industry, the companies within it, or the players involved may be great resources for finding a potential partner. Not only will they have their ear to the ground on the latest and greatest actors, but they may also be tired of writing about the players and want to become one themselves.

Investors

Investors are typically happy to stay behind the scenes offering financial support. But an investor can know a good idea when they see it and may want to try their hand at running the company instead of funding it. Look for investors who focus on your industry. If they are not interested, don't be afraid to ask for referrals.

Learn from Josh

A couple of years after selling his business with Josh, David packed up his wife and two kids and moved to a sunnier location. "I wanted to try my hand at another business, and I came across one with great potential to become a franchise. I'd really enjoyed having a partner, and I knew I wasn't interested in doing another business alone." So once he and his family settled in, he got to work finding a cofounder.

First, David reached out to his college fraternity to see if anyone was interested in going into business. He figured since he found his previous partner at university, he might find his second there too. When nothing came to fruition, David reached out to a handful of other organizations he belonged to. "I sent out an email sharing a brief description of my business idea, the skills I was looking for in a partner, and, should they not be interested themselves, a [request for a] connection to anyone who they thought may be interested." He expected to receive some good potential candidates, but again, nothing came of it.

When the organizations didn't deliver anyone, he tried ex-colleagues, customers, and employees. David even tried a few parents he met at his kids' sports events. "I had a good idea of what I was looking for, so I knew I had to cast a big net to find that one person."

Despite his positive approach, "I was actually a bit surprised how long it took to find the right partner." So when Jillian came into the picture, David was thrilled. Jillian was the wife of a customer he had in his previous company and had all the skills he was looking for. "I met with her on three occasions, and we totally hit it off, with her checking most of the boxes I needed." The only problem was she lived two states away and was too entrenched in her lifestyle to move. "We discussed a long-distance partnership and even identified a few ways [in] which the second location could be an asset."

In the end, David decided he wanted a partner to work alongside him on a daily basis. "I had to let her know that I didn't see it working, hoping that I wasn't making a huge mistake."

Luckily, his concern didn't last long. He received a call from a friend who told him about Jake, a business colleague who had just asked if he knew of any opportunities in David's state. The two connected, and once again, David felt he'd found someone who checked most of the boxes he was looking to fill. Was it luck? Maybe, he admits. "That said, I put out a lot of feelers into my network." He figured it would only be a matter of time before there started to be a return on his persistence.

Jake joined the business eight months after David started it, and together, they have grown the company and launched their first franchise. "I didn't think it would happen twice, but in both my businesses, I have found both a partner and a friend."

David has drawn two lessons from his partnerships. With Josh, David says he is extremely happy he went into business with a friend. "I know people say you should never do it, but I think there is nothing better than being able to build a company with someone you have a history with." However, the one thing David feels entrepreneurs should prepare for is the eventuality that one of the partners will need to rise to become the leader of the company. "When this happens, the friends need to be mature and professional enough to either take orders or lead."

From his second venture with Jake, David advises, "Don't compromise to get the right partner." He acknowledges that finding a partner from scratch can feel daunting and discouraging at times. "You will need to know exactly what you are looking for and know your nonnegotiables." But when you do find them, "Don't be greedy. Do whatever it takes to get them on board because it will be worth it in the long run."

When you're ready and find the right person in any of the areas we discussed, be bold. You never know who is looking for an opportunity or who can connect you to someone else who is.

While searching, this is a great time to practice expressing your confidence in your idea and ability to undertake it. And stay open to working with people who have more money or experience than you do. Don't be intimidated by someone who you think would be a great partner. Those who look too busy, too wealthy, or too experienced are successful for a reason. Go-getters are always looking for the next great thing.

CHAPTER 5

PIKE

One of my favorite cofounding stories comes from the tech start-up crew of Meg, Tyler, and Ravi, who have worked together for eight years. Meg laughed when I asked her how they all met. "I'm excited to talk about this as it's a part of our business that I don't get asked about very often. It's actually a really crazy story. I don't think many people could say that they barely knew the people they started a business with."

Meg first met Tyler while taking on an entrepreneurship program in college when she was working to get her MBA. "I took part in an incubator competition, which paired teams up to try and launch a business." Meg joined up with two other students, and they went to work to determine the viability of their idea. Tyler was part of one of the other twenty teams competing in the program. "We never really worked together, but over the months in that program, I did notice when I would go in on the weekends to do some work, he was one of only a few who I would also see working there. Looking back, it was this memory that probably left the impression that this guy was very able to commit."

At the end of the competition, Meg's team and Tyler's team tied for first place. "Basically, after the program, we went our separate ways, never expecting to see each other again."

Destiny had other plans.

During the incubator competition, Meg and her partners went a long way toward making their idea a reality. "As we were building the business, it became more and more feasible that it could actually be a viable venture." This was why Meg was surprised to discover that when the program was complete, her partners didn't want to carry on. "I was actually quite hurt. I'm actually still a little bitter about it to this day."

Meg decided that it was too good an idea to waste, so she packed her bags, flew across the country, moved in with her parents, and decided to make a go of it on her own. "I had had a cushy job with a big firm prior to getting an MBA, and they wanted me back, but I knew I wanted to give entrepreneurship a try."

Three months later, Meg was surprised to hear from Tyler. "He called me out of the blue and asked me if I was still interested in finding a partner to do a business with." Tyler had stumbled onto an idea that he was working on after the business he and his team had started, which failed. "I thought the idea was interesting," Meg recalls with a laugh, "but I didn't really take him seriously." Tyler lived twenty-one hours away by plane. The possibility of them doing something together seemed unlikely.

They spoke about the business over two telephone calls. Then Tyler asked if she was serious enough to get started together. "I told him, 'If you jump on a plane and move here with me, I'll build the business with you.'" He agreed and let her know he would be there in a week's time.

Meg recalls hanging up and wondering if Tyler was really serious. "I remember talking to my brother and telling him, 'So, I think this guy I barely know is going to move here to start a business that we have only spoken about twice.'" Her brother told her not to go through with it, thinking the whole thing sounded a bit sketchy. But Meg figured if Tyler showed up, he was definitely demonstrating seriousness about the plan. So she figured it would be a sign to give it a go.

A week later, Tyler showed up with a snowboard bag and suitcase and moved in with Meg and her parents. "Yep," Meg laughs, "probably the ultimate start-up beginning." It was this big move, however, that gave Meg the confidence to proceed with the venture. "There was no denying Tyler was serious, and the fact that I moved him in with my family likely showed him I was serious too."

What Meg didn't realize was that, by partnering with Tyler, she was also going to be introduced to Ravi, a software engineer from India. Ravi had worked with Tyler on his previous business, and Tyler was impressed with his work ethic. "When it came time to build our software, Tyler recommended we reach out to Ravi to handle all the technology." Once again, sacrifice and work ethic proved to Meg that she had another incredible partner at the table. "For one year, Ravi worked on our business from India but during our time zone." This meant he worked through the night and slept during the day.

After a year had gone by and the platform launched, Meg and Tyler offered Ravi a partnership. "We asked him to move to our country and build the business with us, together." When Ravi accepted their offer, once again, Meg was left wondering if a business partner would actually show up. Even on the day of his scheduled arrival when she and Tyler hopped in a minivan and headed for the airport, Meg wondered, "Is this guy really going to make an appearance?"

Look for PIKE

Determining the likelihood that someone will make a great entrepreneur is difficult. That said, I believe there are a few factors that contribute to the success of a business and a partnership. These are passion, interest, knowledge, and excitement (PIKE). Each of these provides "stickiness" to a venture as they speak to the core of a person. They give work significance, something I think is just as valuable as wealth and freedom.

The only issue with these four factors is that they are difficult to measure. There is no test or questionnaire, certificate or diploma, or anything that can truly determine or predict whether or not a person has them. The biggest problem is that many people can go through the motions and put up a convincing argument that they are interested in your venture when, in reality, they are not.

Your mission will be to determine whether or not potential cofounders possess these four factors and to what degree. Backed with the assurance that they are passionate, excited, interested, and knowledgeable about the idea, you will be able to move forward confidently toward locking in a partnership.

Let's take a closer look at the big four. At first glance, some of them appear to be similar, but I assure you they differ in key ways. I'll explain each in depth to help you grasp the bigger picture of what each factor looks like so it will be easier to identify it in your potential partner.

Ideally, your partner has all four. In reality, you'll want to find someone who demonstrates at least two or three of the factors. The presence of only one or none indicates they lack what it takes to survive the rocky road of entrepreneurship.

Passion

Synonyms: *fervor, hankering, glorification, thirst, zeal, obsession, devotion.*

You can measure a person's passion by what they are willing to endure and how far they will go to pursue their goal. The old saying "You can lead a horse to water, but you can't make him drink" applies here. This is true when it comes to building a business because you cannot force your cofounder to "want" to work on the business.

The road to success in entrepreneurship is a grind much of the time, and if you or your cofounder are not passionate about what you are doing, you may run out of steam. Your team might be able to go through the motions, but the path will be difficult. It's possible to find someone who has everything you could want in a partner—the skills, the knowledge, and the experience—but if they are not passionate about what you are doing, it will be a tough go.

Someone with passion is obsessed. They are utterly devoted to their goals and have a zeal that can turn anyone to their side. They put the idea or object on a pedestal, and it becomes obvious to everyone within minutes of meeting them that this thing is valuable to them. Hopefully, you and your partner will both hold this zeal for your business as it is jet fuel for an entrepreneur.

Passion, in an entrepreneurial sense, can take many forms. Take the time to learn what it is that both you and your partner are passionate about.

I have come to discover that there are four ways of being passionate about what you do. Let's go through each.

Passion for the Product (Or Service)

The most common form of passion comes from the love of the goods or service that you provide. This would be someone like a fashion designer who gets into business because they have a passion for designing clothes. It may also be the chef who gets joy from serving the dishes they create, the piano teacher who lives and breathes music, or the inventor who creates a product to solve a major challenge. Whatever it is, having a passion for the service or good will often keep you motivated and excited when the peripheral business tasks get more and more numerous. A person with passion for a certain product or service is often easy to spot as they surround themselves with it and build their life around it.

The Entrepreneur Journey

I built data-driven businesses in the credit reporting and identity space. I certainly did not have a passion for credit files and AML/KYC verification. What I did have was a passion for taking an idea and bringing it to fruition. The goods and services were just the vehicle I used to allow myself to do what excited me, which was starting companies. I believed that what I was selling was valuable and could improve lives and businesses, but what I really enjoyed was figuring out the ways to get others to believe that and building products to make it all possible. The passionate entrepreneur finds a cofounder by igniting their potential partner with the possibilities and journey of getting there and finding the excitement in the day to day of building a company.

The Big Picture

These people see a way to make a difference and they don't necessarily need to be enthralled with their product or service. What they are excited about is the way their company will improve the lives of people, leading them to work for the sake of a worthwhile goal. Many business partners have found common ground on building a company for this reason and in doing so are able to make the difficult times seem less painful in light of the significance achieved at the end of their journey.

The Opportunist

This is that person who sees a great opportunity with a time crunch and wants to run with it while the iron is hot. They know that time is of the essence, and the thrill of being first to market with a new or enhanced idea is what drives them. This person has a strong end goal in mind and likely sees the path to get there. They are often in it to take advantage of a trend or a window of opportunity and know that it's likely to be a quick cash out should they manage to make it work. Their passion is contagious to anyone who loves the adrenaline that comes from hustling and gambling on the viability of their theories.

Passion Is Recognizable

Here are six ways to gauge someone's passion level:

1. Are they up to date in their field? Is that chef cooking food from the '90s or dishes that could be highlighted in this month's issue of *Savour*?

2. Listen to them explain why they want to solve this problem. A person passionate about something will be able to share multiple reasons and usually in much detail, demonstrating the thought that they have put into the topic.

3. Have them speak to how this problem you are going to solve has popped up as relevant in their lives. Previous work or personal experience with the issue, a connection to a close friend or relative who has run into the problem, classes they have taken, hobbies they have embarked on, applicable topics they have written about; there are a myriad of ways to demonstrate when opportunity and preparedness come together.

4. Are factors such as money and time commitment major obstacles, or are they taken as a necessary price to pay? In other words, is the focus on the business or on them?

5. Don't mistake energy for passion. Someone who is passionate about something will get things done even if they don't do them with excitement and boisterous actions. Passion can be meticulous, studious, focused, intentional, questioning, serious, and tenacious. It isn't always in your face.

6. Passion is hands on. It's ready to go. It's itching to delve deep and get its hands dirty. Passion won't leave a ball in your court or disappear for days without returning your call.

Interest

Synonyms: *absorption, attraction, diligence, precaution, curiosity, restlessness*.

Where excitement is emotional, interest is intellectual. Interest is when the rational brain overrides the emotional brain and says, "This idea makes sense from an analytical side and may be worth looking into." Interest without excitement will not be enough as it doesn't sustain through turbulent times. You can think something is a good idea but not be inspired (excited) to take the arduous journey to bring it to fruition. But interest is key because it means your cofounder conceptually enjoys the industry you'll be working in.

You can tell someone is interested when they ask the right questions, understand the answers you give, and keep coming back for more. Even a sense of precaution is a good sign. If they didn't care, they would dismiss the opportunity and not linger in a state of nonconfidence. If they keep coming back without you chasing them, they're probably interested.

Knowledge

Synonyms: *insight, familiarity, recognition, ability, awareness, intelligence*.

Knowledge isn't just about finding someone who knows your space, your industry, or the skills required, although those are desirable traits to look for. Knowledge can also be the ability to grasp what you are saying and comprehend your message. It's when someone tells you something and, thinking you didn't understand, asks you to repeat it back to them. They're gauging whether you are tracking together and have a clear understanding of the vision they are setting forth.

This can happen when you reach out to someone who you believe to be a great potential partner even though they have had nothing to do with the industry. If their comments are insightful, intelligent, and demonstrate comprehension, then you know that the knowledge is there.

A word of caution: do not just presume that an expert in your field has all the tools to take on the venture. Knowledge without any of the other three is hollow information.

Excitement

Synonyms: e*motion, energy, enthusiasm, enjoyment, eagerness.*

Excitement is important because it signals that someone "gets it". Half the battle to get people on board with your business in any capacity is reaching the point at which you see their eyes light up with enthusiastic anticipation and understanding. Excitement is the fuel that keeps someone motivated when the challenges and obstacles rear their ugly heads. An excited person isn't bored, finds joy in the prospect, and is eager to get going in some form. It demonstrates that you're onto something and that their getting involved could be a strong possibility.

The issue with excitement, however, is that it isn't durable. Excitement can be fickle and can wither in a moment. So while it does acknowledge a potential working opportunity, on its own, it isn't a good predictor or a good foundation to build a strong partnership on. If a potential partner seems excited, that may falsely convince an entrepreneur to bring them in when in reality they only want to cheer from the sidelines.

More Signs Your Potential Cofounder Is "In"

There are other ways by which to gauge a potential partner's readiness.

They see a challenge as exciting, not a major obstacle. When an obstacle shows itself, they aren't so quick to throw in the towel but immediately begin to brainstorm on the work-around.

You get emails, texts, and phone calls at two in the morning. When you are passionate about something, it can be difficult to get to sleep or concentrate on anything else.

You have long, positive conversations about what can be. When you believe in something, you see possibility, not challenge. That said, healthy debate about the viability of a business model is essential in avoiding overoptimism. Someone who shares real concerns is demonstrating they are putting the opportunity to great thought.

They have a willingness to put their money where their mouth is. Have they invested any hard-earned cash to test viability? Do they cringe at the idea of testing the waters with their own funds? Money is a very strong sign of someone's commitment.

They're telling family and friends and anyone within two feet about the idea. It's one thing to have an idea baking in your head, it's another to open it up to criticism and skepticism from loved ones. If someone is sharing the opportunity with their inner circle, you can bet they are deeply invested.

Are they up to date? Are they sharing data and details that reflect what is happening in the current environment? Likely this means they are doing their research and getting informed to make a decision.

Are they giving stuff up and showing a willingness to sacrifice? Are they willing to put anything aside to keep the discussion going and investigate the opportunity further?

They're reading, listening, and learning about topics related to your industry.

They're doing small beta tests, tinkering, or trying prototypes.

They're also having conversations with specific individuals to feel things out: e.g., potential customers, suppliers, competition, and anyone else involved in the industry.

All these are great signs that your potential partner is taking the idea seriously. If you are still not sure, I have a few suggestions that will assist in determining whether your potential cofounder is considering the opportunity.

Ask, "What do you want to do as our next steps?" This question leaves a door open should they not be interested and want to let you down easily. They can say, "I want to ponder what you've said, and I'll get back to you." Or they could say, "Time is of the essence; let's get on with it!" By putting the ball in their court, you will get a good idea of where they sit (or bounce) with excitement.

Say to them, "If you come up with anything or have any questions, suggestions, or ideas, please ask or let me know." By doing this, you allow an avenue to discover if the idea is keeping them up at night or forgotten by the time you paid for the coffee.

I'm always coming up with ideas for businesses, and every once in a while, I'll reach out to someone I think would be a great partner for one. By not chasing them after our initial meeting, I'm able to gauge their interest by the interactions we have later. A couple of times, the person never speaks about it again, and it falls to the wayside. But in a couple of other instances, I've received texts late at night with their ideas, emails with their insights, and even calendar invites to meet again. This tells me that they like the idea, want to explore and potentially be part of it. It doesn't mean that they will be the one, but it is a good first indicator.

The more times you meet with someone, the more in depth your meetings should be. If you gauge interest as you go, eventually, you should bring out all the details that you have and go through a deeper discussion about the opportunity. Discuss the positives and negatives, the holes and advantages, the vision and execution. If, after everything about the opportunity has been discussed, they are still excited, it may be time to move on to the next phase. On the other hand, if after the third meeting, they are still dragging their feet, it is likely time to move on.

Learn from Meg

Meg was surprised to see that Ravi did show up. And he's shown up every day since. "Ravi has shown his commitment from day one. It took a year and a half before he could finally bring his wife and child to our country."

This level of demonstrated commitment undergirds the incredible partnership Meg, Tyler, and Ravi share. "I'm so lucky to have found these men to work with. There is no doubt each of us is passionate and willing to do what it takes to make this business succeed." When I asked what role their cofounding partnership has played in the success of their business, Meg smiled. "It's been fundamental. I would say that one can have a great cofounder partnership, and your business could still be a failure, but if you have a bad cofounder partnership, I cannot imagine how you could be successful at all."

Make sure you go into business with someone who's as passionate, interested, knowledgeable, and excited as you are. It will make the journey much more enjoyable for all involved.

CHAPTER 6

Assessing Potential Cofounders

"I love starting businesses," Brit exclaims. "I was one of those classic entrepreneurial kids who undertook every conceivable childhood hustle." From the lemonade stand in her parents' front yard to dog walking, raking leaves, even selling candy to classmates in school, Brit showed the early signs of being an entrepreneur.

Brit's first business was a landscaping company. "I started cutting lawns for a couple of families in my neighborhood. When my parents offered me a truck to grow and expand my current client base, I jumped at the chance." Brit hired a friend who was looking for a job, and it was then that she learned firsthand the ups and downs of having employees. "It was difficult because we were friends, so navigating the line between friend and employer was a challenge." In the back of her mind, she thought her friend could become a partner. But after a few months, she knew that would not be a smart move. "I realized the importance of accountability, adaptability, passion, and a willingness to do whatever it takes." None of her later employees modeled those abilities either. She determined that, should she ever partner with someone, those would be the traits she would seek.

That opportunity came a couple of years later.

Brit maintained her landscape business while she put herself through university. However, when she got her degree, she closed her doors and took a position at a legal firm. "The landscaping business served its purpose as a way to make money on my terms and on my schedule. But it wasn't anything I wanted to do long term." She was also ready for a change of pace and looked forward to applying her newly acquired knowledge by charting her own path within the legal world.

After a couple of years working in a law firm, Brit realized she gravitated toward a role in conflict resolution. "I really enjoyed the strategy and discernment that needed to be applied to determining how to help people in the throes of conflict." She saw a growing need for mediation and began thinking about changing direction to focus on providing this service exclusively. As she contemplated once again turning to entrepreneurship, she knew she wanted to find one or two partners to join her.

She approached a coworker at the firm. "Lauren was smart, decisive, and had many of the same career and life goals that I had," Brit recalls. They'd worked on cases together and found that they not only complemented each other's skill sets but also genuinely enjoyed working together. When Brit shared with Lauren her desire to break away and do her own thing, Lauren jumped at the opportunity.

Within a few months, they'd opened their doors and started accepting clients. Unfortunately, not long after, the first red flag went up within their partnership. "We had agreed each shareholder would loan fifty thousand dollars to get the business up and running." Brit opened the account and deposited her share, but it took almost three months before Lauren put in any funds, and it was only half the amount. She had multiple excuses for the delays, and they seemed feasible, so Brit continued to give her the benefit of the doubt. "We were moving ahead full steam, so I really wasn't focused on the funds. I just wanted to get the business up and running."

Over the following weeks, Brit sensed Lauren pulling away. "Her commitment level just tanked. She began to be very skeptical about our business plan and ability to get profitable quickly." She questioned whether the model would make money and started to drop hints that pulling a wage was very important sooner than later. Brit knew that, in their early discussions, they had both recognized that it would take time to build up enough of a client base to cover expenses and marketing, so the push to start drawing salaries sooner concerned Brit. "She was open with her reasoning, but I started to wonder if something was up that she wasn't telling me."

There was. And Brit would find out just how complicated cofounder partnerships could be.

The Cofounder Assessment

Once you have vetted the passion and excitement of a potential cofounder, there are a few more steps you need to take. Up until now, your effort with potential partners has been similar to sifting through résumés. If you ever had the pleasure (or displeasure) of doing that, you will know that all that glitters isn't always gold. Now is the moment when you assess their strengths and weaknesses, test their skills, determine their personality types, verify their experience, investigate their networks, and take a deep dive into their goals, wants, and needs. This is where you do the hard work of due diligence so that you can lay the groundwork for trust and confidence in your partnership. This is the time to do a cofounder assessment.

This step is as crucial as your own self-assessment. It will become an invaluable tool for your own knowledge and that of your candidate too. Armed with an extensive report on each other, you can determine where you will be complementary, compatible, and potentially conflicted. It will enable you to map and delegate the roles and tasks each will need to undertake in order to make your vision a reality.

At this point, you want to find out as much as you can about your partner. Get them to run through the exact process you just did in the self-assessment. I recommend you utilize my online tools to make it simple. This will be an invaluable opportunity to better understand where you both stand and how to move forward in the most efficient way. Remember, the goal is to build your business to profitability quickly and in the most effective way. The founders at the helm of your ship will make or break this plan.

How do you broach the subject and request proof of their expertise, knowledge, and skill? The best way is to share your own self-assessment report. By exposing your strengths and weaknesses, your abilities and skills, you can communicate what you bring to the table while at the same time setting a precedent for transparency and communication. Hand over your own report, saying, "Look, here's me in a nutshell. The good, the bad, and the ugly. I want you to know where I excel and lack, and if you provide me with the same, we will be able to identify ways to boost our efficiency and get our business up and running sooner than later." I can assure you that a dedicated and committed person will see the intrinsic value of such an honest and open relationship.

But First: A Word about Due Diligence

Have you ever watched a singing competition on TV? It never ceases to amaze me the number of people who honestly believe they are good singers when, in actuality, they can barely carry a tune. Not only that, but many of these people are surrounded by folks equally confident that they have what it takes to be the next big star.

Sadly, this is true in many areas of life, including business. At this stage of the game, taking someone's word at face value is extremely risky. Perspective is everything, and now is not the time to shrug your shoulders and hope for the best. This is the time to be intentional and thorough in your due diligence. If your potential cofounder needs to bring something tangible to the table, it's wise to ensure they really can deliver.

The points below may appear to be overkill. They're not. Trust is a huge factor in a strong partnership. This early stage in your partnership is where you lay the foundation for that trust, and you can choose to bestow it blindly or with verified facts. Many cofounders have a history that carried them alongside their partners, so confirming validity is easy. Others may have only just met or never merged worlds, and therefore knowledge of someone's accomplishments may be limited. This chapter is especially important for those in the latter category.

Once you have the completed cofounder assessment, below are a few ways to undertake your due diligence.

Verify the Diploma

Did you know that fake diplomas are a $200-million-per-year business? If a degree matters in your field, do your research. Confirm whether or not the school exists. Is it accredited? Visit the Council on Higher Education Accreditation. Contact the school for proof of enrollment and completion of that course.

Seek Out References

Contact people who have seen your potential cofounder work in action or who relied on them in previous projects to help get the job done. Look for what is called "reference-able, provable skill." That is something more than mere opinion or hearsay. This way, you know that someone is not just paying lip service to help a friend out. Ask for concrete examples of the person successfully putting their skills into action.

Do not ask your cofounder to provide a list of contacts. Instead, be specific. Ask for references from the last person that they worked with, whether at a job, on a project, or in a partnership. This way, they cannot cherry-pick who they present. You can also check LinkedIn, peer reports, previous employers, teachers, and others who know them professionally and who are great resources.

Consider Articles and Awards

Did your cofounder brag about an award? Talk to the journalists who wrote about the award or the award presenters. Confirm the award was received and clear up any coloring surrounding its endowment. Double-check that the award was presented for the actual skill or expertise that you are looking to verify.

Ask for a Demo

An up-front and personal demonstration of someone's skill is the most effective way to confirm what they bring to the table.

Let me give you an example of how much a demo can tell you about a person's skill. Imagine you were looking for a partner-chef for your French restaurant. Ask them to make one of the signature dishes they would put on the menu. You will discover whether or not their style matches the level of quality you envision and the type of food you want to provide, how they execute, even whether they understand food cost. Use this tool in any environment. Partnering with a dentist? Get them to clean your teeth. Starting a concrete business? Have them do a demo patch in your backyard. There may be a cost associated with these small projects but it is well worth the investment for the peace-of-mind and confidence it can accomplish.

Set Up an Interview

Do you know little to nothing about a skill your partner is claiming to possess? Set up an interview with someone who is currently or has previously successfully run in the role your new partner will take on. Pick their brains on what questions they would ask or information they would verify. You could even ask them to do an interview for you. The questions a knowledgeable interviewer might ask will provide true insight into whether or not your potential partner is on point or out in left field.

This is a great option for testing technical skills. Having founded four technical companies without a technical background, I can honestly say that it was difficult not being able to assess the skill level of someone who was to be the architect of our products. This may be the case in many industries in which one person has the business acumen but needs someone with technical or trade skill to build the product. The best way to overcome this would be to seek out someone in the field who can attest to their skills. If you know someone you can ask, great. If not, you may need to go out into the world and find someone you can pay to make the determination.

Testing the skill level of a chef, beautician, lawyer—whatever the business may be—needs to be done early on to determine whether or not they can be entrusted with the early building blocks of the business. Making the wrong decision on a person when time and capital are so precious will cost you more in the long run and likely a *lot* more than paying for a couple of skill tests or hours with an expert early on.

Give an Online Test

The age of the internet has made building a business simpler in many ways. A quick Google search should turn up a few online tests for most industries and roles. Research whichever is the most robust and choose that one, even if there is a fee. Don't cut corners now as it won't be easy to ask them to do another test at a later date should you not get the data you need. Additionally, since you are doing the verification, it goes without saying that it falls on you to pay the fee if there is one.

Do a Mini Project

Depending on your business, determine whether there is an opportunity to partition out a small project to see how you work together. This is an excellent way to do a trial run without jumping in full bore. It is here that you can get firsthand experience tackling a challenge, solving issues, negotiating tactics, expending capital, even whether you can have fun in the process. The takeaways from a small project could save you from an ill-fitting partnership or confirm you have found the right one.

Take a Trip Together

I've met more than a few cofounders who decided to take a trip together while debating a partnership. One great outing could be to an out-of-town conference within the industry you are entering. The trip itself allows each of you insight into how well you get along, navigate travel, deal with minor (hopefully not major!) inconveniences, switch on and off from a personal role to a professional one, and interact with your potential competitors, suppliers, and customers. Really, the exposure to the "real" person becomes very possible when one has to cross time zones and be away from their usual creature comforts.

Note Public Recognition

Have they gone public with their skills or expertise? While there is still an opportunity to be dishonest here, when someone shares their accomplishments or abilities in an online or public environment, this demonstrates that they are confident in what they can do or know. Do a Google search of their name and see what comes up, noting what is served up from outside sources and from their own hand.

Now Do Some Detective Work

On top of verifying the assessment of your potential partner, here are a couple of other things you will want to try and ascertain—things that may not be easily clarified on a spreadsheet or report.

Are They Trustworthy?

The foundation of a partnership is built on trust. You lose that trust, and your business will find itself on rocky ground. You will want to get confirmation that they are straight shooters financially, personally, and in their business dealings. There are three excellent ways to do this.

The first is to ask to see a credit report. This will show up to the previous ten years of personal credit data and their payment habits. Are they up to their ears in debt and leaving a trail of past-due payments? Have they filed bankruptcy in the past? Do they have loans with a cosigner who may have interest in how they make or spend their money? It can also include information on property purchases, liens, foreclosures, court judgments, and divorces, all of which could affect your business in some form in the future. Additionally, keep in mind that credit reports of the founders will be taken into account if you ever need to go to a bank or financial institute for a loan. Should either of you have this liability, you need to address how it's played out within the partnership.

The second is to ask for references who can speak to their character and values, an angle different from that of references who can verify skills. Ask for contact info for friends, teachers, religious leaders, volunteer heads—whoever you feel will be able to provide insight into who they are as a person and how they conduct themselves in day-to-day life.

Again, this may be a time to reiterate that the best way to get someone on board with sharing information is to start off by offering up your own. Give them your list first. Explain why you want them to have a chat with your contacts and why you think it's a valuable exercise. If you start your partnership confident about the character of the other person, you will be able to move forward on decisions so much easier.

Note: if you decide to seek investment, your investors will ask this of you. You will need to provide a list of people who can speak not only of your skills but also of your character and abilities. So don't feel like this is a futile exercise. It's actually par for the course.

The third is social media. Ask to be friended, followed, subscribed to—whatever the SM of the day happens to be. This may give you insight into how they spend their off hours and who they are in their personal life. It also potentially allows you to see their views on topics, what really interests them, and how they portray themselves. What do they post and share about? You can see very quickly what gets them excited and how they interact with the world around them. Who are their friends? Keep in mind, like attracts like. You can tell a lot about a person by the company they keep and who they allow to influence them.

Are They a Cactus or Cockroach?

A frequently studied question is "what do all successful entrepreneurs have in common?" Studies have proven the answer to be "very little." Business starters come in all shapes and sizes. There are introverts and extroverts, rich and poor, healthy and unhealthy, social butterflies and hermits, educated and dropouts of all sexes, ages, and cultures.

That said, the best entrepreneurs do have in common a long list of challenges and obstacles that they have had to overcome. Days and nights of solitary toil, a bombardment of internal doubts, repetitive trips back to the drawing board, and finding hundreds of ways of doing something ineffectively are all common stories among those who have successfully brought their vision to reality. Looking at this, one can see some characteristics that resemble two common life-forms: the cactus and the cockroach. This comparison is attributed to Liam Martin, cofounder of Staff.com, and I thank him for sharing it.

The Cactus

Anyone who doesn't have a green thumb knows a cactus is the best kind of plant to have in your house. They can thrive with little care or attention. They can sit on a shelf and go about their days, weeks, and months with only minor amounts of water.

This is the perfect kind of cofounder: someone who knows what they need to do and can carry on without hand-holding. The cactus cofounder doesn't need constant attention and direction but can solve issues without needing to constantly be guided or presided over.

But be warned: this can show up in a negative way as well. Big decisions need to be made as a team. Someone who wants to do too much on their own may create problems in the future. You will have to decide, be clear about, and possibly even document what will be considered a team decision and what doesn't need a roundtable. Finding someone who can walk that line is a great asset to any business.

The Cockroach

This is the only time calling someone a cockroach is a compliment! The cockroach is extremely tough. Its secret to survival comes from two very interesting qualities that every business starter should have or be willing to acquire.

First, it can survive if you cut off its head, as it has a brain, albeit a primitive one, in its abdomen. This may mean they're not only smart but also have the famous "gut" that can be relied on when logic and a fact-heavy solution cannot be found. Being able to rely not just on your knowledge but also on intuition can give you that slight edge that means the difference between success and failure.

Second, it can survive high doses of radiation (toxic input). Hopefully, your entrepreneurial journey will not be as toxic as radiation, but the principle is still important. A cockroach cofounder is able to tolerate a lot of challenges and negativity that come their way. There will always be naysayers, doubters, and obstacles. A cockroach cofounder will be able to withstand this onslaught and persevere through the adversity. They can tread water through and even thrive within an onslaught of doubt, adversity, and negativity. This is a great person to have on your side throughout the journey.

Are Drugs or Alcohol an Issue?

Remember back to the Google search list at the start of this book? Issues relating to drug and alcohol use are more common than people would like to believe. Recreational substance use can perhaps be harmless, but throw in the roller coaster ride of the entrepreneurial journey, and use could easily increase and begin to affect your business growth. Find out whether the use of these substances is merely for fun or a crutch for dealing with stress. Be ready to discuss where and when they can be used and what stop points can be put in place in case it gets out of hand.

Because of its potential to do irreparable damage, this is one topic to be sure that all parties are on the same page on going forward.

Learn from Brit

Brit had been concerned about why Lauren wasn't depositing her investment and she wondered what might be boiling under the surface.

One afternoon, Lauren showed up to the office with her face swollen and eyes red from crying. She stormed into the office and told Brit they needed to talk. Lauren finally revealed she and her husband had decided to divorce weeks after she and Brit had opened their doors. She explained that this was the reason for the delay in putting up her share of the capital and why it was only half the amount. She let Brit know that she and her husband kept their finances separate, and her leaving her job to start a business meant that she was living on the small savings that she had, which had now basically dwindled to zero.

"It was just bad timing," Brit realizes, looking back. The move from a secure job to go after her goals triggered for Lauren a rift with her husband that couldn't be remedied. Brit wishes that she had asked questions that in any other situation would have been too personal but, in light of their starting a business partnership, were necessary. "If I had probed the status of her marriage and how it might affect our business, I may have discovered that her husband was not on board." She would likely have also discovered that Lauren did not have the $50,000 if her husband did not pitch in. She felt that even if they had chosen to continue with the venture together, their equity or profit-sharing might have been altered to reflect that.

"Lauren and I discussed her options and decided that she would return to her previous position at the firm, and we would revisit her as a partner when she got back on her feet." Brit found herself as a solopreneur and running her small business alone only six months after starting it. "It was not the start I expected."

Within the next year, she found herself speaking once again to someone about joining her as a partner. "The second time around, I was definitely more cautious." When she began talks with her potential partner, she took the time to double-check that all was well. "I didn't want to be jaded and write off ever working with someone again. But I recognized the first time around I was ignorant, naive, and too optimistic." With her second business partner, she added due diligence that included sharing each other's financial status and conducting reference and character checks. Her new partner knew of her earlier horror story and understood her concerns.

Now Brit feels that no matter your history, you need to go deep to confirm everything you learn about a partner. "It's just good business.

And moving forward together while mitigating any future surprises creates a layer of trust that gives you peace of mind."

So what if you have done your due diligence and found something you feel contradicts what your potential partner has claimed? First off, don't be too quick to either call it quits or sweep it under the rug. You need to get more information before you jump ship or start accusing someone of fraud.

Let's say you come across a discrepancy on whether or not they led a team well in a previous venture, or you realize that they lack the skill to take on the major role you were hoping they could fill. The first thing you want to do is confront them with your concern and get clarification on that particular factor. Remember, there are always two sides to every story, and sometimes there is a third that isn't easily identified. You may discover something at play that skewed the results or had someone provide an opinion that didn't actually represent the truth. This is where you begin to dig deeper.

This is also the perfect opportunity to bring forward a situation and see how you both navigate it. Have a frank conversation about the discrepancy and see their reaction to what you discovered. Do they get angry right off the bat or laugh it off like it's not a big deal? Or do they throw out a ton of excuses to try and cover up their role in the situation? What you want to see is someone who owns up to the misguided information they gave or a factual explanation as to why the info you received lacks credibility. No matter what, your job is to keep an open mind, but also an objective one, about the facts presented.

Only you can make the call as to whether it's a risk to move forward or not. Once again, you haven't signed on the dotted line yet. Like a couple heading to the altar, there's always time to run before you say, "I do." It's going to be much easier to back out now than later.

If it all checks out fine, you're on to the next phase: "The Talk."

CHAPTER 7

"The Talk"

Mark, a tech entrepreneur based out of the United States, discovered firsthand the importance of discussing what in most situations would otherwise be a taboo subject. "I was told you should never discuss religion or politics. Boy, was that wrong."

Mark and Ali met at a hackathon in their home state. "We were there to build an app for a local telecom company and had twenty-four hours to come up with a concept and rough prototype." Each man worked alone on his project. When time was up, Mark and Ali each presented to the sponsor company. "Neither of us won. But at the after-party, we sat beside each other and shared what we built," Mark said.

The conversation progressed to other ideas that each engineer had. That turned into a brainstorming session about one idea in particular that appeared to have great potential. "You could say the idea began from Mark, but it was just that, an idea; together, we turned it into what it is today," Ali told me.

Over the next couple of months, they talked daily about their new idea. While they hit many of the "must discuss" topics we've covered in previous chapters, they completely skipped over one big hurdle—religion. Mark was not religious himself, but Ali was a "lightly practicing" Seventh-day Adventist, a Christian denomination. "I grew up in church, but after I moved out on my own, my involvement became minimal," Ali said. His involvement was so minimal that Mark didn't even know he was a follower. "I had no idea about his particular faith," Mark recalled, "nor did I know that there could be some issues that would arise should Ali return to his faith more seriously."

Seventh-day Adventists (SDAs) follow the traditional Sabbath laws, similar to those kept by members of the Jewish faith. Strict SDAs will not work, or require others to work, from sunset Friday to sunset Saturday. "It's not that I didn't believe in the tenets of the church at the time we started," Ali said. "It just wasn't something I followed at that time in my life. But that changed after we started working together."

A couple of years after starting their business, Ali felt called to return to his faith. "I met a young woman in my church, and we began to date, casually at first but then seriously," Ali said. When the relationship turned toward marriage, Ali's girlfriend shared her desire to have a marriage that kept their faith at the forefront. For her, it meant keeping the Sabbath and abstaining from work during that twenty-four hour period.

Ali and Mark's company ran a traditional Monday-to-Friday schedule. But there were times, especially during launches of a new iteration of their software or a new product, when the team had to work into the weekend to hit a deadline. Suddenly, that conflicted with Ali's previously undiscussed faith. Ali frowned as he recounted that tough decision. "I knew that my adherence to the Sabbath laws would mean Mark or one of my team leads would have to step in to take my place."

Ali knew that if he wanted to marry his sweetheart, he'd have to discuss his faith with Mark and find a compromise. And he had to hope the impact of delaying The Talk so long wouldn't destroy their partnership.

Have "The Talk"

So by now you should have completed the evaluation of yourself and through this assessment, you've determined what you needed in a cofounding partner. You set out into the world, searching high and low for that person who fit all the requirements. You met someone and put them through the ringer to see if they had the chops to make it work. You tested their skills, looked at lifestyle differences, and hung out enough to determine whether or not you could stand being in the same room for long periods.

Great. Now, since you have checked those items off the list, it's time to have The Talk.

The Talk is likely to be as awkward as the one you had with your parents about the birds and the bees. You'll choose to have it, though, because this is equally important. It will set the foundation for trust and hopefully allow you to enter into the partnership with your eyes wide open. Think of it as the first real look behind the curtain.

The most important thing to understand is by having the hard conversation now, you may save yourself from a brutal conversation later. Shining light into the dark corners ensures you begin with a clear understanding of what you are working with and buying into.

The pastor of my church declares quite candidly that his goal in premarital counseling is to break up the couple. This may seem harsh, but as he says, "Better to break up now than later, when there is a mortgage, two kids, and a dog involved." I agree. I walk into consulting sessions with the same philosophy. I want to find those issues that the founders have conveniently swept under the rug in the hopes that they will disappear and those that they have never put any thought into. In these two places reside the hidden perils that can make their business lives miserable.

So how do you start The Talk? If you've got a topic that's secretly stressing you out but you've hesitated to bring it up, that's a good indicator of where to start. But in the case of Mark and Ali, they didn't have that feeling because the issue wasn't an issue yet. For teams like them, I've compiled my top six questions you need to inspire The Talk. Covering these six topics is your best chance to bulletproof your cofounding relationship.

This list is my top six, but don't stop here. There may be others you will think of that are specific to your industry. Also, if you find something that on the surface seems negative, don't despair. It may still be possible to work with or around the snag. Knowing is the first line of defense. You can discuss how it will affect the partnership, and that discussion will allow you to determine if the news is a deal breaker or not.

What if you are already in a partnership? These questions are still just as beneficial. No matter what stage your partnership is in, when you keep an open mind and engage in open dialogue, these questions will help you chart the course ahead and find the path of least resistance to team growth.

Again, these questions are just starting points for dialogue. In no way am I suggesting you need to ask each of these exactly as written. The questions run the gamut from those who just met their potential partner at a meet-up the day before to those who are considering a partnership with their sibling. These questions were triggered by conversations with entrepreneurs who could've saved themselves a lot of grief had they been asked before they got in too deep. Determine what is applicable for you. Just don't think, "This will never happen to me." Skipping these conversations has destroyed many businesses.

Question 1: What Is Your Financial Status?

This question is first because it might be the most uncomfortable to ask. No one likes to open their books to people. How we spend our money falls into the none-of-your-business category. It's personal, intimate, and reveals information that can expose us to judgment and critique. Who wants to invite that?

That said, partnering up with someone in financial distress can put you at a significant disadvantage. Finances will affect decisions down the road, so taking the time to ensure that there are no significant issues is a smart move on your part. Remember Brian and Chris in Chapter 1? It was Chris's secret debt that started the downward spiral of their partnership.

If you don't feel the time is right to request a deep dive into each other's financials, there are ways to get a glimpse into someone's financial status by seeking out clues in casual conversation. Comments like, "I'm addicted to shoes," or "My husband is too cheap to buy name-brand beans," or "I can't get a loan" give a lot of insight that can indicate potential red flags.

On the other hand, if your partner is open to it, get an accountant's view of both sides. Get assessed financially and see where you both stand.

From my personal experience interviewing entrepreneurs, I will tell you that the partners who refuse to share financial details are likely not going to be the best option for a cofounder. If they're starting off secretive, there may be other landmines that you won't see until you step on one.

Follow-Up Questions to Ask

- Is there anything that I need to know financially that could affect our business going forward?
- Have you ever claimed bankruptcy?
- What is your credit score?
- Are you in a position to embark on this project for a year without an income?

Question 2: How Does Your Significant Other Feel about Our Endeavor?

This question is also awkward. It mixes the cofounders' business lives with their personal lives. It's here that you start to realize just how much the business will bleed into every other aspect of your life.

However, as I've mentioned before, when you enter a business partnership, you need to be ready to blur those lines. What you do in your business life will affect your personal life. The same is true in reverse. Even within the corporate space, many Fortune 500 companies add an interview of the spouse or common-law partner into the hiring process for high-level positions because they understand when things are not good at home, the effects extend beyond the front door. When one partner divorces their spouse, this can affect the company in some big ways. Additionally, some industries are more straining on a relationship than others simply because of the nature of the business. Love and business complicate each other.

You want to make sure whoever is connected to your potential partner is supportive and fully understands what they are walking into.

Anyone familiar with the famous band the Beatles and how they broke up will understand a Yoko Ono reference. If you sense turmoil behind closed doors, you may want to complete a buy-sell agreement with stronger clauses sooner rather than later to ensure your equity and investment are protected.

Follow-Up Questions to Ask

- Is your spouse/partner on board? How about other people of influence, such as parents, guardians, and dependents?
- Does your spouse/partner have strong opinions on any topic as it pertains to the business (e.g., when you get income, time commitments, investment requirement, etc.)?
- Does your spouse/partner expect to be involved in any part of the business?

Question 3: What Is Your Health Status?

Starting a company requires long days, high levels of stress, and a roller coaster of emotions. It's not an undertaking for the faint of heart. Someone with a faulty ticker, mental health issues, or any other potential health concerns cannot expect them to get any better in an entrepreneurial environment.

Pay attention to your mind and body. Obtaining a clean bill of health from a doctor will mitigate the risk of physical or mental breakdowns when the going gets tough.

Follow-Up Questions to Ask

- Are you physically/mentally ready to take on this endeavor?
- Do we need to make preparations for any particular health issues?
- Do you foresee a future need for time away to address a health issue?

Question 4: What Is Your Religious Status?

We are told never to discuss money, politics, or religion in polite settings. But when you are determining the feasibility of a working partnership, those are the topics you need to discuss. Remember Mark and Ali?

As the global environment becomes smaller and people immigrate more easily from country to country, different cultures come together in new ways. That brings conflicting perspectives and beliefs into contact. Certain religions have tenets and requirements that may affect business decisions down the road. Some of these are nonnegotiable, and those on the other side of the table may find themselves facing concessions they just can't make.

You don't need to rehash old religious wars about who's right and wrong. This isn't a debate or an attempt to convert anyone. Asking if your partner holds any religious or philosophical beliefs that will affect how you will conduct your business should be sufficient.

Follow-Up Questions to Ask

- How do you see your religious faith interacting with our business?
- Are there any behavior or schedule limitations I need to be aware of?

Question 5: What Are You Ultimately Looking For?

This question ties into the purpose of one's life. When it comes to business, reiterating your ultimate goal and confirming theirs will ensure that you are moving forward together with a parallel purpose.

Follow-Up Questions to Ask

- Just to reiterate, what are you in this business for (money, power, impact, stave off boredom, impress a guy/girl, etc.)?
- How can we integrate both our purposes into one mission?

Question 6: What If?

Some of these questions will vary, depending on your industry and situation. Some will apply no matter the subject. Either way, these questions will allow you to better understand how your cofounder thinks about the business, the partnership, and the future. Below is a list that should get you and your partner having some very interesting discussions.

Follow-Up Questions to Ask

- What if one of us becomes sick, is severely disabled, or dies?
- What if one of us hits hard financial times?
- What if one of us gets into a PR issue?
- What if someone wants to spend more time with their family?
- What if we run out of money?
- What if one of us loses interest, but the other still wants to keep going?
- When do you want to put pen to paper and legitimize our business?
- What are one or two things that worry you about our partnership?
- What are one or two things that worry you about our business plan?

Red Flags and Gut Instinct

Ali sat down with Mark and explained the religious situation to him. "I was surprised," Mark remembered, "but fortunately, I knew that Ali was not the kind of person to shy away from his obligations." Mark, while not sharing Ali's faith, figured that for Ali to raise these concerns meant they were important to him and needed to be taken seriously.

The two men worked out the protocol for the new requirement. Then they sat down with their team to explain it to them as well. "I'm very lucky to have a partner who was willing to work with my situation," Ali said. "He could have gotten angry and forced me into an ultimatum. Instead, he accepted my need and rolled with it."

Mark also mentioned the issues that could have arisen. "I suppose this is why one should talk about everything in the early stages of a partnership. We were lucky it wasn't too serious an issue, but I could see where things like this could derail an already fragile partnership."

We all have that still, small voice inside us that nudges us when it senses that something isn't right and alerts us to warning signs that are too subtle for our conscious mind to pick up. Listen to these inklings. They may come from an off-handed comment or something about the way your partner interacts with you. It may be the way they acted one day that was unlike them but may be the beginning of their wall cracking and showing what is behind it. Take these concerns seriously, and weigh them as you consider this person as a long-term business partner. At this point, it's still not too late to walk away.

That said, no one is perfect. Everyone has idiosyncrasies and issues. Being willing and able to weigh the pros and cons of every situation will ensure that you don't act too harshly or abruptly. And asking questions in advance will help you handle the many curveballs that your entrepreneurial journey will throw at you.

Without getting overly pessimistic, you may also want to get responses to the questions above in writing. This way, you have a record of decisions and actions for going forward. Also, these questions are not just for your potential partner to answer. You yourself should also answer them. As a matter of fact, being the first to respond is both an act of goodwill and a symbol that transparency is the foundation you want to build your partnership on.

Remember: trust, communication, and honesty are the hallmarks of a strong business relationship. So have The Talk as soon as possible and establish that foundation.

At the Cofounder's Hub we have put together an extensive question-naire that has all the questions you need to ask. With over 150 questions to discuss, you and your cofounder will be able to walk through a minefield behind hundreds of founders who would have benefited from seeking their answers. This product was meticulously put together to act like a type of insurance policy that protects you from issues that could rear their heads long after you're heavily invested.

Please visit www.thecofoundershub.com to get more information about this invaluable tool.

CHAPTER 8

Factors to Consider (Before It's Too Late)

"Fashion is my life," Jada told me. "It's what gets me up in the morning. I can't remember a time in childhood when I wasn't playing dress-up. And I never stopped."

Jada's passion for fashion carried on through her teenage years. She started to design her own clothes and sew them in her small bedroom. "Looking back, they were not great," Jada laughed, "but they were my designs, and I wore them with confidence."

The fact that she was homeschooled gave Jada the leeway to design without fear of ridicule. "I didn't have to align with the culture's trends in the same way kids in school feel they need to. Even my lack of design and sewing skills wasn't an issue. I was free to explore without judgment."

When Jada graduated high school, she had a decision to make. "I had the opportunity to attend the local community college in fashion design. But I already had such a trove of pieces I felt confident that I could start selling them, if only I could open my own shop." Unfortunately, she had little money to her name. "I knew I needed to get creative if I wanted to go out on my own."

While attending a local fashion show, Jada met a fellow designer, Pierre. "His designs were gorgeous, and I was instantly drawn to his confidence and outgoing nature." They talked for hours at the after-party and ended up starting a romantic relationship. "We were identical in so many ways."

Jada and Pierre had the same big plans for their designs and shared the dream of starting their own fashion lines. The excitement of meeting her personal and professional soulmate intoxicated Jada, and the feeling was mutual. "It clouded us from considering how the pitfalls of getting in business together could be a mistake."

The couple pooled their slim resources, and after months of hard work, Jada and Pierre signed a lease on a small retail space not far from their apartment. "We jumped in. And when I say, 'jumped in,' I mean jumped. We didn't have much more of a plan beyond just getting the doors open."

Opening day proved anticlimactic, and the scope of what they had started began to weigh heavily on the partners. "We had the grand opening party, then kinda looked at each other and said, 'Now what do we do?'"

Jada and Pierre's dream of opening a store had come true, but the business realities of making it successful came crashing down on them. "We were artists. We lived in the ethereal and the creative. The day-to-day practicality of running a business wasn't anything we were equipped for. We had limited inventory to begin with, and quickly realized our own fashions would not be sufficient to cover our costs of business."

The couple began sourcing fast-fashion inventory they could mark up to boost revenue. "We had to compromise what we would like to sell in our store and instead focus on what would appeal to the grand masses." That compromise defied everything the two believed in. "The store became a hodgepodge of what we loved and what we abhorred."

Jada looked sad as she recounted the partnership's struggles. "It's one thing to have an idea and a plan for a business. It's a whole other game to execute. It turns out that we both were full of ideas, but neither of us had the gumption to educate ourselves on the practical skills for running a company day to day."

One partner would have a great idea and chase it, only to let it fall to the wayside when the going got tough. Eventually, many tasks were performed half heartedly or left undone. "Our plan for the store, the concept, and the fashions were no longer clearly thought out."

Jada eventually realized their highly optimistic attitudes were a liability. Challenges they'd thought would sort themselves out didn't. The partners started casting blame at each other. Jada wanted to keep going, but with their business on the brink of folding, Pierre cut his losses and moved on. "It got ugly," Jada recalled, "and ended with us parting ways."

Complicating Factors You Need to Plan For

Hindsight is twenty/twenty. Learn from the mistakes of those who went before you so you don't have to make them yourself.

When speaking to successful and unsuccessful entrepreneurs, I try to figure out the factors that got them ahead or held them back. These elements often go unnoticed in the early stages. But as a partnership progresses, they begin to affect the business's success.

Read these factors, and keep them in mind as you interview potential cofounders or reflect on your current partnership. They just might help you sidestep a potential land mine or, better yet, expedite your success.

Capital Investment

Cash is king. In a partnership, the one holding the purse strings will have the final word. Even in the eyes of the law, the one with the highest financial stake usually carries the power. How you handle the initial infusion of capital will set the stage for your partnership going forward.

Partnerships handle capital in three main ways:

1. Equal financial contribution

    Equal contribution is the simplest capital arrangement. It involves tracking and matching spending or pooling a set figure into an account. In many partnerships, one founder puts in more effort while maintaining an even equity distribution. Those people think unequal work for equal pay won't cause friction. But rest assured, investment between partners is no trivial matter.

    Let's say two partners decide to build a product. They brainstorm its dimensions and functionality. Then they research manufacturing options, distribution avenues, and marketing efforts.

When it's time to build the product, both partners could take completely different paths. A partner with $50,000 will consider options differently than someone with $5,000. The partner with a larger amount to inject may be more open to working with a bigger manufacturer or using higher-quality materials.

Realizing equal investment isn't an option. The partner with more capital may be willing to carry the financial responsibility but will probably want added compensation for the risk. To avoid giving up equity, the partner with less money may need to take on a loan or a DIY project.

I can't tell you the right decision for every case. But imbalanced financial positions often test partnerships. All partners will need to take an honest look at their business situations to find the best solution.

2. Financial investment in exchange for alternative equity

Alternative equity could include a myriad of options like time, skill, network, product, or name. An example of this arrangement is one partner putting in the money and the other building the prototype. Another is one partner purchasing the initial inventory while using the other's name and influence to generate sales.

This method only requires the partners to work out a new cap table once the business is up and running or if more capital needs to be injected. Many businesses use alternative equity to get started. It's an easy way to make the transaction feel fair and equitable for all parties. The key is to translate the alternative equity's value into cash and use that as a marker for the equity that will be attributed.

For example, one local software company quoted start-up founders the amount it would cost if they were to do the work that one of the partners was going to take on. The partners used this quote as a guideline for the financial value the time capital would provide. Once the work was completed, that amount was counted as a legitimate financial contribution, and equity was distributed.

Providing work or intangible resources instead of money is a great way for cash-strapped cofounders to contribute.

3. Silent partner/investor

In this situation, one person invests, and the other builds the business. This type of partnership clearly delineates what each cofounder will contribute, what the day-to-day responsibilities will be, and who will make what decisions within the company.

Just be aware, a silent partner will often remain "silent" only until the first sign of trouble. I've heard of many instances in which a silent partner with little knowledge of the industry parachuted in to "save" the other founder during a rough patch. I've also heard of silent partners being too silent in the face of turmoil because the investment was inconsequential to them.

Any financial route you choose can have a profound impact on your business's success. Be sure to consider all the angles and lay a strong foundation.

Age

Knowledge is your ally in the fight for business success. On the flip side, not knowing all the pitfalls and failures others have succumbed to can free you of limiting fears. Either way, your partner's age can be an advantage or a disadvantage.

It's a common misconception that only people in their twenties can be innovative, energetic entrepreneurs. At the same time, today's youth are often dismissed as lazy, entitled, and aimless without a fair hearing. When considering a partner, objectivity and impartiality are key.

Let me give you an example. Gerry and Baron worked together at a tech firm. Gerry was fifty-nine and had been managing a small team within a company for five years. Baron was twenty-two and fresh out of college, overflowing with enthusiasm.

Throughout the day, the two of them would discuss their passions and interests. It turned out they shared a train-building hobby. They bemoaned the lack of options for accessories in their area and thought an online option was long overdue.

When I spoke to both men, Gerry shared a struggle he was having. "I had to get used to Baron's late-night schedule and resist the temptation to treat him like a child. It took work to give him the proper respect that he deserved as my partner."

Baron faced his own challenges: "I needed to trust his experience and fight the urge to dismiss them as old school."

Age divided Gerry and Baron, but their shared passion sufficed to bring them together. With their mutual willingness to keep an open mind and stay focused on the business, the two were able to build a successful company.

Experience

Experience can be an asset and a liability. You're unlikely to fall for the same entrepreneurial pitfalls twice, but using the same tactics that have worked before may prove ineffective.

Industry veterans may have hard-to-break habits and might struggle with the need for new approaches. Having years of experience doesn't necessarily mean one is familiar with the latest advances in a field. Technology changes at lightning speed, and what worked eighteen months ago may not work today. That said, a newcomer may waste valuable time and money trying to reinvent the wheel.

Vet candidates' experience by asking how they would apply their knowledge to your business. If their tactics are obsolete, reconsider involving them. But be sure to keep an open mind.

On the other hand, someone new to your industry may do well to sit at the feet of someone who knows the ropes. Experience often comes with a valuable network and expertise that can expedite the entrepreneur's journey. It's imperative to separate the wheat from the chaff.

Business Mentality: Entrepreneur, Employee, Big Corp

Partners whose prior experience is limited to employee roles may lack the entrepreneurial mentality necessary to launch and run a business.

The employee mentality is the opposite of the entrepreneur mentality. An employee, if you will allow me a broad stroke, is more conditioned to prioritize personal benefit over the company. Because employees do not bear full responsibility for the business's success, they tend to value security and shun necessary risks. Entrepreneurship brings little or no security, especially in the early stages.

Employees take getting paid for granted and aren't required to invest unpaid time. The business owner is often the last to get paid and has to put in the time and money to keep the doors open. Making the leap from employee to entrepreneur requires a complete mindset change.

"The more my potential partner and I talked about our plans to open a restaurant," says Peter, owner of an upscale restaurant in San Francisco, "the more red flags began to appear. Especially as we discussed expectations."

After two decades of employment in high-end restaurants, Peter's partner and executive chef didn't understand the risk and sacrifice required in the beginning stages of a business. He wanted the same guaranteed income and vacation time he'd enjoyed as an employee.

Peter tried to explain the need for everyone to accept a minimal salary at first so their capital could be used for operations. "Even after explaining my position, I got the impression he felt I was just trying to cap his earnings." It became obvious a partnership wasn't going to be feasible.

I ran into the Big Corp mentality many times while hiring for my businesses. Some people loved the idea of starting a company, but years of working in a large corporation instilled attitudes that conflicted with the start-up and small business mentality.

Big Corp mentality can foster the following bad habits:

- In a big corporation, individuals take on specific roles. Wearing multiple hats is not only unnecessary but often frowned upon. In a partnership, cofounders must often handle many tasks themselves.

- Large companies allocate budgets and preplan how to spend them. In entrepreneurship, capital expenditure can look illogical from the outside. Entrepreneurs' Big Corp counterparts might even see it as gambling.

- Big Corp minds focus on their own roles to the point that they can lose sight of the company's vision. An entrepreneur needs to know the big picture and be able to break it down into its necessary components.

- Big Corp minds are more structured. Start times, break times, and end times are seen as absolutes. In a start-up, you do what needs to be done right now. The time of day or day of the week doesn't matter. Your hunger or fatigue levels don't matter either. You do the work.

Be sure to have a frank discussion with a partner who comes from a Big Corp career about the necessary time investment and commitment.

Significance

Some people want to use their work as a way to give back to society. The inspiring book *Halftime: Moving From Success to Significance* by Bob Buford, guides already financially successful people as they move from self-rewarding work to that with a higher purpose. It's a business that may look less at profit maximization but instead impact maximization.

If you or your partner have this outlook for your business, make sure you are both on the same page. Seeking to build a legacy may entail an unconventional approach to scaling your company, profit distribution, building corporate culture, and choosing partners and clients.

Political and Religious Affiliation

Political and religious affiliation doesn't matter until it really matters. Your support of a certain political party could drive a wedge into your partnership. The same can be said of faiths that affect how adherents undertake their business. Be sure to discuss how you will grow your business in light of these affiliations.

Outside Support and Influence

In season one of *Dragon's Den*, the Canadian version of *Shark Tank*, four university students saw their investment from the Dragons go up in smoke when their professor botched the deal. It was a textbook example of how well-intentioned friends or family can influence a business, even if they are not directly involved.

Don't underestimate the power of close friends, colleagues, and opinionated acquaintances. The opinions of people you least expect could curtail your business plans if they are whispering into your partner's ear outside office hours. Negative Nellies, Ignorant Igors, and Jealous Jerrys may think they are acting out of love, but their lack of insight into the full picture makes them terrible guidance counselors.

If necessary, gather with anyone who may have influence and let them have a Q&A meeting. It may be frustrating to have to explain yourself, but you need to turn these foes into allies.

Aversion to Risk and Need for Security

Security and business ownership do not mix, at least not early on. Many say they want to start their own company, but precious few are willing to do what it takes. Fear of financial risk is often the biggest obstacle between people and their dreams.

Be alert to signs that a potential partner is risk averse. Demands to be paid immediately, lack of willingness to invest money, and a desire to work limited hours may be red flags.

You might make an exception for a sole breadwinner with a mortgage who absolutely needs to be able to put bread on the table. Look for a clear desire to go all-in as soon as possible, and do what it takes to compensate for their financial requirements. Do your best to distinguish between legitimate needs and lack of confidence.

Family Business

Being married to someone who grew up in his family's construction company, I've seen the challenges of having a family business firsthand. Going into business with family requires striking a delicate balance between your professional responsibilities and your personal life.

Contrary to common wisdom, your family can be an excellent talent pool for finding a cofounder. After all, you know how well you can work with a family member, and you know each other's priorities.

Just be sensitive to these issues that can arise within a family business:

- Tensions with family members you choose not to partner with
- Learning to draw appropriate lines between work and family
- Conflict with a business partner who'll also be at every family event, which can make for a lifetime of awkwardness
- Family involvement further complicating tough business decisions
- Work/life balance being even more difficult to maintain

Bringing in sons and daughters, nieces and nephews, can put family unity at risk even further for generations to come.

All of the above applies even more to spouses. Working with your better half can be a joy, but it can also invite the worst possible disaster. If you are thinking of working with your significant other, pay even more attention to expectations, boundaries, work compatibility, and legal documents. Try a mini project together first to see if you can carry a challenge through to the end.

Likability

Could you be trapped in a room with your prospective partner without wanting to claw your way through the walls?

You and your partner need not be besties. But you should enjoy each other's company to some degree. You will be spending a lot of time together. Having a great rapport is crucial.

Take a weekend trip with your potential partner. Go to a conference, and see if you come out as friends or itching to get away.

Life Stage

The average life expectancy is about seventy-eight. And the vast majority of people follow a similar life trajectory: high school, post-education or job, marriage, family, career, empty nester, retirement. Other stages exist, but these are the most significant. Your daily life varies greatly during each of these phases, and which stage you're in can greatly affect how you run your business.

When you are single, your ability to dedicate time to your venture is practically unlimited. You can spend eighteen hours at the office, travel at the drop of a hat, or invest your life savings as you see fit. But as you move on to another life stage, that kind of flexibility and unbalanced work life becomes less feasible. People with families must balance their time and financial contribution more carefully.

An entrepreneur seeking a partner should account for a cofounder's life stage and how it will affect that person's involvement in the business.

Consider each of the following life stages and their complications.

High School/College

What is your prospective partner's level of academic commitment? Will the degree be applicable to your venture? How much time is needed to complete it? Who is paying for it? Are you OK with your partner dividing time between business and school? Can it be put on hold until the business is on a more solid foundation? Can your student cofounder contribute financially to the endeavor? Can this person forfeit partying and social engagement for the sake of work?

Ask all these questions. Hard decisions might need to be made on both sides.

Single/No Family/Empty Nester

How much time and money does your partner plan on committing? If the answer tilts the scale more in one direction, should the equity or pay agreement recognize it? Is your cofounder's life stage expected to change, and will it trigger a shift in commitment that might need to be reflected in equity or pay?

Family

What needs does this person have? Are there family situations that call for special consideration? Is the spouse on board? Is the expected sacrifice understood by all?

It is likely that someone with a family will be more risk averse than someone without. How is this factor taken into account?

Family can be a full-time job. And the more kids, the more obligations. Is your potential cofounder looking to be a stay-at-home parent with your business as a part-time job? If so, can you accommodate that arrangement?

On the other hand, if your partner has money to invest, and you've got the energy to do the work, you might be able to make other financial arrangements. And no one will be more committed to making a business work than a parent with children to feed.

Mid-Career

Will your partner be walking away from a solid career? Are you both clear on the demands of entrepreneurship and ready to take the plunge? Does your cofounder have an employee or Big Corp mentality? What about an independent streak or baggage from a previous partnership? Did they cut ties with their previous venture? Are they leaving open a back-door to go back, or have they burned their bridge?

Retired

Does your partner have relevant experience? Is there sufficient money and energy to embark on the journey? What's your contingency plan should your cofounder fall ill or pass away?

Don't be afraid to ask the hard questions about the stages of life. And don't be afraid to get creative in working around them. Chances are your needs will change down the road, so being open to flexibility and change will set the tone for negotiation in the future.

Romantic Relationships

My opposite-sex cofounder and I worked together for over twenty years. Many times we were asked if we were in a relationship or would be told, "You know, I always thought that maybe you guys were an item."

I can honestly tell you that my partner and I always kept our relationship professional but we still had to navigate the perceptions and questions that came along. Many have asked me whether I thought our situation negatively affected our ability to raise money, interact with employees, or have personal relationships outside the business. My response is always that it was something that we paid attention to and always worked to ensure it wasn't an issue.

Being in a romantic relationship as cofounders creates a level of complexity not found in those that are purely professional. Even the mere perception of a relationship creates its own set of issues. It is my recommendation that if you can avoid it, do so. As a matter of fact, I would recommend going out of your way to ensure that your partnership remains platonic. Why? A failed romantic relationship will spill over into the business, and seldom is it easily rectified.

Managing Potentially Romantic Relationships

Where there is the possibility of a romantic relationship, consider these eight steps you can take to protect your partnership and avoid negative perceptions:

1. Set boundaries between you and your cofounder. Decide and commit early on that while you are business partners, your relationship will remain professional.

2. When dealing with investors, clarify your relationship up front and make a comment early on that answers this question. My cofounder would often mention something about my husband in a nonchalant way to signal that we were not a couple.

3. Be professional. I've known my cofounder since high school, so we can be quite familiar around each other. Inside jokes, hello hugs, or just "too close" seating can be misread as flirting. We learned that we needed to be extra professional to avoid sending mixed messages.

4. Be sensitive to your significant other and your cofounder's. Never give them any reason to distrust your fidelity because once that door opens, it's hard to close. Your significant other needs you to maintain transparency in your private and business relationships. Make sure everyone knows everyone and feels comfortable. The last thing an entrepreneur needs is a jealous lover resentful of their cofounder relationship.

5. Always get separate rooms when you travel. Nothing feeds imaginations or sends tongues wagging like the optics of cofounder's sharing a room. Even in the start-up phase when the capital was tight, my cofounder and I always made sure to get separate rooms to avoid scandal and set clear boundaries.

6. Avoid being partners with benefits. The cofounder partnership is difficult enough to navigate. Adding "benefits" brings a whole other level of complexity. Remember, if your romantic

relationship goes sideways, the business will be affected, guaranteed. Your first priority should be the business, not each other.

7. Investor bias is a concern as a partnership ceasing to be "just business" can put an investment in jeopardy. That said, if your business idea is strong, it won't be an issue. Just be sure to clarify the positive attributes that make you, together as a team, the right combination to lead.

8. Finally, don't make it a big deal. People love scandal, and there is nothing more enticing than an office romance. In the end, it doesn't matter what people think. You need to stay focused on your business and the road to success. Let the gossips and busybodies have their petty distractions.

Managing Married and Committed Partnerships

Many businesses are founded by those who are married or in a committed relationship. While precarious, it can also be the perfect recipe for the right leadership team of an organization. That said, I highly recommend that you take extra care to keep both your personal and professional relationship strong.

Here are four ways that you can do that:

1. Put in place legal protections that can be utilized should your relationship come to an end. All your legal documents should take into consideration the possibility of you and your cofounder getting a divorce. How will equity be handled? Will there be the opportunity for a buyout on the basis of a relationship break down? Who will handle mediation? Note that few people ever expect to get a divorce or separation, but most who do, often regret not having a plan in place to protect themselves and their business from the fallout. Presume success but plan for failure.

2. Don't let the comfort you have in your relationship display itself in your business. Public signs of affection, conflict management, and communication styles should all be professional, seeking to avoid awkwardness in the workplace.

3. Consider making your home a "no work zone". Entrepreneur-ship is 24 hours, however you need a place where you are able to refresh and replenish to avoid burnout. It's very easy to take work home when both of you share a space so set a boundary that you will not talk shop.

4. See a counselor together regularly or at minimum, intermittently. Having a sounding board to mediate issues that arise in both your personal and professional lives will assist in keeping your partnership strong and negative feelings at bay. It's the greatest insurance policy you can have for your business.

Learn from Jada

Jada's failed fashion boutique broke her heart. But she's able to laugh about it now. "At least I can say I saved myself the pain of a dramatic romantic breakup. We didn't even have a formal 'it's over' conversation. It just ended."

The stress of a failing business and reality dashing their dreams incited arguments. Their partners-with-benefits relationship went down with the ship. Jada and Pierre couldn't afford to move out on their own. They were forced to stay in the same apartment but rarely spoke to each other. Pierre finally left, and the pair haven't spoken since.

Jada ended up meeting Tyrell at a dinner party. "Tyrell was telling someone at the same table that was looking to get into the retail business but wasn't sure where to start."

Jada struck up a conversation, and the two spent the evening discuss-ing her business and his aspirations. "He wasn't a fashion designer, but he had a passion for the industry and a background in management that seemed to highlight skills I felt that I could use."

For the next couple of weeks, Jada and Tyrell explored the idea of working together. She applied the lessons from her failed partnership with Pierre and asked the hard questions up front. Within a month of meeting, she and Tyrell signed a partnership agreement.

Tyrell's skill set merged into Jada's perfectly. "Where I had a big vision, Tyrell was all details."

Tyrell stepped in to optimize the processes Jada and Pierre had put in place but also trimmed away tasks that were not helping the bottom line.

"The business had so much potential," Jada said. "It just needed someone to come in and streamline."

The pair used Tyrell's capital investment to hire an up-and-coming fashion designer and even offered him a small equity position should he stay with the company for a minimum of four years.

"We hired the role I thought I needed in a partner," Jada said, "and I partnered with someone with a skill set that could translate into boosting the entire business."

Jada's takeaway: "I don't think it pays to get into business with a romantic partner. Adding the element of business ownership could put it at risk and cloud your judgment." Jada recommends that people who work together pay close attention to big ideas and details. "You need both. It's magic if you can complement each other in this way."

Now you know the biggest factors that can affect your partnership. Weigh them carefully, and keep them in mind as you go on with your journey. Remember, communication is the best method for heading off unexpected problems. The better you are at communicating concerns, ideas, and solutions with your partner, the faster you will reach your goals.

CHAPTER 9

Expectations Defined

An entrepreneur named Cary shared his business horror story with me one fall afternoon. "[My three college friends and I] worked in construction on a part-time basis and were discussing how our work clothes lacked practicality, style, and a modern fit."

They decided to design clothes with their trades' unique requirements in mind, such as strategically positioned pockets and moveable fabrics. They decided they would seek to discover how to combine function with designs a younger generation would want to wear.

Hearing complaints in the workplace about the lack of functional yet on-trend style workwear, the group knew they had a customer base poised to purchase these clothes. They went straight to work. "In the beginning, each person was committed 100 percent." Every evening after classes, they would gather in Cary's apartment and discuss how to design each clothing piece. "Sebastian's girlfriend, Violet, was a seamstress and went to school as a fashion designer. She would sit in on the meetings and would alter our own work clothes as prototypes for what we envisioned."

Violet would take the group's ideas home and cut and sew the pieces to match their intentions. Cary, who had taken on the leadership role, reflected, "To be honest, Violet actually worked the most on the venture in the beginning, but since it was a business between the four of us, she was never considered a partner."

This was the first lesson Cary learned. "Commitment is demonstrated, not just talked about."

Over the subsequent months, as research into manufacturing and sourcing fabrics brought some big challenges to light, two of the friends shared their skepticism about the business's viability. Cary noted, "Mark and Kole doubted their ability to navigate a path to achieve their goals in a cost-effective way. They were not optimistic about the risk-reward balance, and you could tell they were both losing their excitement and passion for the project." The partnership started to reveal cracks in the foundation.

Fortunately, Sebastian, the fourth member of the team, was still excited. But his recent breakup with Violet cost the group their main seamstress and design contributor. Cary shared, "In retrospect, we should have offered Violet shares in the opportunity because she actually believed in what we were doing. Even though she and Sebastian were through, they were still friends, so a working relationship would likely have still been possible."

The second lesson Cary learned: "When you find someone dedicated to the cause, jump at the opportunity to involve them in some capacity."

When it was time to put in a capital investment, everyone except Mark contributed. He said he wasn't comfortable contributing the money, time, or effort to get the business off the ground. "Looking back, I'm actually appreciative of Mark for being honest and bowing out when he did." Cary appreciated that when Mark knew he didn't want to continue, despite the fact that it would be a difficult conversation, he was honest and acted on his true lack of interest.

Kole, on the other hand, invested but continued to lack involvement. He popped in and out of planning meetings and took on only the easiest and simplest of tasks. In an attempt to avoid conflict, Cary and Sebastian let the issue go in the hopes that Kole would step up in the future.

Cary's third lesson: "Don't sweep issues under the rug. They find a way to grow under there."

These unspoken issues would eventually reach a breaking point that threatened everything the team had built.

Laying the Groundwork

Expectations can be standards to live up to however they can also be uncommunicated assumptions. In my experience, the majority of cofounder partnerships fail because expectations are not handled appropriately and therefore are not communicated and met in real life. For example, one can assume that a partner is totally devoted to a venture and expect their actions to reflect that, but until that expectation is discussed and confirmed, it is just a hope.

The same goes for the areas of investment, salary, equity, responsibilities, roles, and all other aspects of cofounding. Without clearly defining where the partners stand on each of these topics, you could be setting yourself up for a disappointing reality check.

Setting expectations can be daunting, but it can also be exciting! You get to pull up your sleeves and say, "OK, let's get serious." It's when you take an idea, start to create a road map, and put in concrete your thoughts and considerations. Setting expectations lays the foundation for your partnership and helps you delegate the work required to realize your goals.

The expectation-setting phase is not the time to be sly, secretive, or vague. Your cofounder partnership needs to be built on complete transparency and honesty. If you cannot have a raw conversation sharing your concerns and ideas, then you need to rethink your partnership. This is the time to get deep, because either A) you haven't inked an agreement yet, or B) your current partnership could derail if you are not able to clarify plans and expectations. If there is any chance you are ill suited as a team or failing in transparency, this is when you will find out.

You and your partner need to engage in countless conversations over the course of starting and building your cofoundership. Many will be specific to your industry and business model, but there are some topics that are universal no matter what space you are in. I have compiled a list of those that are most important to your partnership so you can navigate them without conflict.

This list of questions is important, not only for those looking to set up a partnership but also for those already working within one. I recommend partners refer back to these questions and review their previous answers to them, at minimum, on an annual basis. This will ensure that any misunderstandings or desired changes can be addressed before they become issues.

Let's begin.

Investment (Time and Capital)

Most partnerships find it challenging to broach this subject and navigate the process of making investment decisions. The great thing about this topic, however, is that investment conversations allow all parties to truly gauge each other's interest and commitment. Deciding who, when, and how much each partner will inject into the company can reveal a lot about the confidence each person has in the business model.

When you start discussing how you will handle capital and investment and put in motion a plan to act on your decisions, you solidify your commitment to working together in the future. Few other factors carry the weight of responsibility as much as putting your money where your mouth is. These conversations take your business to the next level, whether it be ideation to reality or early stage to large scale. Conquering this major hurdle should be celebrated as it signals that you are moving forward as a team.

To get your business off the ground, grow revenue, and achieve profitability, you will need to figure out how to allocate your time and capital. Converse with your partner to create a detailed plan for financial investment down to the minutiae. Also, have one or two backup plans to deal with sudden obstacles and any shifts in direction that you think might occur. If your partner balks at investing or committing to anything in writing, it may be a warning sign and something you should explore deeper before moving ahead.

When it comes to plans, the more detailed, the better. And remember: you can always go back to the drawing board should conditions change.

Let's break down the investment topics you and your partner should discuss.

Capital Conversation

Questions to ask a cofounder:

- How much money does each of us have to invest in this venture? Should we each provide proof of funds prior to moving forward?

- What amount do we want to invest now? In six months? Upon reaching a certain milestone? Is there an investment required that we should prepare for long-term?

- How will a partner who has more to invest be compensated? Will they receive more equity? Will repayment come from revenues or profits?

- Will we seek a loan? If so, how much can we get approved for? Each partner should meet with a banker to learn the answer. Even if you do not plan to seek a loan, you never know what is around the corner. This tidbit of information could be valuable in a time crunch.

- Will we seek investors? If yes, when? Will we solicit investments from friends and family? Business development banks? Venture capital? Other sources? Who will undertake the task of fundraising? How much do we need and at what valuation? Should we travel to raise money?

- If we run out of money, what will we do? How long is our runway? If the business fails, how will capital investments be repaid?

- Who will manage the funds? Do the banking, taxes, and payroll? When should we hire a bookkeeper? What are our checks and balances to ensure transparency and accessibility for all partners?

- How do we handle spending? Is there a minimum amount that requires both partners' approval?
- When should we revisit this discussion?

(A note about this last question: I have found that many cofounders come to a time in their partnership when they have an issue that they want to bring up but find it difficult. This question, which sets a date to revisit previous decisions, can be a "scapegoat" that you can use as an excuse to bring up any concerns that may arise in the future. It allows you to be intentional with your communication but is also there to help you navigate potentially difficult topics. Be sure to set a date to revisit all that you have discussed and follow through to keep it.)

Time Commitment

Questions to ask a cofounder:

- How much time do we have to invest in this venture?
- If the time commitment is unbalanced, how will we compensate?
- When will we make a full-time commitment to this venture? When will we each leave our jobs?
- How will we log time invested?
- Is a partner spending more time than they expected they would at the beginning of the partnership? Does this increased involvement need to be compensated? Is a partner spending less time than expected? Does a change in equity, salary, or role need to reflect this?
- Can both partners be working on other opportunities at the same time?
- When should we revisit this discussion?

Time is money, and sweat equity can be a valuable asset. Depending how you structure your partnership, compensation should reflect the time commitment given to the growth of the business. That said, the cash or stock value of time spent working in the early stage of a company may be difficult to quantify. Do your due diligence to ensure that fair market value is being attributed to the time each partner is spending.

Your company's status can change quickly in the early stages. If time commitment becomes unbalanced or less equitable than previously set, be sure to revisit what this looks like between partners as soon as possible. Instances like these are ripe for creating resentment and frustration.

Salary, Raises, and Bonuses

Discussing salary will help you determine whether a partner is employee minded or entrepreneurial. It will also give you insight into a prospective cofounder's ability to commit financially. The salary discussion will likely affect all other business topics, so it is a good one to have throughout your partnership.

Putting salaries, raises, and bonuses on paper will set expectations that provide clarity for both sides. The details needn't be ironclad but need to be specific enough to ensure everyone is thinking in the same ballpark.

Here are some salary questions to ask a cofounder:

- When should we start pulling a salary?
- How much should we earn?
- Will salaries always be equal for all partners?
- How much will a partner who wants to forfeit a wage for equity get? Can the money be banked until the business earns revenue or reaches other milestones?
- Will partner compensation be a salary, a dividend, or a loan?
- When should we revisit this discussion?

Role and Job Description

Decide who will do what early on. It may seem obvious that the software engineer will build the prototype, and the chef will build the menu. But in a new company with a limited labor pool and capital, your team's skill sets may not fit every job perfectly.

Giving everyone a detailed job description is the best way to divide up labor. Someone will need to handle hiring, corporate culture, social media, and even office cleanup outside their main workload. By dividing up jobs, you can ensure a balance of work so no one person has to shoulder all the weight. Down the road, you can delegate or reassign certain tasks. But setting expectations early on avoids confusion and friction.

Questions to ask a cofounder include:

- What are the obvious tasks each of us will take? What tasks does that leave out?
- Do any tasks have milestones attached (e.g., one partner will create a budget when revenues start to come in)?
- Are there any tasks we should undertake together?
- Will some roles require additional compensation?
- Do any tasks create inventions that will belong to an individual partner?
- How will we determine a partner's effectiveness in a role?
- How do we remove someone from a role?
- What is each partner's "dream role" within the company?
- When should we revisit this discussion?

Try and match up roles with those who are more wired or better skilled to achieve success. Don't be surprised if someone who's not detail oriented shirks legal tasks, or someone bad at numbers lags behind on payroll. Partners should still step up to difficult tasks no matter their competency level, but it's helpful to have grace when a lack of enthusiasm for a role is evident. The best thing you can do in these instances is to be proactive in undergirding efforts in these roles in any way you can.

I once interviewed two cofounders of an insurance start-up who found a great role mismatch work-around. In their words, "When I finally had a heart to heart with my partner about how I honestly struggled with holding our staff accountable for arriving late or not being thorough in their job, we brainstormed and researched alternatives together and found a peer accountability program that we could initiate that didn't require a face-to-face confrontation on my part but still allowed me to retain responsibility for that role."

Work Schedule

Turning an idea for a company into a reality can be overwhelming. You can easily spend eighteen hour days devising ideas for your business, as well as researching, testing, and creating products and services. Running and scaling a business can be even more daunting, potentially requiring a higher commitment level and self-sacrifice than previously expected.

Setting a work schedule is a vital part of clarifying roles and communicating expectations. Taking the time to schedule work will help determine if you have a fair-weather partner or a cofounder who's in it for the long haul. Especially in this environment, when more and more people seek the flexibility of working from home, specifying where and when partners will work within the company could allow you to mitigate confusion, uncertainty, mistrust, and resentment.

That said, it can be hard to set or predict the exact time requirements for each partner. Sometimes a partner will still have a day job or family responsibilities that they need to work around. Or a role may not be totally fleshed out and the time commitment uncertain. Either way, a ballpark figure, along with a method for tracking logged hours, is a great way to infuse trust into a partnership.

John and Massoud, cofounders of a software firm, would seldom work in tandem because of their locations. John told me, "Massoud is from Iran and doesn't speak English. I came to the US when I was young and came up with a great idea for a software company."

On a trip back to his home country, John shared his idea with Massoud, his cousin. "Massoud is a brilliant engineer and understood immediately what I wanted to do and got very excited about it. There was no doubt that he would be able to deliver the technology necessary to deliver our service."

They agreed to be long-distance partners. John would handle vetting and early business development, then hand over his concepts for Massoud to build. "I worked for one year, evangelizing the idea, seeking feedback from potential clients, lining up investment, and conceptualizing the first iteration of the product. Massoud and I had conversations regularly but ninety percent of the work was being done by me in the early stage."

Massoud took over when the time came to build the first concept. "For about eight months, Massoud worked tirelessly day and night building the technology, and my tasks were greatly reduced during this time." These two men found a schedule that worked not only for their situations but also for the stages of their business.

Questions to ask a cofounder:

- When should we set a concrete work schedule?
- Where should we work? Do we need to acquire office space?
- How do we handle time zone differences or opposing schedules?
- Do we have a mode of communication that allows us to track our progress and stay up to date when apart?
- Will our roles require a specific work schedule?
- When should we revisit this discussion?

Few of the entrepreneurs I interviewed insisted on an exact balance of their responsibilities. Some had even split the workload sixty-forty, if not seventy-thirty, but ultimately, the main desire was that no one would shirk their duties. Sometimes you cannot quantify how many hours of work will be necessary, but instead, it is about just doing what it takes to get the job done.

Sometimes the role itself requires a deeper level of commitment and involvement, like that of the CEO. "I spend more time on the business than my cofounder, but I expected that when I became the CEO," says Colin. "The responsibility weighs on me as the leader of the company, and therefore I tend to do and take on more."

Some partners do more work, regardless of their roles in the company. "I go crazy if I'm not doing something," says Alex. "I never really stop. It's who I am, and I certainly don't expect Karl to be the same. I would never resent the fact that I am up at four in the morning working on a presentation because that's what I enjoy! It's what fuels me."

Determining a balanced workload may not be expected in your partnership, or even possible. But entrepreneurs should discuss division of labor in advance so everyone knows what to expect.

Equity

How will you distribute shares in the company? The possible equity splits are endless. Many have tried to build a formula, and a Google search may help you find one that suits your partnership.

Formula or not, you should carefully consider a few key factors when dishing out equity.

- Time: Is the business a full- or part-time gig? For everyone or just one partner? The equity split should reflect respective time spent.

- Capital: How much money is each partner putting up? All founders' initial investment might be equal, but if one partner's capital contribution increases later, the equity split could change accordingly.

- Idea: Which cofounder had the initial idea? How long did they work on it before the other cofounder was brought on board? Equity compensation should take into account legwork already completed.

- Miscellaneous: Notoriety, a significant network, equipment, a team of staff, and/or a robust customer roster could all justify additional consideration when deciding the share split. Basically, any factor that one partner brings to the partnership that expedites the path to success is up for regard.

Vesting

When starting a company or at the onset of a new stage in your business, consider a vesting period when doling out equity. A vesting period is an agreed-upon amount of time during which the founders "earn" their shares by staying and working in the company—typically, this term is four years. That means if a partner were to leave within a year, they would only receive 25 percent of their total portion of agreed-upon shares; two years would equal 50 percent, and so on. This ensures the equity received reflects the time in operations but also gives the founders peace of mind should the partnership not work out.

You can also choose to recognize work or capital that one partner has committed to the venture prior to deciding shares and deduct time from the vesting period to reflect their contribution. You may use this feature if someone has gotten the business past a major hurdle or has injected money into the venture when no one else has. Where all the partners have a four-year vesting, this partner might have only two or three.

Other criteria can be utilized to trigger receiving the entire portion of one's shares, such as when the company begins to receive revenue, investment is secured, or a major deal is signed. This approach encourages commitment but also makes exiting cleaner. If one partner leaves prior to reaching one of these milestones, the business retains their pool of shares and can give them to another potential partner or to the partner(s) who stayed.

Whatever your situation, a vesting period may be a sound option when working with someone for the first time or as a general safeguard against the unknown.

Questions to ask a cofounder include:

- How should we divide up ownership?
- What are some significant factors we should account for in our decision?
- Should we have a vesting period? If so, how long should it be?
- Does anyone outside the partnership deserve equity?
- Should we set any equity aside to give to employees, contractors, or advisers?
- How should we handle disbursement if a partner leaves? Will there be a buyout? Will the buyout amount vary based on the value of the company?
- For what reasons would someone receive additional equity? Who would it be taken from?
- When should we revisit this discussion?

Title

Whether titles matter to you or not, they carry a message, and I've seen more than a few partnerships struggle because of job title disputes.

Typically, partners have two titles to begin: a designation for the creator (e.g., founder, cofounder, owner) and a title that represents a role within the company (e.g., CEO, COO, president). You should pay more attention to these titles than you think is necessary since they communicate a lot, hold significant weight, and require great care to change down the road.

Founder versus Cofounder

Many entrepreneurs find their companies become extensions of themselves. They come to regard their ideas as their children, birthed in their minds and raised with much effort.

Being part of the early stages of a business creates a connection rarely shared by later contributors. The founder title identifies someone who saw a need in the marketplace and decided to fill it. That term symbolizes Herculean effort made against great adversity.

Here are some ways to decide on the founder or cofounder title:

- The person who had the idea for the business is the founder; all others are cofounders.
- The single person who took the business to a certain level retains the name founder; a partner brought in at a later date is a cofounder.
- Despite one person having the idea, if someone is brought in early on and both partners develop the business together, then both parties are designated cofounders.
- If the business is the brainchild of two people, both are considered cofounders.

Once titles are decided, they should not be changed unless all parties agree. Changing a partner's status from cofounder to founder implies that person is solely responsible for bringing the idea to life. It's altering history.

I have seen partners change titles on a few occasions, and the personal damage can be irreparable. The only time a change from cofounder to founder may be acceptable is if the business evolves, and someone earns recognition for successfully taking the company in a new direction.

Questions to ask a cofounder:

- How should we assign the titles of founder and cofounder?
- Should these titles change in the future for any reason?
- How do we want to memorialize this stage of the business?
- If not as founders, how can we recognize others who contributed from the beginning? (Think about co-contributor as an option, as mentioned in Chapter 1.)
- When should we revisit this discussion?

CEO/COO/Big Boss

You will often hear a business owner's title stated as president and janitor. This practice pays homage to the number of hats an early-stage founder must often wear.

It may be smart to wait till the business has grown before formally assigning titles to the partners. A title defines expectations and responsibilities that may not have gelled in the early stages. The eventual chief financial officer may oversee social media along with finances at first. Someone taking on tasks typical of a CEO may not have faced a test of leadership yet.

How should you and your partner define yourselves within the company? Unless your role is obvious, I suggest you create one. Try to make it whimsical, but keep it humble. No need to jump to the C-suite right away. Even the titles President and Vice President are presumptuous. Cofounder or founder is more than acceptable and will help everyone fall into their natural titles as they settle into their roles within the company.

Questions to ask a cofounder include:

- Is there any need to apply a title beyond cofounder or founder?
- When do we want to assign titles?
- What title do you ultimately see for yourself?
- How much do our job descriptions define our titles?
- Does compensation need to follow title distribution?
- Are there any titles we need to build into and fill within our business?
- When should we revisit this discussion again?

Corporate Culture

Your corporate culture will define your entrepreneurship journey more than any other factor. Deciding how your business will function and choosing a philosophy for dealing with employees and customers will have lasting effects. Even ignoring this topic will create a corporate culture, so why not be intentional about it?

Questions to ask a cofounder:

- What does our workspace look like? Is it structured or malleable? Typical for our industry or unique and ever changing? Will we work in an in-office environment or from home?
- How is hierarchy demonstrated? Glass offices for leaders, cubicles for newcomers?
- When everyone is giving 100 percent, how do we handle occasional days off?
- How will we deal with medical status in the era of pandemics?
- How will we build camaraderie within the organization? After hours get-togethers and corporate parties?
- How do we handle family? Do we involve them or keep work and family separate?
- What about our office wardrobe? Do we want a business formal image or a more relaxed, individual style?

- Will we allow pets? Music? Prayer? Will we offer stand-up desks or even free beer? The sky's the limit, and only the founders can decide.
- How will we handle HR issues like diversity, equal pay, and hiring transparency?
- When should we revisit this discussion?

In all likelihood, you will spend more time in your business than any other area of your life. Make it an environment that feeds your spirit rather than sucking out your soul.

Exit

What does your business's finale look like? Many entrepreneurs are so focused on starting their business that they neglect to discuss how they will exit. Understanding where each of the founders see themselves five, ten, or twenty years in the future is important. Knowing your exit strategy will affect every decision you make within the company, so ensuring that everyone is pointed in the same direction is paramount.

Shannon and her partner were in the early stages of developing their ice cream business. Months in, when it came closer to pinning down investment requirements, Shannon discovered her partner only wanted to stay within the farmer's market demographic. Shannon, on the other hand, had her sights on growing into grocery chains with national reach and exiting with an empire. It turned out neither wanted to compromise, and the business fizzled.

Like it or not, your company will come to an end, on your watch or some future generation's. So discussing an exit strategy from day one will ensure that those invested are working toward the same end.

Questions to ask a cofounder:

- What would you like to get out of this venture?
- Where do you see yourself in relation to this business in five, ten, twenty years?

- How can we make sure your exit plan is accounted for throughout this journey?
- What if you meet your exit plan goals before your partner?
- Who could potentially acquire our company?
- What is the minimum acquisition offer you would accept today?
- What business metrics must we attain to retire, sell, or fold?
- When should we revisit this question?

A Corrected Mindset: The Triad

At a speaking event in Vancouver, I stated that having a business partner has been like having a second husband. Throughout my career, I spent most of my days with my cofounder and made life-affecting decisions with him. He knew more about my life than anyone, with the exception of my spouse. It's this reality that makes people parallel a partnership with a marriage.

However, after interviewing many cofounders about their partnerships, I had an epiphany: a business partnership is not like a marriage, at least not in the traditional sense. There is another central character involved that actually requires more of the founders' devotion than what is given to one another. That central character is the business, and it's the third "person" in the proverbial triad. ("Quad" if there are four cofounders . . . you get it ☺.)

In a traditional marriage, the spouses focus on each other. They strive to put the other person's needs and wants ahead of their own. It's "us" focused, and in order to flourish, the couple has to make one another the main priority above all else. In a cofounder partnership, the business is the one central figure, and the two or more cofounders need to focus their attention and commitment on it. Technically, they don't even need to build a strong bond with each other. As long as they do what's right for the business, and as long as they are amicable, the endeavor can flourish. The founders both "marry" the business and need to make decisions based on what's best for the company, not on what will improve the cofounders' relationship.

The cofounder relationship should never be more valuable than the company. Instead, the partners have to meet the business's needs first, even if their personal relationship could be jeopardized, as the survival of the business should take precedence over the relationship. However, that said, without a good working relationship, the road will be harder and more likely come to an end.

There are good reasons for this being the best way to put your partnership in perspective. By agreeing that the company's needs will come first, the cofounders can depersonalize the partnership. That way logic, not emotion, will guide difficult decision-making. Decisions like whether your cousin should work at the company can be based on tangible merit and not familial obligation.

A properly prioritized partnership can allow you to forge a unique friendship that will last a lifetime. While the main goal is the company's success, uniting to make that happen and enjoying each other's company along the way can make the partnership, on the whole, one of your life's greatest relationships.

Final Words

If you or your partner comes to an impasse in any of the discussions above, don't be afraid to discuss an alternative path forward. While the partnership may not be feasible, moving someone into an employee or adviser role may be a viable option. Again, the idea of a co-contributor title, coupled with an equity position, signals that you value a departing person's input but recognize that your business relationship has borne all the fruit it can yield.

Learn from Cary

As Cary's business progressed, it became clear that Kole was not willing to put in the work necessary to warrant his equity position. Sebastian and

Cary offered Kole his capital investment back plus 10 percent interest. "He accepted, but it ended up destroying the friendship. Even though all parties felt the buyout was fair, we were never able to recover from the awkwardness that ensued."

Cary's fourth and final lesson from the experience: "Be prepared to lose a friendship when you enter into a partnership. I think ours was a worst-case scenario, but I can imagine it's difficult to exit any partnership without some hard feelings."

And he's right. That's why establishing clear boundaries and expectations up front is the best practice. It prevents hurt feelings because both partners are operating from an agreement they created together. At a minimum, it protects your legal interests; at best, it allows you to create a working relationship that you will forever cherish.

Set your expectations on day one for lasting peace of mind.

CHAPTER 10

Lawyering Up

When best friends Celina and Amara came up with an idea for an online pet store business, they were giddy with excitement. Celina already had a small brick-and-mortar pet store but wanted to find someone who could expand her offerings online. Amara, having digital marketing experience, thought it would be fun to try her hand at e-commerce and, even better, get to work with her closest friend.

They came up with the look and feel together, but ultimately, Celina wanted Amara to take full control of the online portion of the business. Amara told me, "It was great because I could access Celina's product line and take advantage of her knowledge on what sold in the past and what hadn't." It seemed like the perfect match.

Early in the research stage, Amara asked Celina what she felt the equity split should be and what kind of capital commitment she wanted her to bring to the table. "Celina told me she didn't want to bring in any financial investors. She was willing to fund the entire enterprise to keep full control with just us. And she would do a generous profit-sharing deal with me." Amara, fresh out of university and having only completed a short stint at a local start-up, was grateful for the opportunity to get the business up and going without having to scrounge up the funds. "I really didn't want to go to my parents or the bank for a loan. I accepted her offer knowing that I was probably leaving something on the table since I wasn't contributing financially." Amara was willing to forfeit some equity for the expected high profits. "I figured there would probably be a chance to revisit the equity split down the road when I'd proven myself and my worth to the company."

At the time, Amara didn't worry about the lack of legal documentation because they were such close friends. "Looking back, I can't say if she intentionally held back on writing up a formal contract. But we could have saved ourselves a lot of trouble had we done it at the start. The partnership was pretty casual since we knew each other for over fifteen years, and we were close friends."

Amara never dreamed that the decisions they were making verbally would not be followed through on. "We talked so much about our goals and the revenue potential and what that would mean for the business. I figured I was safe from her going back on her promises." With their years of friendship as collateral, Amara jumped in with both feet and got to work without an agreement in place.

Launching the online portal was challenging but also exhilarating. "I was learning as I went, but I loved it. It was very easy to put in sixteen hour days." Within four months, she had a working e-commerce site and sales started to come in. "I remember highlighting a very exciting product that we promoted heavily through her existing client base and on social media. It sold out completely within the first four days!" This product was an expensive, high-profit item, and it was then that Amara began to question how her profits would be calculated. "I know it's hard to believe, but I really didn't give it much thought. I just assumed it would be a simple case of profits from sales made online."

Unfortunately, Celina presumed something else.

A couple of weeks after launch, Amara approached Celina on how she would be paid. "I asked her for the profits from the first couple weeks of sales. She told me she would look into it right away." When she came back with a spreadsheet showing a small profit, Amara questioned her data. Celina told her that because the sales from the first month likely came from the client base she had already captured, she didn't feel it truly represented new sales from the online business.

Amara was crushed. "I felt sick to my stomach. I knew right away this was not headed in a good direction. While she was likely correct, that poorly communicated factor opened up a huge can of worms." The two partners had not hashed out a method for determining where sales came from, and now Amara's opinion of what that looked like differed from Celina's. "When I told her we'd never discussed the customer base split as a factor of my profit that we would consider, she got quite upset." The pair agreed to take a couple of days to come up with a solution for determining how they would calculate sales going forward.

The resulting conversation became the hardest the friends had ever faced.

Send in the Lawyers

We've come so far! You took a good long look at yourself, identified your strengths and weaknesses, and assessed what you need to look for in a cofounder. Then you began the search, keeping in mind the various factors and stages that needed to affect your decision as you planned for the future with each candidate. You assessed their passion, tested their skills, and had potentially awkward conversations to ensure there were no serious skeletons in their closet. You defined expectations going forward, and now a clear and decided winner has risen to the top. Congratulations! Sifting through the muck and mire is a tough job, but you've made it out alive. And you've got a fantastic cofounder to show for it.

Now put it all on paper. Right now, before something goes wrong.

After going through the above steps, it's easy to think that you have fully exhausted all the loose ends and filled every hole. And in many ways, you have done the bulk of the work. But the act of getting it all in writing is a whole other ball game. And you can't skip this step if you want your partnership to survive for the long haul.

Entrepreneurs are typically optimistic people by necessity. They need to see possibilities where others cannot, bring an idea to fruition despite much opposition, and presume success in an ubiquity of doubt and skepticism. But optimism can also cloud your judgment and make you overlook warning signs and ignore common sense. Documenting certain decisions and plans is a crucial way to maintain commitments and promises. It's about putting your money where your mouth is and stating that you and your partner(s) are really going forward in this endeavor together. It's formal, structured, detailed, and predictable—all things that run contrary to most entrepreneurial spirits. But it will be worth every dollar and minute spent.

I've included a list of documents you need to draft together. I cannot stress enough the importance of these documents. Putting the particulars of your partnership on paper is the only way of solidifying how your partnership will look going forward.

So, where to begin? Depending on your industry, some documents may be more important than others, but the list below is general enough to cover most bases. As a side note, laws governing contracts vary from country to country, state to state, and province to province. Be sure to confirm with a legal practitioner that all your contractual bases are covered. Additionally, as with all the suggestions found in this book, you do not need to complete all these contracts before you embark on your partnership. But know this: 90 percent of issues between partners I've interviewed could have been averted, mitigated, or softened if the corresponding contract had been in place.

Buy/Sell Agreement

This document is your ultimate exit strategy. It lays out an eject button should any one of the founders decide it is time to leave the business. This enables you to have a starting point for negotiating how you will leave the company, what it will cost, and any time frames or milestones that need to be met.

Having an exit plan in place from the start sidesteps the claustrophobic feeling that can come from embarking on a partnership that could last decades. It enables parties to achieve their goals and walk away or to depart should unforeseen circumstances such as illness, disease, or lifestyle changes come into play. An exit plan also protects the founders should a marriage dissolve or a founder die because it can lay out the procedure to purchase the stock from the widow/widower or ex and ensure that the company is always protected.

A buy/sell agreement never has to be written in stone and can and should be revisited and revised as you see fit or when milestones within your company are reached. A great time to do this is when the valuations of the company changes, the roles of the founders are adjusted, or the principals contribute additional investments. Additionally, a reworking of the buy/sell agreement would come into play if you bring on a new key member or partner.

Partnership Agreement

A partnership agreement, also known as an operating agreement, sets forth the guidelines for how your partnership will be conducted and divided. Whether you are getting into business with a spouse, close friend, family member, or near stranger, this document is essential for defining the structure, expectations, compensation, contributions, and courses of action required when inevitable issues arise during the course of running a business. Your partnership agreement is the closest thing to an insurance policy and will be a valuable fallback reference to keep things moving in the agreed-upon direction when problems happen.

That said, the document can be as vague or as specific as you choose. And while a more detailed contract may be more expensive, you gain greater peace of mind the clearer your partnership becomes.

Consider putting in a clause that the contract can be revisited after a certain period of time, perhaps annually, or once a milestone is reached, such as becoming revenue positive. At the least, provide a course of action for either cofounder to trigger a conversation should its terms no longer reflect the company's current situation. Many things change during the course of building a company, and the ability to reevaluate is important. If the time comes and you don't feel the need to revisit or revise it, great! But the option is there should someone feel the need.

Here is what is typically defined in a partnership agreement:

- Contributions. Identify what all partners will be bringing to the table at the onset of the business. This includes labor, financial, property, time, customers, et cetera. It can also define what will not be contributed to the business, whether because of intentional withdrawal or previous commitments. And it can define broadly or specifically how future contributions will be handled (e.g., capital infusion or time commitment).

- Compensation. Identify who will be paid what, starting when, and for how long. Lay out equity structure with any nuances that suit your particular situation. Consider a vesting period for everyone's stocks. You may want to revisit this part annually or when a certain milestone is obtained. Determine when profits will be paid out and whether they will be paid to the individuals or back into the company. Compensation is another element that will change as the business grows. Be sure the agreement reflects the current situation since whatever is in writing will trump a verbal agreement.

- Structure. Clarify titles, roles, advisers, methods for making decisions, and any other peripherals that may be necessary. Needs and wants should be addressed here.

- Exit. Define the process if and when a partner wants to get out. Situations such as death, bankruptcy, disability, relocation, family changes, divorce, retirement, or simply a lack of desire to continue should be addressed. This portion of the contract can reference a separate buy/sell agreement or may be applicable only until a term sheet is signed should you raise investment. Either way, know that this section makes or breaks the ability to close a partnership amicably, fairly, and with as little confusion or trouble as possible. Be sure to clearly define your responses within the document.

Intellectual Property Protection/ Invention Agreement

When you are creating a new product or process, you want to make sure that what is created within the confines of the business stays in the business. An IP agreement makes it clear that none of the founders have the exclusive rights to the invention or IP. This ensures that, should a founder leave, they cannot take an invaluable part of the business along with them.

That said, if something created within or brought into the company will be retained by a founder, this agreement would lay out the parameters of what that looks like going forward. That can include licensing and noncompete agreements.

Side note: if you haven't already, make sure employees sign a similar agreement for the work they contribute in their roles.

Employment Agreement

Most employment contracts within a company are used to lock in key personnel and lay out the parameters for length of employment and compensation. For cofounders, this agreement could be a tax and financial planning tool. In some jurisdictions, it may be possible to use an employment agreement as a way of legitimizing deferred compensation until the company can afford to pay it. Many entrepreneurs forfeit a salary for months or even years, and an employment agreement enables them to claim that salary with a formal employment contract stating roles and compensation. Additionally, if a company raises venture capital, it may be a way of justifying a portion of that investment going to repayment for work completed to date.

Check in with your financial adviser to ensure that an employment agreement works for your situation.

Noncompete Agreement

A person with total access to the inner workings of a company can be extremely detrimental if they place that knowledge in the hands of the competition. A noncompete agreement ensures that, should a cofounder leave the company, they face a serious penalty should they take valuable insider information to an organization that directly competes. It also stops one angry cofounder from establishing themselves as a direct competitor with identical practices. The contract can put in time stipulations, geographical boundaries, or specific names of companies a partner would be prevented from working, partnering, advising, or contracting with.

A noncompete agreement can be a stand-alone contract or a clause written into the partnership agreement.

Written on Paper, Not in Stone

Now that you have lawyered up, there are a few things to keep in mind. Once you have the documents in place, schedule an annual meeting to review them and make any changes that are necessary. Get a legal sign-off each time to prove authenticity. All these contracts need to be admissible in court should the necessity arise. Thus, you should ensure they reflect the current understanding of all parties involved. Additionally, an annual review can be a way to facilitate conversations that might otherwise be difficult to initiate.

Use all these documents as tools to build the strength of your partnership, add value, and clear the air when problems arise.

Learn from Amara

Amara found out too late how crucial these documents are when Celina disagreed over fair profit and equity distribution. They were forced to have that conversation after tensions were already high.

"Honestly, it was the conversation we needed to have before we started working together," Amara told me. When they finally discussed equity, Amara had a list of questions and concerns that she wanted to go over in the hopes that they'd never again feel so at odds. "For that brief period, I think we both felt that each was taking advantage of the other, and it set a bad tone in the partnership."

They were able to get over the issue, but it has made them both careful to get in writing any decisions they make regarding the business and the partnership. "Clarity and accountability are so important in a partnership, and emails, contracts, and agreements help facilitate that."

Today, Amara is clear about the importance of documents. "At one time, a handshake meant something. My grandfather used to talk about how he would accept IOUs from merchants who purchased from his vegetable stall, who would then pay promptly on the first of the month." Amara figured that these types of business interactions would transfer into modern-day partnerships and therefore didn't prepare herself for the strife and complications that would come from not inking her deals. After her near disaster with Celina, she's careful to get everything in writing so no one's feelings get hurt.

Learn from thousands of cofounders with broken hearts and broken companies. Get your documents in order as early as possible so you never have to face uncertainty in your partnership.

Visit www.thecofoundershub.com for templates to help you work out the details of these documents and save time and money with legal.

PART II

How to Strengthen Your Partnership

CHAPTER 11

Building a Foundation with Communication

"**W**ho knew a cookie would be such a point of contention?" Ingrid laughed. She and her partner Erling sat with me and recalled their first big blowout. "Looking back, we both realize it was a ridiculous topic on the surface. But it was an inevitable reaction to a major issue: lack of communicating our expectations."

The bakery that the two partners owned was a collaboration between Ingrid, a baker, and Erling, an operator. Ingrid loved being in the kitchen, and Erling had had success in two other ventures running operations. "We knew our roles, and slid into them easily," Ingrid told me.

Everything ran smoothly until one issue popped up—chocolate chip cookies. "Erling would come in regularly and take a dozen cookies for himself." It didn't affect them much when it came to costs, and they often had more than enough cookies for their customers, but it began to rub Ingrid the wrong way. "After a while, it was a dozen every few days, either for his family, as gifts, or his other partners. I felt like it was getting out of hand." Erling wouldn't pay for the cookies as he deemed them a perk of being in the bakery business. Ingrid also took some bakery items home but was cognizant (in her own eyes) of not being "excessive."

Ingrid let her resentment fester. For months. Then years. "It went on for a long time, until finally one weekend, I had enough." That fateful day, Erling came in and asked Ingrid if she could make an extra twelve dozen cookies for his son's end-of-year school party. "I snarkily said, 'It must be nice to have a private baker.'" Erling noticed the tone and asked her if it was a problem. "So I unloaded. I let him know that I felt his taking cookies and baked goods on a regular basis made me feel taken advantage of. And while it seemed minor, it was lost profits that ultimately affected my pocketbook."

Their argument over cookies brought to light areas of distrust, resentment, frustration, and underappreciation. All because of unspoken expectations, those cookies nearly cost them their business.

Building a Foundation

Just like going through the process to find the right cofounder is essential, laying a strong foundation is imperative to keep it strong. That's the next phase and Part II of this book: creating systems for healthy interactions.

The reality is that even if you find a cofounder who ticks all the boxes and looks perfect, your relationship can die if you leave the partnership to fend for itself without attention or intention. Many people have partnered up with great individuals and built large companies only to find themselves unable to stand being in the same room and struggling to agree on anything. This isn't because the people or the work changed. It's that they failed to address issues that popped up and left conflicts unresolved.

I cannot stress enough that right now is the best time to make your partnership a priority. It's like a home. You can maintain it by keeping the yard trimmed, doing repairs as they pop up, and even throwing on a fresh coat of paint every once in a while. Yes, you have to work on it consistently, but at least the issues are minimal or, at least, manageable. Your other option would be to let it all go and focus 100 percent on other things. In this way, you may have more free time in the beginning, but the compounding damage is often more costly and sometimes irreparable. Like a home, a relationship doesn't have to be a ton of work every day. But it does require you to be attentive to your words and actions and to follow a strict plan for how you will engage with your partner. Once you have those things aligned, navigating the ups and downs of working together will be a lot less difficult. In fact, it might be downright enjoyable.

Remember, this person is or will be someone you likely see and interact with more than your spouse or family. Maintaining a great relationship with them is worth its weight in gold.

Communication

Communication is the most important tool in maintaining a strong partnership. Over and over again in my conversations with those in past or present partnerships, the biggest challenges stemmed from miscommunication. For those who failed in a partnership, it was almost invariably when communication broke down or failed to exist that the partnership fell apart. Those who made it work succeeded because they knew how to express their thoughts, opinions, and concerns.

If you take anything from this book, I hope this is it: taking time to communicate frequently and effectively is the best defense against the breakdown of your partnership.

Because communication is key, I'm going to share practical ways I have found to improve it, as well as tips from others who nailed that skill. It won't hurt to integrate all these in some form or another to improve your chances of mitigating issues. My hope is that these suggestions will help lay a foundation for robust communication between you and your cofounders.

Let's get started.

Look at the Data

Take the time to do the self-assessments discussed in this book, and ask your cofounder to do the same. These assessments are not trivial, and doing them is not busywork or a waste of time. Being able to understand what makes you and your partners tick will replace years of trial and error. Knowing if your partner is detail oriented or big picture, moved by emotion or data, able to work under a deadline or crippled by it allows you to deepen your relationship and become more effective as a team. I call it a hack for relationships as it allows you to permeate your words and actions with the right tactics to be heard and understood. That saves both time and headaches.

Remember Hannah in Chapter 2? She took a personality assessment and was able to determine that perfectionism, adaptability, and easygoingness would be key traits that she needed to seek in a partner. Or Rodrick in Chapter 3? He considered his strengths, weaknesses, and personality style before seeking a cofounder. He knew exactly what he needed to take his company to the next level and went in search of it. Both these founders understood the importance of complementary traits and what it meant for the success of their venture.

Action Items

Pull out all the assessments and tests that you and your cofounder have done and reiterate the points that are true of you. Highlight where you are exceptional: either high or low, positive or negative. This is where you will excel or falter and clash with or complement your cofounders.

Sit down and discuss ways in which both you and your cofounder can communicate more effectively based on what you learned in the assessments. Aim for transparency, vulnerability, and authenticity. There is no point to this exercise if it's built on false pretenses or unspoken expectations.

Strategize how to maximize efficiency to get through issues and challenges, keeping in mind you and your partner's personalities and work styles: for example, methods of bringing up concerns and dealing with them effectively or finding a person who can act as a third party to help put issues in perspective.

Create an environment that works for both of you. For example, hold meetings early for the morning person, reiterate conversations by email for those who need reminders, or put together a customized work schedule for those who get easily distracted. These are all ways of avoiding the bad feelings that can arise if one partner thinks the other is shirking their responsibilities.

Once you have had these discussions, do not be afraid to speak up when your partner misses the mark in an interaction. It isn't petty to say, "Hey, last week when you sent me that email about the sales cycle, adding a simple graph would have been super helpful. I wasn't clear on what you were trying to get across." Even an "If you could bring up concerns about timelines privately instead of in front of our employees" could be all it takes to avoid the buildup of resentment. Just remember to offer your partner the same grace when they bring up a way that you, too, could interact more effectively.

Meetup Sessions

It surprises me how many business partners do not get together to hash out the current status of their business and what they are working on. I know that the entrepreneurial journey is riddled with surprises and involves a to-do list longer than your arm. This is why I know it's possible to have enough fodder to warrant regular conversations.

Taking the time to plan for the future, deal with present-day issues, and reflect on what worked and what didn't in the past is immensely valuable for staying united in your partnership and vision for going forward.

To do this, I would recommend planning for both daily/weekly meetings and monthly and annual connections. Here are some suggestions on how to do this:

Daily

Daily updates are optimum. It's very difficult to have issues with miscommunication when partners are touching base throughout or at the end of a workday. It doesn't need to be an intensive deep dive; it's the habit that is valuable. I recommend tools such as Slack or similar apps as they allow you to keep track of where you are and to look back more easily than searching for emails or scrolling through texts. For a daily update, communicate the following:

- Notable highlights
- What you got done
- What's on your schedule for the next day
- Questions that have arisen
- Musings about previous discussions
- Meeting/phone call reminders for the next day

The great thing about this routine is that the information will be just as valuable for you as for your partner. Consider it a to-do list, a calendar, and a journal all in one. Refer back to it regularly and keep it for future reference.

Weekly

A weekly wrap-up is yet another opportunity to communicate important information to your partners. Slightly more in depth, it can communicate what is still outstanding and what has been put to bed. It helps measure efficiency and can detect potential bottlenecks before they get too constrictive. Sit down with your partner or email and share the following:

- What got accomplished
- The overall plan for the following week
- The status of your projects or jobs
- Meeting/phone call reminders for the next week
- Bank account totals and review weekly financials
- Any notable events that occurred over the week

Monthly

There are twelve months in a year. These chunks of time are a great summation for determining whether or not you are on track to reach your overall goals. Communication is accountability. If you are able to stay on top of what is happening in your business, you will be able to catch when there is a deviation from the plan and bring it back into alignment.

Every four weeks, pull out a white board, carve out two hours, and discuss the following:

- The current state of the business from each founder's perspective
- The business strategy for reaching your goals and key milestones
- What's exciting
- What's challenging
- What's upcoming and what did or didn't work since your last meeting
- A quick rundown of financials: revenue, expenses, receivables, account balances, next month's large payments
- A quick update on employees

Take time to share about what's going on in your personal life.

- On a scale of one to ten, share how you are handling the stress that is coming from the business. Discuss ways that everyone can mitigate the effects and enjoy the journey more.
- Update on holidays and needs. Don't spring these on your partner!
- Bring up any other issues, concerns, or challenges that are occurring or that you foresee in the future.

Acknowledge each other's strengths and compliment one another on jobs that were well done. Celebrate your wins! Perspective can easily be lost when you are constantly focused on improvement and damage control.

Take a picture of your white board as both a reminder of what you spoke about and a memento. I have a couple of pictures of these sessions from the early days of our businesses, and it's amazing to see how closely our paths followed what we had discussed and planned.

Annually

If there is one activity that can ensure the longevity of your partnership, this is it. It's the one opportunity to sync your minds and actions toward the vision you have for your business. It's the pinnacle of intentionality within your partnership, and it has the ability to strengthen your partnership's effectiveness and the growth of your business.

The annual meeting is not to be taken lightly. It requires planning and preparation. I would suggest taking a weekend, preferably away from your usual surroundings so that you are not distracted by your working environment. Create an agenda with clear outcomes that you want to accomplish. Every year, make time to discuss the following:

- Do an honest assessment of the business plan and current execution strategy. Do you need to pivot? Are you missing any key elements?
- Review budget and financials.
- Review sales and marketing related practices.
- Review employees, board, advisers, et cetera.
- Do an honest review of your working partnership relationship. Is there anywhere there can be improvement? Are there certain habits or exercises that work extremely well?
- Review your legal partnership documents. Make any changes you see fit. Be sure to sign each revision.
- Be open and specific about what was awesome over the last year. This is a great time to encourage one another with what worked. Starting and running a business are tough but made much easier when you have a cheering squad in your corner. Again, remember that when you encourage your partner, you are also helping yourself as you are both on the same team.
- Have fun! Do something that creates an epic memory that you can look back on and laugh. All work and no play makes Jack a dull boy. Make this event something to look forward to, not to be dreaded.

Putting It All Together

Does this seem like a lot? Maybe. But it's necessary for a good partnership. This is what I mean when I say being intentional. Every set of business partners I've met who did some form of these exercises had a strong partnership. Trust and even good feelings were significantly greater between them than between those who thought the exercises were a waste of time or not a priority.

Think of the potential ROI of the following:

- Daily: Ten minutes out of 1,440 minutes in a day
- Weekly: Thirty minutes out of 10,080 in a week
- Monthly: Two hours out of 730 in a month
- Annually: Eight hours out of 8,760 in a year

Your partnership will either be an asset or a liability for your business. It is also the one thing that doesn't have a pressing urgency, which is why it can be easily ignored. But if it's strong, your business will flourish, and the journey will be more enjoyable. If it's not, your business is at risk.

You decide if a short time commitment is worth it. You're the one who has to live with the decision.

The Core of Communication

Beyond the practical exercises above that allow for clarity and effective management of your partnership, there are additional elements that can kick your communication into overdrive. After interviewing multiple partners about what worked and what didn't, I've identified a trend. While few partnerships were actually intentional about making their partnerships a priority, those who were successful often had four important factors present within their relationship that seemed to mitigate their struggles. With further investigation, I noticed that almost all the partnerships that were having issues or that had failed lacked these four factors, or at the most, only had minimal occurrences of them.

The four factors are vulnerability, authenticity, transparency, and truthfulness (VATT).

Practice VATT

These four factors need to blanket every component of your relationship. They should permeate all that you do in order to lessen the drama, miscommunication, and lack of efficiency that can occur when doubt, emotions, and struggles come into play. They are there to ensure cohesion throughout your journey. When cracks in the relationship begin to form (and they will, no doubt about it), they can be handled as soon as they are detected.

Let's dissect each of these factors and discuss why they are so important.

Vulnerability

If you treat your cofounder like the enemy, they'll become your enemy.

Vulnerability is the ability to open up and trust. It's exposing your back to your partner knowing they won't stick a knife in. There is always risk, and much of this book is about teaching you to manage the risks that can be managed. But there are some that just can't. The way you treat your cofounder regarding those unmanageable risks determines whether or not you really trust them.

When you give your partner the benefit of the doubt, you're choosing to be vulnerable, not a blind doormat. And when you're honest with them about your own fears and shortcomings, you're trusting them not to laugh at you. Vulnerability is choosing to trust someone in a way that means they could hurt you; it means acting on the belief that they won't.

Cathy and Michael started their partnership on the right footing. They discussed at length their goals and expectations and worked together to plan the next five years in their business. But not long after they launched their company, Cathy began to recognize certain traits in Michael that reminded her of her ex-husband. The result of this association meant that almost everything Michael did, Cathy second-guessed. She looked for hidden meanings in his words and questioned many of his decisions. And when Michael confronted her about her peculiar behaviour, she lied and said there was nothing wrong. She didn't feel like she could tell him about her inner struggles. She knew that how she was acting was misplaced, but she wasn't willing to be vulnerable and share the source of her mistrust. In time, being treated like a criminal and not knowing why made Michael want to end the partnership.

Do not invite confusion and uncertainty into the relationship with your cofounder. Learn to be vulnerable.

Authenticity

Brené Brown may have the greatest and most simplistic explanation of what authenticity looks like: "Authenticity is a collection of choices that we have to make every day. It's about the choice to show up and be real. The choice to be honest. The choice to let our true selves be seen."[1]

This type of authenticity is important in a partnership because in business, everything you do together builds on what you built before. If you fail to be who you are in your cofounder partnership, you will find yourself falling into a role that may leave you discontented and bitter. If you think one thing but say the opposite in order to keep the peace or not potentially look foolish or ill informed, know that inauthentic action informs how you make decisions. If you do not act as your authentic self, you will stifle your creative and productive energy.

John and Colin were eyeballs deep in their early-stage start-up. John agreed to take on marketing despite the fact that he had never marketed a product in his life. It was the one task that made him feel like a fish out of water. This was why he was often defensive and closed off when he was emotionally struggling with the task. He started getting short with Colin when Colin would touch base to see how things were going in this department. Colin saw this as John neglecting his role and began to get annoyed. This introduced a crack in their relationship.

---

1 - Brené Brown, *The Gifts of Imperfection: 10th Anniversary Edition* (Center City, MN: Hazelden Publishing, 2022), 67.

So many times I've heard a partner's frustration about what they felt was the apathy and disregard the other partner had for their responsibilities. What I went on to discover was that often, it was more of a lack of confidence in the role and fear of failure that paralyzed them, not a laissez-faire attitude. Had there been more honesty and authenticity between the partners, they could have tackled the issue together through collaboration or even by redesigning roles.

In entrepreneurship, you cannot always choose the tasks you have to undertake. However, when you can, take that moment to align them with who you are and how you were designed. Your partner and your business will be better off for it.

Spare yourself the frustration. Always be authentic.

Transparency

Transparency means uncovering the good and bad so people can see it for what it is. When you could act in secret, even if it wouldn't be a big deal, but you decide to make your actions open and clean anyway, that's transparency.

In business, transparency means documenting everything you do and making your half of the company visible, even when nothing shady is happening. It differs from vulnerability in that it keeps the other person from having to rely on trust. They can see with their own eyes what you're doing. The fact that you're so completely open breeds more trust because it speaks volumes about your commitment to right actions.

If you manage the money, frequently walk your partner through the financials without waiting for them to request it. If you are in charge of HR, share any notable event and how it is being handled so your partner isn't in the dark about employee relations. If you are in sales, find a way to communicate your workload and its progress. Give them open access to your sales funnel so they can not only have confidence in your activity level but also keep an eye on how the company is progressing.

Transparency is also crucial when it comes to your spouse or significant other. You're going to be spending a lot of time with your cofounder. Make sure your spouse knows the door is always open, so to speak. They can poke their nose in at any time and check to make sure nothing "offside" is happening in the office. Being transparent helps your spouse relax because they see that you're proactively taking steps to ensure their confidence.

Jeff and Sarah started off with clear expectations. Jeff would manage their money, and Sarah would handle running the shop. Sarah told Jeff she trusted him, and since she was so busy, she didn't need to be regularly updated—only if there was something major to note. Over time, the reason this arrangement was dangerous began to show itself.

One day, Sarah asked Jeff to purchase some new supplies, but Jeff told her they didn't have the money at the moment, and she would need to wait a couple of days. When she questioned why, he brushed her off and told her not to worry. When it happened again a couple of weeks later, Sarah started to wonder what was really happening with the books. Finally, after a third incident, she snapped at Jeff and asked where all their money was going. Jeff was shocked. When they sat down together and he opened the books, Jeff's numbers were all correct. A regular client, who had fallen on tough times, had requested an extension to pay their invoices, and because of that, capital had to be allocated differently on their side. Without this insight, Sarah was left to come up with her own conclusions, and as a result, she'd started to grow suspicious. Lack of transparency had opened up gaps for doubt to fester.

Spare yourself the heartache. Strive to be transparent.

Truthfulness

The saying "The truth will set you free" can often seem easier said than done. When you make a mistake or a wrong decision, it may seem like a better plan to lie or fudge the facts about who was responsible or how the issue came to be. These tactics may soften the repercussions of poor choices in the short term, but in the end, they can lead to even more serious consequences.

Truthfulness is *essential* for maintaining that precious trust factor that must be present in every partnership. A lie, even the smallest, has the potential to shake a strong foundation and put in jeopardy everything that has been built. Even a smudging of the facts, when discovered, can put in question every word and deed that is said and done going forward.

Do not put your partner in the position of having to question your integrity. In all matters, be truthful, even when it's hard, embarrassing, or shameful. When you understand how much partners are intertwined, you will get why lying to them is not much different from lying to yourself; it isn't effective, and it doesn't help you.

Additionally, always be that partner ready with grace and empathy when the truth has to be said. Don't make the environment difficult for truthfulness—ready to punish every mistake your partner makes. Be ready with understanding and gratitude and even acknowledge their willingness to be honest. A simple comment like "I'm glad you told me exactly how that went down. It probably wasn't easy, but I appreciate the honesty, and let's figure out the plan together for moving forward from here" is incredibly effective in building an environment for trust.

Let your relationship with your partner be built on actuality and fact. Strive to always be truthful.

Parts of a Whole

VATT is not about the feelings you have toward your cofounder. VATT is the actions you need to take in order to maintain a strong partnership built on integrity.

With that in mind, there is a mentality that I suggest you use when making decisions in your business and interacting with your partners: you and your partner(s) are two/three/four parts of a whole. What affects one part or what one part does will always affect the entire group.

Nothing you do now as a cofounder happens in a vacuum. You're not going to be a tree falling in the forest without anyone hearing. Instead, what you do and what your partners do will invariably have an impact on everyone in the partnership. Your words and actions in the business will directly affect them for the basic reason that together, you form the founding team. Investors, clients, employees will all presume you move forward in agreement and therefore everything said and done by the company will automatically be attributed to the shared beliefs and decisions of you and your partners. Everyone will be held responsible for how all the members individually handle finances, HR, customer service, culture—basically every matter within your company. So, speak and act accordingly.

This is why it is so important to choose your partner wisely and to be intentional in your partnership. Integrity is an invaluable virtue to build a business on, and vulnerability, authenticity, transparency, and truthfulness within the partnership are ways to ensure it happens.

Learn from Ingrid

Erling was shocked that Ingrid was so angry over the cookies. He genuinely thought that it was not an issue and even presumed that Ingrid did it herself. And she kind of did, though her expectations about the acceptable amount had been kept secret.

In response, Erling explained that he considered much of the gifting as marketing, as many times, it led to sales from new customers trying the product. While often it was just his family and friends who benefited, he knew the perk kept them excited about his work, which he also saw as an advantage.

Ingrid hadn't considered that angle before. She was surprised to hear that he'd been thinking of the business all along.

The outburst triggered a conversation about expectations. In this case, there was a happy ending. Both partners agreed that in the future, any food taken from the bakery would, at a minimum, have the cost of goods covered.

Now Ingrid can laugh about the experience. "I never thought this would be an issue and just expected we would either not take goods or would pay for them. I guess these are things you need to think about when you start a business with someone. Even something as little as taking a cookie."

Discuss your cookies with your cofounder. Don't leave anything to chance.

CHAPTER 12

The Long Game Trifecta: Mindset, Expectations, and Trust

Rufaro is a veteran in building businesses. His experiences have garnered him a reputation as "the man who's done it all". He laughs at the nickname but acknowledges the sentiment. "I've built many different kinds of businesses, but I've also done so with the help of many people." It is for this reason that his advice on partnerships has been sought out by so many in his sphere.

His biggest piece of advice is this: "When someone asks me what is the most important thing in a partnership, I always tell them: trust. If you cannot trust the people you've linked arms with, you'll be plagued with misery."

Of the twelve businesses Rufaro has started, ten involved partners. "I have always found myself gravitating to a business model where someone else has begun the ideation process." Either through seeking out operating partners or being sought out himself to join someone else's idea, Rufaro has had the opportunity to experience multiple ways of partnering. Many of the lessons in this book could be drawn from his expansive business history. According to Rufaro, most of his partners have been good, a few have been bad, but all were experiences he would have repeated, if just for the lessons learned. And the bad experiences have not soured him on partnering. "I will always prefer to start a business with someone. I'm not a lone ranger."

Rufaro shared with me that his emphasis on trust stems from the few bad partnerships he's experienced. "I've never started a partnership expecting trouble. I always do my due diligence on the skills and capacity of those I get into business with." While he focused on hard skills like sales, marketing, operations, and design, early on, he never gave much thought to the "soft" skills. "I especially didn't consider the signals that could come from how someone lived their personal life or how they spoke about themselves and others and how these factors could point to potential trouble ahead."

Rufaro shared with me the story of one partner who, in his opinion, was the main reason the business failed to thrive. "Oftentimes, it's a culmination of many different factors which lead to the demise of a business. But in this instance, I think that it was his lack of trust that ultimately did us in.

"We met after I had had success already in previous ventures." Rufaro now believes this prior success made his partner feel insecure. "He, too, had a successful business prior to ours, but he would often overstate the heights it actually got to." There was a feeling of one-upmanship that infused their conversations. Rufaro found it uncomfortable swapping stories as doing so often developed an air of competition. "I never let it bother me, but I certainly steered our conversations away from any opportunity to fall into the trap."

In their newly formed partnership, Rufaro was to be the financier as well as the one to seek out the large corporate clients necessary to grow their business. "My partner was to be the operator and basically rebuild the same business model he had in his previous venture, only this time in a new industry and with more capital to build bigger." Unfortunately, this division of roles created problems early on. The sales process took approximately eight to twelve weeks, so in the beginning, the flow was slow. Then the customers started pouring in, and the business exploded. During this time Rufaro was seldom in the office because of all of the customer meetings, so his partner was alone at the factory handling operations and expansion. "It was a lot, but by no means was I MIA. My role was just different. And for some reason, he resented me for that."

Rufaro began to face little comments like "While you hobnob with the executives at XYZ, I'll just be here working in the office." Or "I'll just be here doing the grunt work while you eat fancy lunches." At first, Rufaro thought he was joking. After a while, the tone got more and more accusatory. "He began to accuse me of doing 'nothing.'" Rufaro remembers that it made no sense to him as it was clear that he was signing deals. "I suppose because he did not actually see the work taking place, he presumed my role was leisure and filled with days of minimal hours and jet-setting."

It got so bad that his partner began to only communicate through email. "I tried calling him and leaving a message, but he would respond only via email or text." Not only did communication stall, but his lack of trust increased. "He actually hired a private investigator. I found out later." Fortunately, the outcome of the investigator's report brought his partner back to the table. "He told me that he realized that our roles were just different, that everyone was pulling their weight, and that we should let everything go and just focus on the business."

Rufaro wasn't harboring ill will. He took the gesture as a chance to start over on a better note. Still, the lack of trust continued to rear its ugly head. "The comments never let up, and while this time they weren't as accusatory, the experience got old really quick."

Partnerships Require Your Best

Too many founders underestimate the distructive capabilities that issues they know and recognize within themselves or their cofounder can have on their partnership. I don't mean problem areas that can be managed through conversation and structure, like punctuality. What I am talking about are those that may lay lurking under the surface; the ones that may require professional intervention or therapy. For example, trust or anger issues. Deep-seeded issues like these, will likely cause someone to struggle to be a confident business partner and therefore set up the partnership for struggles down the road.

Unfortunately, there's often no getting around these points of concern. You've got to face them and be honest about whether or not you can work with, or through, them. In Rufaro's story, his partner hired a private investigator, yet even documented proof of Rufaro's honesty still wasn't enough to fix the lack of faith. The suspicious partner had a broken mindset, secret expectations, and an inability to trust.

I want to break down three key factors (that I call the Trifecta) that can lead to painful dead ends for your partnership and your business if not managed correctly. You need to address these factors both within yourself and with your potential or current cofounder. Without a healthy outlook on them, struggle and conflict are just a disagreement away.

Get Your Mind Right

The cofounder relationship is unique among partnerships. It's intimate without the intimacy. It's personal while needing to be professional. The paradox is enough to make your head spin. So how do you walk this fine line and build a partnership that lasts?

After interviewing hundreds of cofounders, I've found a collection of similar rules, tasks, and guidelines common among the best. I have also heard stories from those who were struggling or who had failed a partnership and found common threads that ultimately played a role in the partnership's demise. All these relate to your mindset and mental state. I have divided them into sixteen steps that you can take to ensure your partnership flourishes.

Note that while they are all vital, you may recognize one particular area where you are failing miserably. If so, don't feel bad—we all have challenges to overcome. Don't shy away from the issue. It could be the one thing that, if turned around, will result in the strong partnership your company, employees, and customers need you to have.

Start with a Strong Mind Frame

The best place to start when building a relationship is with the person staring at you in the mirror. This is the easiest place because no one else is holding you back from taking action. You are fully responsible and able to change your thoughts, words, and actions. You do not need anyone's permission to do it, nor are you on anyone else's time frame. You can choose to commit 100 percent or 0 percent. And your decision will have a huge effect on your return.

I have found that when one person in a relationship decides to make changes within themselves, the other person tends to step up and make their own changes without any prodding. It may not be a complete turn-around, but it will be some change for the better. And that is better than nothing, isn't it?

Within yourself is the place where you will see the most dramatic impact. You will make the changes in your own life, so you will be the most affected. By changing your perception and perspective, you will be the sole recipient of a new way of life. Sure, your cofounder will feel the effects as you speak and act differently toward them. So will your romantic partner. But you will feel the impact in the boardroom and while you're alone at home.

So what kind of mind frame should you have? I've broken this down into five sub-steps that will create the one you want to achieve.

Where Is Your Focus?

When starting a company or running a business, it's easier to see what's going wrong than what's going right. A workday is seldom designated to tackle those tasks which are moving along nicely, but instead, it's directed toward those that need attention and repair. However, many veteran entre-preneurs say a balanced approach toward noticing and focusing on what is working in your business and what is not is a better methodology for determining the output of your time.

The benefit of the cofounder relationship is that both of you can share the load when dealing with the good and the challenging. Keep in mind, though, leaving one partner to put out all the fires and the other to focus on the growth of what is winning can lead one feeling overly optimistic and the other overly pessimistic. Don't overload one with trouble and leave them dreading coming to work. Have all the partners share in the responsibilities where possible.

Benefit of the Doubt

Sometimes things get rocky. When they do, remember that you picked this business partner for a reason.

If your cofounder is a relatively normal human being, you can guess that whatever their actions, words, or decisions, the intention was not to purposely plummet the company into bankruptcy or to make you look bad. There may have been a method to their madness. As their partner, you owe them the chance to explain their side of the story.

Each of you will have roles. You will both be making decisions that may or may not need to include the other person. Therefore, recognize now that not all of the decisions you make will be perfect. Entrepreneurship is 90 percent feeling your way through the darkness, so a poor decision, action, or choice of words will happen. Both of you will make mistakes. When your partner is the one at fault, approach the situation with the same grace you would want your partner to have with you. Remember, you are both aiming for the same goal: success for your company and for yourselves. Getting more information about mistakes allows you to know the full picture before you act, as well as take measures so they aren't repeated.

Additionally, if you happen to be the recipient of that benefit of the doubt from your cofounder, be sure to acknowledge that they held their tongue until they had spoken to you. Be grateful. Their pause for more information shows maturity and respect, two things that should not be ignored.

Mistakes happen. Anticipate frustrations, disappointments, and hurts. Be gracious when your partner is at fault. You may be in need of that same grace sooner than you want to admit.

Be OK with Disagreement

Some people are so fearful of conflict that any disagreement feels like the sky is falling.

I can assure you that you and your partner will not agree on every decision. If you do not engage while disagreeing, you will build up resentment and eventually explode. Trust in the power of communication to help you work through your conflict and see a better way on the other side. Choose to trust or choose to fall apart. There's no way around it except to lean in.

Know that it is OK to agree to disagree. As long as both people feel they have been heard, you should be able to come up with a course of action that is, minimally, palatable to both sides. Accepting that sometimes that will have to be enough will get you further than requiring that each party always gets exactly what they want.

Prepare for the Marathon

Your company journey will have many twists and turns. You'll see staff come and go, your product will adapt and change, suppliers will be traded in and out, your endgame altered, and who knows what else.

What will (hopefully) stay constant is your cofounder. The plan should be to build a cofoundership that stands the test of time. That's the goal of this book, right? You need to see your partnership as that permanent fixture that comes with you throughout the entire journey. When you realize your partner isn't going anywhere and will always need to be factored in, you will be more able to make concessions for the sake of the relationship. Ultimately, that means making concessions for the sake of the business.

Prepare yourself for the long haul in this relationship. Make decisions for the long term, not to make yourself feel better ten minutes from now.

Drop the Ego

This is such a big one that I could probably dedicate a whole chapter to it; however, I'll do my best to summarize it here because ego is a mindset. It's how you see yourself and those around you. Being able to view yourself and your cofounder as two parts of one whole instead of two parts competing for the most glory will help you act in a way that isn't selfish or self-promoting.

A damaged ego is typically the cause of overreaction, jealousy, and insecurity. If you don't hold captive these negative feelings that come from a self-centered ego, you can hardly expect your partner to do so. Every action has a reaction, and ego, imposed on others, seldom elicits a positive one.

To combat this, you need a "them-focused" mentality: by taking care of your partner, you take care of yourself. Looking outward, acknowledging that together—not individually—you are creating something great will help you see your partnership as a team effort. Being conscious of protecting the relationship, ensuring that everyone gets acknowledged for the role they play, will go a long way in strengthening your teamwork. Don't let ego ruin the relationship you need to rely on.

When you start strong, it makes the whole journey easier. These five sub-steps add up to the first step you should take to begin your partnership with the strongest mind frame. That mental balance will help with the next fifteen steps.

Take Action

Having a great mind frame is wonderful, but it's useless without action.

You can have all the points above nailed, but if you fail to demonstrate where you stand, your partner will feel unsteady. They may take nervous steps to figure out how you feel. You may even drive them into unhealthy behaviors by sending the wrong signals. The responsibility falls on you to show that you have made the partnership a priority. That includes using good communication skills and being clear with your partner about how you feel.

Remember, you cannot change others or make others act the way you want. You can only effect change through yourself. That said, I haven't met any business partners who didn't enjoy a great partnership or see an improvement in it when they took the actions listed in this section.

Proper mindset plus action leads to a better life.

Develop Conflict Resolution Skills

Disagreements and arguments cause a particularly vulnerable time for the partnership. These can occur because of different points of view; actions someone failed to take or do appropriately; or behaviors that are annoying, offensive, or hurtful. Conflict is actually an important part of a relationship because it makes clear how each person feels, and it can also flush out solutions to a problem that need to be addressed. The problem is that it can be dangerous because there is a strong possibility of saying hurtful things that can make you or your partner feel devalued or misunderstood.

To avoid this, arguments need to focus on the specific issue at hand. It is especially helpful if you find ways to intersperse positive comments about what is working in the situation even though you are expressing disagreement. The following examples state the area of disagreement but also acknowledge your partner in some way.

- "I know you want the office to look nice, but I'm concerned about the expense."
- "I know you feel this employee is effective, but from where I stand, I see missed deadlines and incomplete work."

People are different, and their priorities vary. The goal here is to discuss the differences and be clear that while you do not agree with your partner's priority or opinion, you respect it because you respect them. And you know they aren't acting out of stupidity or malice.

You can disagree in an agreeable way. In fact, some good relationships are characterized by an ongoing expression of differences. Sometimes the best partnerships are a combination of the most different set of partners, so disagreements are bound to happen. The success of these partners is most likely attributable to the way that their "fighting" is done. They disagree strongly but take the time to ensure that their thought process is heard and understood while maintaining respect for one another and staying solution focused.

Get good at conflict resolution; it separates those who succeed from those who don't.

Avoid the Blame Game

Blame gets you nowhere. Yes, it's natural to want to point to the cause of a problem. But blame's effectiveness as a tool for constructive criticism is greatly overshadowed by its effectiveness at building walls.

Blame says, "It's your fault." No one responds well to that. That's an attack. No one likes to be attacked, especially by their business partner. If you turn blame attacks on your cofounder, expect them to feel hurt and close their doors against you.

Where blame says, "It's your fault," partnership says, "This decision had some negative consequences; how do we fix them and ensure they don't happen again?" It's not a personal dig at someone's abilities or smarts but instead a recognition that many factors contribute to a poorly executed plan. Choices are made after a series of events, conversations, and involvement of other people. Owning the issue together and finding a solution as a team means you're not calling the other person out as the weakest link in the chain. It's looking at the problem, not the person.

Choose Your Battles

Building a business is a marathon, not a sprint. Even if your goal is to flip the company, the amount of time you will spend with your cofounder warrants a thoughtful approach to what is and what isn't worth the fight.

One way to look at this topic is to go back to your honest self-evaluation. Look at the nonnegotiables and use them to draw the hard lines. This is where knowing yourself is going to be invaluable. Knowing what you absolutely cannot live with or compromise on will enable you to determine whether it is worth the conflict.

Determine who will be most affected by the issue or who is the most passionate about how it is addressed. Sometimes, partners jump out of their lane and draw a hard line on an issue that really doesn't affect them in the same way it does their partner. Consider allowing a partner to make the final call when they carry the weight and responsibility of it. Even a deep belief in a course of action is an opportunity to let go and show trust in your partner.

Just remember, when you do argue, stay respectful. Fully value each other even if you don't agree with or are unable to see the other side. The wise adage says, "Do you want to be right, or do you want to be happy?"

Show Solidarity

Never talk down to, yell at, or disrespect your cofounder, either in private or (especially) in public. Even if they are wrong, never air your issues out in the open. When the doors are closed, you can argue, but when you're among others, you're a team. If you break this rule, there's a good possibility you will break your company culture. No one wants to invest in, support, or work for a divided team.

Balance Your Social Life with Work

One set of cofounders I interviewed for this book said, "One thing that worked for us is that we never hang out outside of work."

Another set of cofounders said, "One thing that worked for us is that we often hang out outside of work."

Who's right? Well, both of them because their approach worked for their needs. Do I have the perfect answer for how to approach your social life together? No. But a balance is likely better, at least to begin with. During the building phase of my own businesses, my cofounder and I often had to travel. We always made sure to tack on some fun time to experience the location we were visiting. It built memories and was a way to blow off steam, never mind that it turned the journey into something as special as the desired goal. That said, we also chose to eat breakfast on our own time, take breaks to ourselves throughout the day, even sightsee all alone when it was an interest that wasn't shared. Balance was the key.

Talk about how much private time you and your cofounder want to share, and make sure you keep some boundaries in place. Also, should the time come, respect your partner's decision to pull back from hanging out socially. It is not likely personal but more the result of a need to take a break from the elements that make up their work life. If it is you who wants to pull back, consider having a specific conversation about it. Clarify why you're choosing to limit interaction and put their mind at ease that your distance is not because you are angry with them.

Be Honest

Trust is your most powerful ally. If that is gone, it will be difficult to rebuild. And without trust, your business is doomed.

In the absence of camaraderie, the way you spend money and make decisions become the only way to determine trust. "I may not like you, but I trust you because I can see your choices." Any other combination doesn't work. A business can be sustained if there is trust between two people who cannot get along. As long as you can be cordial and professional, you can build a strong business based on trust. But where trust isn't present, even the best of friends will find themselves in conflict.

Hear and Be Heard

The most broken cofounder teams I interview say things like, "She doesn't listen to me," or "He does what he wants, no matter what I say."

All of us want to feel that we have influence over our partners. Which means we have to feel and know we are being heard. The goal is not to control your partner but to communicate clearly your thoughts and expectations and be willing to let them do the same. Only when this is achieved can progress be made.

Make an effort to truly listen to your partner and find ways to make sure that you yourself are also being heard.

No Nagging!

It is essential to understand that nagging does not work. When you are frustrated or angry about an issue and you constantly repeat to your cofounder something they already know, it will have a negative effect on the relationship.

Nagging doesn't get you anywhere. For example, restating the obvious: "You have to complete the corporate taxes or we will be fined," or "You really have to fire that person or else we can't rehire" will often result in a counterattack or withdrawal into angry silence.

Instead, state your concerns with a solution. This way, you move more swiftly toward resolution and demonstrate the team effort your partnership entails. So instead of "You have to complete the corporate taxes," you might say, "Do you want me to help you get some of the receipts together so you can complete the corporate taxes?" Or "I know it's going to be a difficult conversation; do you want me to be with you when we fire that employee?" An attempt to help with the solution rather than stating the obvious gives the other person options for moving forward.

The more options people feel they have, the less defensive or angry their response is likely to be. And the less you remind them of obvious basics, the less they will feel like you're calling them stupid.

Avoid Judgments

It's crucial to have verbal exchanges that are nonjudgmental.

Judgmental types of communication can be triggered when one partner is feeling hurt or angry. These words, when they come from a space of negative judgment, can make one feel diminished and devalued. People stop listening and instead focus inward and protect themselves, resulting in defensive or passive-aggressive responses. The problem is that words said in anger or defensiveness cannot be taken back, even with an apology. It can take a lot of work to fix the damage done by disparaging statements.

Try to focus on the task, not the person. When you do this, judgment can turn to positive criticism, and change will become more likely.

Now, with all this new information, there's a final set of mind states that one can aim for to grow in a partnership. The aim here is not to maintain a good relationship but to create something far better: a relationship built on trust and fine-tuned for efficacy.

Get Over It, Quickly

Moving on from conflict and disagreements needs to be part of your intentional practice with your business partner. Because all the emotions that come with conflict can permeate every movement you make within your company, you cannot afford to taint the decisions and actions you take with bad blood. A decision made out of spite or pettiness can have long-lasting negative ramifications. You need to learn to forgive and forget and to move on without seeking vindication.

Confront Personal Issues Head On

This is where the intimate, personal side rears its ugly head in a partnership. It's when one of the cofounders says or does something that hurts the other(s) in a personal way. Having experienced it myself (and done it myself, to be honest) and after hearing about it from others, I've realized how unavoidable this is. You're both working long hours on something that means a great deal to you. Mistakes will be made. You'll both be stressed. Odds are good that one of you will do or say something that hurts the other partner. It happens in romantic relationships, so why would business be any different?

Hiding the pain caused by your partner can quickly build it into a festering volcano in very short order. Many are capable of brushing things under the rug, and while that can actually be a great skill, there are times that it can be a bad move.

Instead, confront these issues head on. Sometimes the best way is to go to your cofounder and say, "I'm feeling very hurt. Maybe you didn't mean it this way, but this is how I'm feeling. We need to find a way through this." That acknowledges that your cofounder is not a villain, yet the situation is serious to you, all while leaving the door open for them to apologize and make amends.

Become Your Partner's Biggest Champion

How to Win Friends and Influence People is among the top three books ever written. In it, the author talks about the power of overhearing a compliment. Your partner needs to overhear you complimenting them. They should feel like you're their biggest supporter in the world. When they're away on a hard business trip, they should be able to picture you leading a cheer for their success. When they handle a project through to success, make sure they know how much you appreciate and respect the work it took to complete.

Create a culture of compliments. Your partnership will benefit as will your corporate culture as it will trickle down to your team as a model of how you expect everyone to interact.

Honor Your Partner's Decisions

Staying in your lane goes hand in hand with honoring your partner's decisions. If you are communicating frequently and effectively, the decisions your partner makes should align with yours. If they don't, you should first take the time to reflect: "Why do I really think this was a bad decision? Is this an emotional call or something based on fact?"

When decisions don't align, it's a sign you need to meet up and see why. Has someone's vision for the company changed? Has one of you changed their plan for execution? Asking for their reasoning in a respectful manner and with an open mind will allow you to understand why they made the choice they did. You may even come to see they made the wrong decision for the right reason, like turning down a contract so as not to violate their principles. If you still disagree with the decision, you can have a conversation about shared goals for the business and get back on track.

Once again, you need to respect your partner and recognize they're making decisions according to a plan, rather than out of malice or stupidity.

Life as an entrepreneur can get so busy that your partnership and its health can be easily overlooked. It may sound trite, but having physical reminders around you that help you see your partnership in a good light can be a great way to maintain a positive relationship. Maybe you can keep souvenirs from your trips together in the office lobby or trophies and plaques of achievements you have conquered together. These reminders will trigger feelings of happiness and success and can remind you to do something that day to work on strengthening your partnership. Do whatever works for you, but find a way to alert yourself to check on your relationship and keep it strong.

Note: at The Cofounder's Hub, we created a free tool to help you keep your partnership front and center. Sign up to receive daily or weekly emails with tips and tricks designed to help you strengthen your partnership via quotes to consider, exercises to try, and questions to ask or ponder, each with the goal of helping you stay intentional with your partner. Go sign up . . . it's free!

Managing Expectations

In Part I of this book, you were asked to clearly define your expectations on a myriad of different topics, from time and capital investment to job roles and titles. As time goes by, those expectations may need to be altered to reflect the current state and direction of the company. When this happens, you'll need to manage and communicate those changes.

A business is like a living entity, shaping itself and taking on a life of its own as time progresses. The role of cofounders is to guide the direction but also to bend with the twists and turns as they come up. Rigidity and arrogance will not be rewarded. When it comes to your cofounder partnership, there needs to be a level of openness and grace to ensure that the relationship moves through the obstacles and challenges while maintaining trust and comfort.

Raising a business is a lot like raising a child. Parents have a fixed idea in their heads of what this little person will do, say, and become. Quickly, though, every parent realizes that they have a lot less control than they think they did. The same is true in business. As a founder, you may have set a one-month, ninety-day, half-year, and yearly goals. You might even have a plan laid out for exactly what the business should look like in five years. You will realize that forces outside your control and feedback from the marketplace will often alter those plans. So you need to be adaptable, both in your execution and your expectations.

To help you manage expectations, let's talk about what you can look forward to in each stage and how to talk to your cofounder about what you want.

Early-Stage Expectations

In the first twelve to eighteen months of your start-up, I suggest you keep a keen eye on the roles and expectations you have set for yourselves as cofounders. Expectations like who is handling payroll, who will hire employees, even who will take out the trash all have answers that could be very different from one partner to the next. The more expectations you discuss at this stage the better because you are laying the foundation for your partnership and the road map for your business.

When it comes to your relationship and partnership, watch especially for any breakdowns that may be starting to occur. When I interviewed cofounders, I often heard that the start of a partnership dissolution began early on. If they'd dealt with breakdowns early, many felt issues might not have gotten so big later on. That's because issues disintegrate your future plans when left unchecked. Those teams that addressed the issues early on tended to work through the challenges quickly and efficiently.

The truth is you don't know what your entrepreneurial journey is going to look like. One minute, you are focused on customer acquisition; the next, you are scrambling to build your technology or product. In one month, you are desperately trying to grow your team, and in another, you are looking for ways to cut overhead. Through all this, it's easy to expect your partner to play a certain role or rise to a particular standard. If you don't discuss this, it's very easy for them, or you, to let the other down unintentionally. No one is a mind reader. Use your scheduled check-in times to clarify who, how, and when tasks and roles will be taken up. In an early-stage business, cofounders need to wear all the hats they can;

it's easy for things to slip through the cracks or for one of you to expect they'll be tackled by the other.

It's during this time that the cofounders find out who's on this trip for the long haul. When it gets hard, people start to get discouraged and frustrated. This is where doubt and disappointment start to creep in. People begin to question not only the validity of the business idea but also their own ability to execute it.

The great thing is, this is what a cofounder is for! Your business partner should be there to pick you up when you are feeling down and pump life into your soul again. My cofounder Stephen and I had moments of discouragement, but fortunately, we never felt them at the same time. When one was down, the other was there to encourage and shed light on the positive. Later down the road, those roles would be reversed, and this time, it was the other person's turn to lift up and be the rock.

This is one of the biggest perks of having a cofounder. Your role is to encourage and be there to support one another as things get tough. To do that, however, you need transparency, vulnerability, and authenticity. You build these by maintaining clear expectations and having frequent discussions about goals and issues early on.

Phase Two Expectations

After a while, as your business starts to find its groove, it may be time to have an honest discussion about roles going forward. You and your partner may have settled into particular roles in the start-up phase based on skills or because you just had to do it. But now may be the time to stop and say, "Is this really the best place for me?"

This is a perfect time to remember that you are in this together. And if one of you isn't happy, you're probably both going to end up unhappy. Work together to find the fit that helps the team to work in the most optimal way. Don't rely on unspoken expectations.

As you clarify your expectation in this phase, blurring lines a bit can also be helpful for the longevity of the business. Sharing responsibilities and trying what the other is doing allows partners to get a taste of what's on everyone's plate. It also provides a bit of redundancy should you be hit by the proverbial bus. You don't want to be irreplaceable when a health or personal issue strikes. Sharing some roles keeps you both in touch with all the working parts of your business, not just your own, so you see the whole picture. It also allows for a fresh set of eyes to assess what is going on and provide new insights and suggestions.

With this in mind, I'm going to make a special note about the roles of CEO and COO as I've heard similar sentiments in enough cases to take note. For the COO, it is typical that the list of roles and responsibilities is huge in the start-up phase. However, as time goes by, they begin to defer tasks to people with more time and expertise. The role of operations becomes a to-do list of what has not yet been assigned instead of a holistic position that dabbles in everything. The CEO's list of responsibilities tends to stay steady over the course of the years, but the COO, who once handled financials, marketing, human resources, product sourcing, and a myriad of other tasks, can find themselves suddenly feeling like their value and contribution are diminishing. If and when this occurs, recognize that the role may need to be tightened and specified.

Additionally, in this phase, when capital allows for roles to be hired, all partners may want to reassess their positions within the company. Let each partner share what role they would like to ultimately settle into for the future. This should even include the CEO. While the expectation may be that they stay at the helm, your cofounder CEO may have another plan in mind.

To ensure the passion and excitement for the venture continues long term, be sure to make space for partners to work toward their dream job.

The Trust Issue

The Hollywood producer and talent manager Shep Gordon says that we should conduct ourselves in such a way that, when hard conversations happen, your partner knows that you are working toward a win-win situation, and they don't need to fight to get a morsel.

Trust is the ultimate factor that decides whether a cofounder partnership succeeds or fails. When trust is lost, every action, every word, and every decision are marred by doubt, skepticism, and suspicion.

This is hardly a conducive environment when trying to build a business. Cofounders need to put extra care and attention into ensuring that trust stays intact throughout their partnership.

The idea of what trust is, I believe, has lost its depth and scope in our modern world. It's become this thing that has been relegated to the equivalent of a gut feeling, something that either you have or you don't. Trust is an action word. While it is a feeling that one has toward someone, it requires work to give it. When you come across a situation that causes you to call the trust in your partnership into question, you may need to ask yourself whether or not your partner really has broken that trust.

Trust, as defined by *Webster's Dictionary*, is "Reliance on the integrity, strength, ability, surety, etc., of a person or thing; confidence." This is more than just a feeling that comes and goes. This definition lays out the foundation of a successful relationship. There is so much in this definition that I am going to unpack it right here to help you see why you cannot succeed without it.

Reliance

When a thousand tasks line your to-do list, reliance becomes an essential component of your partnership. One of the main reasons for partnering with someone is to be able to divvy up the unending to-do list that your entrepreneurial journey will create. Reliance is that trusting dependence that allows you to pass on a task and gain peace of mind so that you can forget about it and focus on your own list.

Reliance is damaged in a partnership when one or all partners experience repeated disappointment. This happens when tasks are not completed, deadlines are not met, or standards are not maintained. When one partner cannot rely on the other, that person cannot fully defer the task but instead begins to feel the need to handhold and control. This is the opposite of trust.

The way a lack of reliance shows up most often in a partnership is micromanagement. Many cofounders have complained that their partner micromanaged. In reality, it may be that their partner felt they couldn't rely on their cofounder and, therefore, had taken it upon themselves to stay on top of them to ensure the task was completed. This excessive attention to minor details, constant checking up, and task control are often the outcome of a loss of reliance. It is typically followed by feelings of resentment and frustration, which can lead to feelings of lack of appreciation and discouragement.

So how do you activate reliance in your partnership? First off, communication. When you and your partner are staying in communication, there will not be any big surprises or balls getting dropped. By communicating effectively, both partners keep the other abreast on the status of projects, and issues can be handled when they sprout up instead of when they drop like bombs.

Second, honesty. Letting your partner know that you feel ill equipped to complete a task or that you cannot meet a deadline isn't a sign of weakness. It's acknowledging where you are falling short of what is required and utilizing your partnership as a way to get through the obstacle. Instead of trying to push through as though you are alone, seeking aid from the one person who is there to do just that isn't a letdown. That's the point of a partnership. It's why you got join together in the first place.

That said, this also goes back to the role of entrepreneur. It's not an easy undertaking. Being reliable means doing what it takes to get the job done. I've seen more than a few cofounders mistake lazy partners for ill-equipped ones. Yes, that's harsh, but you need to decide now that you will demonstrate reliance when real, difficult challenges require you to lend aid to your partner.

How do you return trust to your partnership through reliance? The only remedy is time. Time spent consistently proving you're worthy of trust in your role in the company. Reliance isn't something lost with a one-time slip-up. It's broken down through repeated failures to complete what you are responsible for. That's why it takes the same process to build up again. The only way to earn it back is through demonstrating over and over that you are 100 percent going to get the job done.

Integrity

In a world where so many think that the way to the top requires doing whatever it takes, integrity can be found in only a select few. You want to find those few and partner with them.

Holding to ethical principles ensures that you and your partner know you don't have to be looking over your shoulder or questioning everything in the hope that you will not be screwed over. Integrity ensures that your partnership will conduct itself in a way that will stand out in a world of skepticism and wariness. When found within a partnership, integrity will automatically overlap the reputation of your business as a whole. Because integrity is top-down behaviour, it starts with the founders and filters into your team. That behaviour comes across to your customers, suppliers, and investors. They can see the integrity in every action your company takes.

Having integrity in a partnership means you conduct yourself with character and a soundness of principles. It means if you mess up, you come clean and accept responsibility for your mistake. Lying and cheating are obvious destroyers of integrity, but so are fudging, exaggeration, white lies, and weaseling out of responsibility. As a matter of fact, when someone is willing to violate their integrity over something small, it's almost worse. It demonstrates a lack of understanding of the value of their word and the price of their reputation. And when they violate their integrity in small ways, you can be sure they'll violate it in big ways too.

Integrity means not taking shortcuts or doing the bare minimum. Instead, you'll do what you promised and even go over and above. You can never have too much integrity. It's something that when overflowing can mitigate the damage of genuine errors. When people respect you, they want to make sure the relationship continues.

Integrity, when lost, has a profound effect on your ability to grow your business and sustain a strong partnership. You do not want to lose your integrity.

Strength

Strength as it pertains to trust doesn't mean your cofounder has your back in a bar fight or can help move a sofa. Those things are cool, but you can't build a business on them (unless your business is in winning bar fights and moving sofas). Strength in trust means you've got the mental power and vigor to see this endeavor through. It means you have the energy and vitality to get the work done and not fall victim to the emotional and physical demands of the journey. A business partner who recognizes a lack of strength in their helper may feel compelled to limit the scope of what they can accomplish for fear of overworking or overwhelming their partner.

That's one way expectations become skewed, and the divvying up of assignments is altered, whether or not it is necessary. Communicating about expectations is helpful here. But your partner needs to know you're strong enough to shoulder your part of the load. It is the responsibility of both partners to ensure that they do the work to keep themselves both mentally and physically able to complete their tasks and support one another.

If strength is an issue, it may require a heart-to-heart conversation sharing the struggles and the need for support in coping. It isn't anything to be ashamed of. The journey is taxing even on the most seasoned entrepreneur, so making one another's mental health a priority is vital.

Strength is also a type of courage. It's a willingness to say or do hard things even if it means disappointing, angering, or alienating other people. Your cofounder has to be able to rely on you not to back down when you need to stand your ground, to fight for what you both deserve when the world seems against you. If one partner feels the other lacks courage, the onus then falls on them to take on all the difficult work, which places an unnecessary burden on them and can cause them to have to switch lanes when it shouldn't be required.

Having the strength to do hard things means partners can rely on one another. It may mean role-playing conversations, strategizing, planning, researching, experimenting, or calling a whole other host of tools into play to help you arm yourselves for whatever comes your way.

Ability

When two people come together to build a company, each person brings a unique skill set to the table. Trust is present when competence in those skills, training, or other qualifications is demonstrated.

Most importantly, whatever you bring into the partnership, you need to be honest and clear about the level of proficiency and expertise that you possess. You should confirm this before the partnership begins if possible, for total transparency. If a partner fudges their capabilities, it comes as a surprise to the other and leaves a cloud of doubt over the relationship. They ask themselves, "What else isn't what it's supposed to be?" and the foundation of trust begins to crack.

This isn't to say you aren't allowed to mess up, find yourself over your head, or get lost in uncharted territory. It means that you need to make sure you are honest about what you are capable of doing, come up with a solution for what you are not, and always keep your partner in the loop when you are struggling with a challenge. Don't try to sort it out or fake it. That can lead to an even bigger catastrophe and rift between you than if you just let them know early on that you need help.

Trust in one another's ability is strengthened when you see each other keeping your skills honed and sharpened. When you see your technical cofounder brushing up on the latest in coding or your sales partner heading to a sales convention, it gives you confidence that they can rise to the occasion when needed. It also demonstrates a recognition of the responsibility they have within the company.

Surety

Surety is about position and relationship. It means that a person has made themselves responsible for another, like a sponsor, godparent, or bondsman. It's the ultimate "I've got your back" proposition. And it demonstrates an unwritten code that you are in this thing together, 100 percent on the same team. Surety is what makes the cofounder partnership as intimate as it is.

Few times in life do we step into this kind of role. Taking on a cofounder position communicates a level of responsibility that will be kept through honor, not by contract (although I do suggest contracts). While partners are often contractually obligated to support one another, surety is like a "pinky promise" that enacts a more personal commitment that can be a powerful component of trust.

A breakdown of surety results in an even graver wound as it is felt at a deeper level than any other aspect of trust. It will be perceived as betrayal or deception and is extremely difficult to repair. Anyone who experiences a breakdown in surety will say, "My problem isn't the fact that they (fill in the blank); it's that they betrayed me."

To rebuild this type of trust requires mediation, whether through a counselor or trusted business adviser. Additionally, it means an honest, heartfelt conversation followed by some kind of reconciliation. It demands humility from both sides and a mutual desire to continue the relationship and get back on track. I have seen partners who rise out of this type of mire forge powerful partnerships, but wow, did it take work.

The best way to ensure that you preserve surety in your partnership is to have the mentality that your cofounder is your greatest ally and friend. You must be willing to see all their actions and hear all their words through that lens. It means when you mess up, you immediately go to your partner and ask forgiveness, finding a way to demonstrate your continued commitment. It also means when your partner does something that calls their commitment into question, you do not jump to conclusions but instead seek their perspective and reasoning for the actions and words.

Protecting Trust in Your Relationship through Finances

The best way to preserve trust is to act according to your principles, always be honest, and stay humble when you make mistakes. There is one way above all others that these principles need to be the most evident, and that is through your financial dealings. The following steps will go a long way toward preserving your relationship and fostering deeper trust through your finances.

- Double-check all numbers together. This can be easy as the person in the financial role sending over the monthly expense chart and saying, "Just so you have this." It's going above and beyond what you need to do so the other person never has to wonder. And if they want to double-check, they can do so because your door and books are open. And making an agreement to go over the numbers together prevents anyone from feeling weird about asking.

- Be honest in all your dealings. And I mean all of them. Bragging to your cofounder about how you're cheating on your spouse at home is a warning to your cofounder that you'll betray them next. Cheating a supplier out of a few bucks is still being a thief. It's almost impossible to respect or trust someone when you see them being dishonest in other relationships. And telling lies means your word is worth zero. If that's the case, you may find yourself at a place where you need to bring documented proof into every conversation because no one will believe your claims.

- Know your partner's financial values and your own. Consider whether as a company you want to focus on quality or quantity in your products of services, or whether or not you will practice delayed gratification in distributing profits. Also, it will be good to find out whether money, in each other's hands, spends itself the day it's earned. Bad surprises result when you don't know these things about each other early on. If it looks like an issue could be on the horizon, make arrangements now so no one gets tempted or makes poor choices that hurt the trust component of your partnership.

- Follow the plan. If you build a business plan together, don't deviate from it on a whim. Stay true to your agreement with your partner. If you want to make changes, talk to them first. They'll trust you to stay consistent and treat them like a full partner.

- Double sign checks. This prevents arguing over where the money is going. Do this until you cannot procedurally do it any longer. Decide what the threshold is for double signatures. Then run all expenses by each other and look at the numbers together. Maintain total transparency. Always.
- Stay knowledgeable. Both partners should be involved in all conversations with accountants and lawyers. This also holds true for your roles. Stay up to date on your field so you're ready to act in your position in the best possible way. That conveys great competence and builds trust.

Relational trust is also key. Treat your partner like someone you actually care about. Don't talk behind their back or undermine them. Instead, let your word be strong. Don't make molehills into mountains. And take your own mental health seriously so your issues don't become their issues. If it would be bad to do to your spouse or child, don't do it to your cofounder. Period.

Learn from Rufaro

Even after a private investigator cleared Rufaro of any wrongdoing, his cofounder remained suspicious. One day, his partner requested access to Rufaro's calendar, and a few weeks later called a few customers to verify their meetings had happened and what was discussed. Rufaro heard about the calls and finally decided enough was enough. "It wasn't worth the emotional stress. It really bothered me, the constant skepticism and distrust." Rufaro approached his partner and gave him a generous price to purchase his shares in the company. "In some ways, I was the replaceable one because he handled day-to-day operations, and I was glorified sales, which anyone with the right training could do."

Rufaro sold his shares and walked away with a valuable lesson. "I now consider the person's personality and how they handle themselves before I start a partnership." Looking back, Rufaro reflects on how his partner always struggled with the success of others, never celebrating it. Rufaro often heard him presume someone's success came from drug money or was inherited. He struggled with jealousy in his personal relationships, too, often doubting the fidelity of the women he was involved with. "It was a pattern, and I have learned that who people are in their personal lives will often transfer over to who they are professionally."

Address all mindset issues, expectations, and trust issues up front. Then take steps to safeguard all three from problems. These are the core areas in which I've seen cofounder relationships break down. By addressing them in advance and checking in on them continuously as you progress, you can bypass the majority of dangers that bring down entrepreneurial teams.

CHAPTER 13

Relating
to Employees

From an early age, JD was involved in the family photography business. "I grew up hearing the inner workings of the company and saw firsthand the hard work and dedication it took my parents to get their business up and running." As a child, he would assist his father with photo shoots, usually carrying equipment or holding lighting. "Like any kid in a family business, I wanted to spend my weekends playing with my friends, but I was free labor." He laughs. "And even with my grumbling, I guess it was worth it to my parents to have me involved."

As time went on, JD was given more responsibilities within the business, sometimes small projects he could handle on his own. "On these occasions, I got a taste of what it was like to work for myself and reap the profits from a job well done." JD began to see a future in the business and to think ahead about what that could look like. "I started to get excited about the prospect of working in, and eventually taking over, the business. Eventually, I decided that sooner than later made the most sense." At sixteen years old, JD left high school eighteen months shy of getting his diploma. He never looked back.

However, not everything was set up to be sunshine and rainbows. "My father and I did not get along." Whether it was because they were too similar or too different, they constantly butted heads. "My father was all business. Growing up, it was clear that the company was his top priority, and his family held second place." Additionally, JD himself was an independent thinker with a strong personality. Taking orders and accepting processes he did not agree with went against his nature. "I knew I still had a lot to learn about running the company, but I'm also wired to take and be in control. So, unfortunately, we clashed often."

Despite their conflicts, after a few years, JD found himself running more and more of the business while his father took a back seat. "I was managing the company, but he still had the final say and chose its direction." However, when his father decided he wanted to retire, he offered JD a sixty-forty equity split of the company. "At the time, I knew partnering with my father would get me one step closer to my goal of owning the business, so I figured I would just bite the bullet and give it a go. But I should have known it would never work as long as we stayed together."

Besides the tension between him and his father, once his leadership position was solidified, the other obstacle to JD successfully taking the helm was the employees. Many who worked at the company had known him since he was a kid and seemed to struggle with viewing him as an authority figure. "I think it was hard for them to see me as anything more than the young kid that used to tag along on the weekends." JD found the daily struggle of running a business was made even more difficult by the pressure to prove himself to the team. "There was just too much history with the long-term employees. It was difficult to shed the old persona. It created a type of stress, which I don't think is found outside a generational business."

Allegiance was another hurdle for JD. There seemed to be an air of Team New Guard and Team Old Guard between those his father had hired and those JD had brought on board. "I would often get pushback from those who had worked with the company over many years." Sometimes he would discover that they would run his decisions past his father first before implementing them or even disregard his requests completely.

For this reason, the day-to-day operations of the company proved to be yet another stumbling block to success. "Our family business was started in the late 1980s and was still run in much of the same way from when it started." Many of the office processes were antiquated and not scalable. The long-time employees were comfortable with the way they did their jobs and resisted any new technology or process that JD tried to implement. Comments like "This is how we have always done it," or "Why fix what's not broken?" were seen by JD more as excuses for not learning a new skill or trying something new. While it can always be difficult to get employees to consider changing a system or protocol, it became even more difficult when his father would back them up. "I started to get the impression that my father saw my new methods as an affront to how he ran the company and was taking it personally that I wanted to change things."

JD tried to discuss these issues with his father but was told that it would "just take some time to earn everyone's respect." JD realized that if he and his father were to continue working together, the chances of the company ever being united were slim to none. "The people I hired were fully bought into my vision for the company and were excited for the plans that I had. The others continued to fight to maintain things the way they always were." It became clear to JD that having the duality of vision between the teams was holding the company back and that he could not continue in any leadership capacity with the old guard still in place.

Eventually, all this, combined with the regular arguments between JD and his father, made their partnership unbearable. "Running a business is difficult enough. But the psychological battle I was having with some of the team made it that much more."

The tension would eventually crack the company in half.

The Three Mistakes

You may be the backbone of your business, but your people are the muscles. They make the body move. Without people, it's just you alone trying to do every job yourself. And that's not possible for most business owners.

The employee relationship needs to be strategized as early on as possible. From the start, before you hire your first employee, it pays to decide what kind of corporate culture you and your cofounder want to create. This culture will be defined through how you interact with your partner and then through how you engage with your team. This, in turn, will set an expectation for how they should interact with each other and, ultimately, with your customers and suppliers. It's the trickle-down effect, a top-down process in which the leadership's attitude and behaviour creates similar responses from their team. It all starts with you.

This isn't a trivial lesson to learn. I haven't written a throwaway chapter telling you to be nice to your employees. Employee relations are a crucial piece of your business. It's the groundwork for the reputation of your organization and will have an impact on the longevity of your business. It also has the ability to affect your partnership in both positive and negative ways.

I will start by showing you the three big mistakes cofounders make in their employee relations. If you own a business, you may be making one of them right now. Avoid these three traps if you want your company to be unscathed by the pitfalls of a poor employee/cofounder relationship.

Don't Get Labelled

I've heard of many cofounder situations in which the staff deem each partner the one to go to for certain situations. Need financial approval? Don't go to Jack; go to Lisa, who is much more lenient. Need a dispute handled? Lisa is slow to react, so go to Jack. Children do this with parents when they want something, but only if the parents don't form a united front.

When your cofounder partnership isn't tight and consistent, employees can see this as an opportunity to cherry-pick the person from whom they have the best chance of getting what they want. Usually this means specifically *not* going to the one who may be most against allowing said act to happen. And if the other partner agrees to it, anger can flare up. The partner can feel betrayed. You and your cofounder must pay attention to this reality and guard against it.

Good Cop, Bad Cop

You've seen good cop, bad cop on television, and I've seen partnerships create this scenario within their organization: the image of one founder being hard nosed and the other lenient. They believe that a "hammer" personality will help get things done, and a "mender" personality will maintain good relations, and they mistakenly believe that both styles cannot exist in one person.

The problem with this style of leadership is that it sets a precedent that is hard to shake. With the "bad cop," employees will always be ready for a drill sergeant, making it difficult to have positive relations or develop good morale. On the flip side, when the "good cop" needs to be firm, their response seems harsher than it really is, or they are not taken seriously. I have seen founders pigeonhole themselves into a persona and struggle to shed it when the need arises.

By choosing not to take on these split roles in your partnership, you give yourselves the flexibility to adapt to situations as they are handed to you. Leadership can be tough or amiable as the situation arises in order to build healthy relationships with the team.

"Just Ignore Them"

The worst thing cofounders can do when it comes to employees is disrespect and undermine their partner. Because the founders are parts of a whole, when one partner dismisses another to their team, the strength of the leadership is diminished; both partners lose influence and eventually respect.

When I see a partner making fun of, dismissing, gossiping about, or ignoring their partner, I know it's only a matter of time before a serious violation occurs. Even when "It's only a joke" bookends the comment, the damage is done, and negative consequences may ensue. When basic civility is nonexistent, and resentment is beginning to permeate the leadership team, the company as a whole begins to break down. Staff members join in on the mockery, build allegiances, or even leave the organization because the culture becomes unhealthy.

Do These Instead

Now that you've learned the three big mistakes, it's time to talk about what you can do to improve your employee relations and your public bond with your cofounder.

Speak and Act with Absolute Respect

Treat your cofounder in the way you would want your employees to speak and act with you. This sounds basic, and it is. But you'd be surprised how many cofounders lack this common sense. Strong partnerships are built on respect, so always make it a point to model regard, esteem, and courtesy to one another.

Encourage and Compliment Publicly

Dale Carnegie, in his book *How to Win Friends and Influence People*, summed up one of the most practical ways in which to build a person up: "Give honest and sincere appreciation." A compliment or encouragement not only uplifts the spirit of your cofounder but also mitigates feelings of underappreciation that can so easily creep into a partnership.

Complimenting is not meant to be a manipulation tactic to placate or influence. It's a simple way of making the journey that you are on together more palatable. Who doesn't like being recognized for a job well done or given a word of encouragement? And when done in public, the positive results are exponential. When you declare, "John's a killer engineer; he always finds a solution," or "Kim has such a way with people," you send a message that will have an impact on the minds of all who hear. You have both clout and a history that makes you the perfect person to state what is true about your cofounder. It also builds confidence and trust with your partner because they hear you claim your opinion in front of others and hang your reputation on what you say.

The other great thing about a public affirmation is that it reminds your team and those around you of the things about your partner that make them a great asset to the company. Appreciation builds trust and strengthens optimism about the future. And hearing cofounders praise each other in public makes investors, employees, and clients feel secure in trusting your company. It's a win-win.

Stay in Your Lane

The cofounder partnership is built on trust. The most valuable outgrowth of that trust is the ability to distribute tasks in a way that elevates the contributions of those involved. Being able to trust your cofounder's decisions and relaxing in the peace that comes from knowing that someone else is "on it" are among the most enviable aspects of a partnership.

So practice that trust. By not sticking your nose into your partner's work, you not only silently compliment their capabilities but also free yourself to focus on the things that you do best. I don't mean you just ignore your partner and the things that they are responsible for. Just be cognitive of how your overinvolvement could be interpreted as meddling. Use the weekly meetups, monthly meetings, and annual sit-downs to dig deeper and gain a better understanding of your partner's processes and decisions instead of looking over their shoulder all the time. This is a much less adversarial way of getting information and creates great excuses to have these meetings (which you should be doing anyway).

Honor Your Partner's Decisions

When your cofounder tells an employee one thing, you need to be cautious about overriding that decision and saying something different. As the authority figures of your business, you maintain your influence through cohesiveness. When you say or do the opposite of your partner, you diminish their authority and create confusion within your organization.

Think about two parents who argue and override each other. What does that do to the kids? Whom do the kids listen to? How easy is it for blowups to occur when something goes wrong?

When you split like this, your team starts to determine for themselves who they should listen to. Or worse yet, to avoid the tension, they may begin acting on their own accord and could make uneducated decisions that derail your efforts at growth. If you do not like or agree with any decision your partner made, you first need to make sure not to contradict them in front of your team. Have a private conversation instead and discuss the issue. Come up with a plan in the office behind closed doors. Then allow that same partner to present the idea to the team so as not to look like they were overpowered or are a less capable leader.

The goal of good communication is having your day-to-day words and actions reflect that you and your partner are on the same page.

Argue in Private

Nowhere have I seen this ignored more than in family businesses. There is a significantly hazier line between business and personal in these kinds of environments, and often the leadership involved doesn't take the time to recognize that what works at home is inappropriate in the workplace. It also can occur between those who have known each other for a long time and have a relationship that can handle a less-than-professional form of communication, not realizing that those around them may not know the background and thus be negatively affected.

When founders argue in front of their staff, it creates an environment of instability and uncertainty. Leadership is built on trust and confidence in your partnership, and heated arguments in front of your team diminish their trust in the founders as a unified team. It also can force your staff to pick a side, which, when left unchecked, can create a sense of animosity within the organization and allow rifts to form.

Also, it's awkward. We've all been stuck with an arguing couple: in an elevator, in a line, or in a friend group. It's downright uncomfortable for those caught in the crossfire. Don't do that to your employees.

Your culture should be one of respect and solution focus. You and your cofounder debating decisions in front of your team isn't likely to promote that. Keep the dirty laundry behind closed doors.

Hire Together If Necessary

This team belongs to both of you, and both of you will have to manage it. At the very least, you should hire key people together so you both have input into the process. And at a minimum, you need to discuss a core hiring process for other roles so everyone has their say.

I saw a trend of failed partnerships in my cofounder interviews where hiring was used as a tool to turn the tide to one founder over the others. When key hiring was done individually, it was often to boost loyalty to the cause of that founder. The other partner(s) felt alienated and mistrustful of the new hires' allegiance, which hindered an effective working relationship.

This is why I always suggest key hires be a shared task, placing the cofounder relationship over the "right" candidate. Sure, there are times it's appropriate for one to have more say. Consider the rule that one partner can hire for a role within their department without shared approval. Or maybe you have a short meeting with a quick rundown of why you want to hire someone. Whenever possible, loop in all cofounders so it doesn't become an isolated process.

Shine Green Lights

You need to decide what the process will be for approving vacations, task assignments, and anything else that pertains to employees. At the bare minimum, this prevents you from approving too much simultaneous time off and running short on staff. At best, it can help you stay on the pulse of your team, its culture, and how your company is being run.

Do It for the Optics

While you may both be 100 percent on the same track, your employees need to see that. Your words mean one thing, but your physical cues will confirm what you say. People need to see the proof.

One set of cofounders I interviewed talked about how important optics were when there was a potential acquisition looming. They made sure whenever they spoke of it, they were together. One of them said, "I was going to be staying on with the new company, and my partner was going to move on. We wanted our team to see that we were both OK with this arrangement and that we were not parting ways with any bad blood or because one of us was upset."

Optics are more important than you think. That's why companies hire whole teams to manage them. Be smart and pay attention to your optics as a founding team.

Remember That Employees Are Not Friends

I'd like to believe that my former cofounder Stephen and I were pretty cool as far as bosses go. We always recognized that the people we work with would be spending a lot of time with us. Because of this, in the early years, we brought them in as though they were family. We gave a lot of trust and used a hands-off form of management in the hope of creating a positive environment that would make the employee want to live up to expectations. We treated them as friends, expecting the same from them. We quickly learned that wasn't always possible.

We realized that treating our employees as friends made it very difficult when all of a sudden, we needed to be all business. Friends and employees are treated differently. You are not in a position to tell a friend what to do, but it comes with the territory when you are the founder of a company. When you blur that line, bad things can happen. It gets harder to ask employees to do their job. It's difficult to have drinks on a regular basis with someone, then one day tell them that they cannot be late anymore or, even worse, that they are no longer needed at the company. It takes a very mature person to walk that line, and we have found that it very rarely can be done.

So over time, we limited our after-hours events with our team members in order to keep our working relationships manageable. We realized that these boundaries made it not only easier for us to manage but also less awkward for our team.

You also have to ensure you don't put your employees in the position of having to do things with you because you're their boss. I knew an entrepreneur who would hang out with their employees after work, sometimes late into the night, thinking they, too, were doing so by choice. I asked them if they ever considered that maybe these people didn't want to stay but instead didn't know how to say no. I reminded him that, as the boss, he was in a unique position. I gave the example that if the boss decides to call everyone together to talk about clowns, every one of those people would sit there and listen to them rant without saying a word. Not one of them would put up their hand and say, "Excuse me, but I've got work to do." The same goes for an invite for drinks, a request to stay late, or being asked to check out a movie; few people have the courage to say no to their boss.

Your employees are not your friends. Don't put yourself or them in a position of having to choose between a professional and a personal relationship.

Over time, I've experienced every type of situation one could have with an employee. While I have built incredible relationships with many of them, I've also had employees steal from the company, depart to competitors, deal with drug addictions, and face criminal convictions. I've had people not show up, ignore deadlines, do less than the expected minimum, talk behind my back, and walk out without notice. I've had to mediate team arguments and fight interoffice politics. Like I said, I've experienced it all. The thing is that every time, my employees started off as excellent candidates (Often the best out of many!). I never would have imagined being betrayed by any one of them in the beginning. If I'd made them my friends, dealing with these issues would have been much worse.

This is why I do not recommend having team members as friends. Just don't do it. Find your friends somewhere else, where you don't hold their job in your hands.

Learn from JD

JD's situation with his father degraded until he couldn't stand it anymore. Finally, JD had to make a choice: leave the company and start his own business or begin the process of buying out his father. "In the end, I realized that the company was in my blood and a part of my identity. Leaving it didn't feel like a viable option. I needed to buy him out."

This decision, JD knew, was likely to set in motion a huge shake-up within the team. "I knew I'd see disruption most in the office and sales department once I took over." For JD, this was actually a welcome outcome because it meant regaining control of those old guard strangleholds. But he knew he needed to be strategic so he wasn't left with gaping holes in the company. "I started interviewing people for key roles that I knew would become vacant from people who had their allegiance to my father and would not want to stay when it changed hands."

When JD announced that he was taking over the business, the employees he expected to give their notice did resign. "Fortunately, I had done the legwork to find their replacements. And I hired them quickly enough that they could be trained by the old team."

Looking back, JD doesn't begrudge the employees who stayed faithful to his father and exited along with him. "It means something when your team has total buy-in, not only to the business but also to the leadership. I strive to build the same commitment and earn the same respect from my employees as my father had with his."

Your relationships determine how your company runs. Keep this in mind when you build your employee bonds.

CHAPTER 14

Handling Disputes and Disagreements

Dayson and his brother Logan founded a small marketing firm twelve years ago in their childhood home. Dayson told me, "Being eighteen months apart in age meant that we shared everything and did everything together for most of our young lives." They got along quite well because of their complementary personalities: Logan is creative and outgoing while Dayson is serious and detail oriented. "In that way, we complement each other really well."

Their first business was a small T-shirt venture that they started in high school. Logan had the idea, came up with the design, and roped Dayson into sourcing the product and figuring out how to get their styles into their customers' hands. "Online marketing was just becoming a viable option for promoting one's business, and we were early adopters of the new form of promotion." When their formula for marketing their T-shirts proved successful, they used it to help grow the businesses of friends and a couple of family members. From that day forward, the brothers never looked back. "We kinda fell into it. Before we knew it, we had a full-out marketing company with a handful of employees."

Because the business grew so organically, Dayson and Logan never had any serious conversations on how to structure their partnership. For the first few years, their roles were clear and their responsibilities obvious.

"I settled into operations, and Logan became client facing and drove strategic growth." They worked well together in many ways.

But as brothers, their familial relationship established a leadership style that walked a fine line. "Professionalism was a priority in front of our clients. But within the office, we continued to relate and interact with one another in the same way we always had." The pair argued openly, even yelling at one another when there was a dispute about how something should be done. Within most family dynamics, members can often argue louder, speak more boldly, and filter less when dealing with each other and not face consequences. But over time, for Dayson and Logan, it created a habit that stuck.

On the flip side, they also joked around with each other in ways only brothers could. They fought and laughed together and seemed to make it work. "Again, we got away with it because we were brothers, but it wasn't necessarily appropriate in an office setting."

The real problems began to arise when Logan decided he wanted to get involved in a side venture with a friend. He needed to work at the marketing business in a part-time capacity. Their organization had a strong management team, so Dayson agreed that Logan could take a step back. However, what that looked like was never discussed in detail. "He just started to delegate out the vast majority of his responsibilities until it became unclear what he actually did within the company."

The disruption affected the whole team. Accountability declined as employees struggled with who they needed to report to. And Dayson became increasingly annoyed. "Logan was still a manager, but it felt more so by title than by actual deed." Additionally, in order to fill the gaps left by Logan's absence, Dayson had to shuffle around key employees. He also made some executive decisions on upcoming projects as well as the direction of the company. "The actions that I took were minimal, not all in one fell swoop. But after six months of small constant changes, the company had clearly veered from its previous course."

One day Logan was at a team meeting and realized just how much of a transition had taken place without Dayson consulting him. He became very upset and confronted his brother. "He felt I should have spoken with him about the new direction we were going. But I felt that because I was the one in the day-to-day, ultimately it was my prerogative to make those calls."

While Logan eventually conceded and backed down, it left a lingering resentment between the brothers that threatened their business and personal relationships.

There are better ways to settle conflict, as you might imagine, and we'll cover them shortly. First let's zoom out from Logan and Dayson's story and explore why cofounders fail to get along. I believe that once you understand this, you'll be well on your way to knowing how to resolve these partnership-breaking disputes.

The Three Types of Conflict

In my work with cofounder teams, I've identified three main types of conflict that lead to legally mired breakups at worst and the silent treatment at best. We'll briefly review each type, look at ways most people handle them, then close the chapter with hope and action—specifically, how you can resolve disputes and disagreements in ways that feel good to all parties involved.

Role and Responsibility Conflict

These tensions often involve concrete issues related to in-office work assignments. They can include disputes about how to divide up resources or manage capital, differences of opinion on procedures and policies, managing expectations at work, or judgments and interpretation of facts. This type of task conflict rears its ugly head when partners presume and don't clarify.

Relational Conflict

This form of conflict arises from differences in personality, style, matters of taste, and even conflict styles. When your personalities just don't mesh well, and when you haven't taken the time to address your differences, this can happen. It may stem from a misunderstanding or inaccurate perspective, but mostly, it comes from ways in which partners communicate and interact.

Value Conflict

The last type of conflict can arise from fundamental differences in identities and values. This can include differences in politics, religion, ethics, norms, and other deeply held beliefs. When your principles are in conflict or when one person's principles are destructive, it becomes hard to relate to or trust each other.

Now that you know where problems stem from, let's talk about why they tend to go badly and what you can do about it.

The Dark Side of Disputes and Disagreements

Entrepreneurship is difficult. And people are . . . people. In times of difficulty, we tend to justify, mitigate, or blame away our bad actions instead of owning up to our errors and communicating like adults. And too many of these bad choices can chip away at any partnership.

There are multiple ways in which we can tear down our relationship with our cofounder. Often, it starts with a one-off comment or action that, when left unchecked, is repeated at greater frequency until it becomes a common occurrence in our daily life. The issue grows when there is a lack of apology, repentance, or acknowledgement on the part of the perpetrator.

Let's talk about some of the most destructive behaviors I've seen in cofounder relationships. We are all guilty of them to some extent. We all screw up and have bad days, but knowing and recognizing them is half the battle.

Blaming

Blaming gets you nowhere. It's a total dead end and stops solutions from getting made. And yet, we all do it.

He said. She said. You did. You didn't. I could've. You should've. These phrases begin some of the most unproductive conversations a human can have. It's not that stating facts is bad; it's that these accusatory statements stop us from entering a constructive setting that would allow us to conduct business in a useful way and in an evaluative environment. Tone, verbiage, timing, and body language all convey messages, and when used to accuse and shift blame, those messages lead to deeper problems than existed in the first place.

You need to be able to sit down and look practically at the situation and how it came about without condemnation; only then can you solve the problem. Own up to your role in a situation and be willing to make amends.

Anger

Learn to control your anger. Period. Anger has no place in business. If you cannot get control, take a class or speak to a counselor to find ways to channel your emotions. Words spoken and actions taken in anger destroy business partnerships. Unlike in a marriage, where there is intimacy and attachment to act as a strong salve, anger unleashed in a business setting can do irreparable damage. Fix your anger problems or get out of the partnership.

Silent Treatment

We know these kinds of people. When they get mad, they shut down. In order to punish the other person, they go forty days without speaking and only communicate through the office manager. But let me tell you, the silent treatment is a great way to destroy your business as it stifles growth, puts the company in neutral, ignites resentment, and fuels egotism. Who will be the first to speak? The action turns into a game with one person winning and one person losing.

Additionally, whether you think so or not, it draws those around you into your drama. Your lack of communication will be noticed and felt by your team, and it puts them in a position of having to navigate the stress. What seems secret because it is quiet is actually quite obvious. Silence sparks rumors and can easily make those around you uncomfortable. Don't pull your partner or your team into this type of drama.

Undermining

Webster's definition of this word perfectly explains its effects: "to weaken or cause collapse by removing underlying support, as by digging away or eroding the foundation." Undermining slowly breaks apart the trust and respect that is needed to undergird your partnership. By playing off one another, you subvert and thwart the progress you have achieved as a team. Failing to build up and support each other makes the journey unattractive and potentially not worth the effort.

Pessimism

It's good to be realistic, but it's important to believe you can accomplish things together. It makes more sense to assume success than to assume failure. If there are genuine concerns, find a solution as a team. But don't assume it will end badly from the start. That kills morale.

Avoidance

Never avoid an issue as it puts you in a weakened position and can easily be perceived as laziness. A trait that doesn't evoke feelings of trust and competence from your cofounder. Face issues head on and get through them. You will gain respect in the long run for not running off or lagging until the last minute. Difficult challenges, when dealt with quickly, will build trust and confidence that you are able to handle whatever comes along.

Dishonesty

Everyone has lied at some time in their life. Hopefully, however, we learn early on that lies are not worth the trouble they create down the road. Lying in business can look as simple as

"Yep, I called them."

"We have the product you need."

"That wasn't my fault."

Yet even little lies like these, to your partner or to the marketplace, can be death to your reputation. Insincerity is the hardest thing to come back from because no one can trust you anymore. Once you develop a reputation for lying, only other liars will want to form relationships with you. When that happens, you're sunk because you can't do business surrounded by phonies.

Don't start down that dark path. Always tell the truth as a strong reputation can go far toward helping you rebuild from any harsh truth you ever find yourself having to tell.

Disrespect

I talk *a lot* about respect, but that is because respect is the glue that holds any relationship together. Talking over your cofounder, mocking, eye rolling, saying "Don't listen to them," even displaying disloyalty to the company are all signs that you aren't serious about your role, your partner, or your mission. When you disrespect your partner, it communicates that you don't care about them and creates a rift that can trigger the start of your partnership's dissolution. Take care not to start down this path; it's one you cannot easily correct.

Irresponsibility

You don't want a reputation for being inconsistent or untrustworthy. No one will do business with you.

Be a person of your word. Be dependable. If you cannot meet a deadline or goal, be honest and seek help. Remember, entrepreneurship is difficult, and often you and your cofounder will be saddled with tasks and responsibilities that you have never had a chance to practice or undertake. Sometimes conquering a challenge will require your having to learn a skill in a couple of months that would take others years. The last thing you want is for your cofounder to think they have to shoulder not only their role and responsibilities but also yours.

Martyrdom

The martyr takes many forms, but sometimes, you can distinguish them through their comments and words. "Never mind, I'll do it myself," or "I'm the only one who can handle or properly complete this job" can be signs that a martyr is at work. Be careful not to mistake real concerns over workload and responsibility, and take the time to honestly assess whether there is reason for someone to complain. But if there is plenty of help and a screwed perspective is at play, then tread carefully as you navigate resolving this issue.

Martyrdom never ends well, so don't fall into that trap. Share responsibilities knowing that there will be times when one partner will be taking on more than the other. Just be clear that no matter what, at any time, you all should be able and willing to help and ask for help.

Neglect

It's crucial to accept reality and not brush issues under the rug. If you must, it is important that you understand that you only have the power to brush *your* issues aside, not your cofounder's. Never dismiss your cofounder when they want to discuss or address a struggle. Additionally, should you decide to let something go on your own, you need to make the decision to no longer speak of it or bring it up and instead count it as a learning lesson and accept it for that. Then, should your partner do the same, you can both draw a line and move past it. If it continues to bother you, you need to sit your partner down and say, "I'm sorry, but this issue isn't resolved for me. Can we go back to the drawing board and see if we can find another solution?"

At the same time, you need to be a bigger person. If you manage to let something go and then your partner comes to you still concerned or troubled, you have a responsibility to the relationship to go back to the table and find a solution that works. Remember, what you give, you will get back. Failing to address someone else's concern builds resentment and sets the stage for an explosion.

Properly handling partnership issues requires a lifestyle decision that involves self-knowledge, moral integrity, and a commitment to maintaining one's individual identity and values. Let's talk about how to build that next.

How to Handle Disputes and Disagreements

How are you going to handle disagreements and issues between you and your cofounder? Because I promise you will have them. Both life and the entrepreneurial journey are notorious for throwing out curveballs, and you need to be ready with a solution that mitigates the damage to your relationship as much as possible.

In a perfect world, you would enter disagreements devoid of emotion and lacking selfishness, arrogance, ignorance, pettiness, or self-righteousness. Instead, you would enter filled up with compassion, understanding, empathy, and wisdom, all wrapped up in an honest search for truth and a fair outcome. Unfortunately, we don't live in a perfect world. We all bring certain biases, perspectives, understandings, expectations, beliefs, and values with us into every disagreement.

So how do you walk through the muck and mire and come out unmarred and ready for the next battle? You create a process encapsulated in a bubble of grace that will walk you through identifying the root issue. Then you find the solution and apply it.

That's what I've created in my dispute process. Let me show you what that looks like.

Begin with the Right Frame of Mind

If you're out for blood, you're going to draw it. If you're out to move past an obstacle, you're going to find a way.

Which do you want? Get that straight first. Everything proceeds from your intent.

Did you know that when a person is in fight mode, the prefrontal cortex in their brain goes dark when viewed in an MRI? This is the part of the brain responsible for planning, goal setting, prediction of outcomes, contemplating future consequences of current activities, and social control. How important do you think these things are when trying to deal with an issue in your company, such as losing a client or a missed deadline?

That's why barging into your partner's office or deciding to address the issue in the heat of the moment is the least effective way for you to identify where the issue stems from and how to handle it now and prevent it from happening in the future. When your blood pressure is high, your brain isn't working correctly. You need to take time to calm down.

Anger also sets in motion brainwave activities in the recipient. It shuts down their prefrontal cortex and triggers their fight-or-flight response. Fighting counters the anger with anger and also tends to blame back and justify actions. Flight builds up walls and locks out information, triggering stonewalling and a passive-aggressive response that will never enable a thought-out solution to the problem.

So what is the right state of mind?

The right state of mind begins long before you confront your partner. It starts today, with the decision to never lash out in anger or shut down. It hops into action the moment you hear the news that they didn't return an important call or forgot to mail the cheque to the government. It takes a moment to gather itself, then sifts through the possible solutions, always giving your partner the benefit of the doubt. Aim for this mindset, and your disputes and disagreements will be mitigated and manageable.

Look in the Mirror

When your middle finger finds itself in the air facing the driver who just cut you off, stop. Take a breath. Identify the issue with the situation. Maybe it's your fault; did you check to confirm? I know I have gotten mad at someone only to discover it was *my* misunderstanding or mistake. And what about your reaction? You may not be in the wrong, but you're about to escalate the situation. Is that really what you want?

In a business setting, odds are good your partner isn't aware that they just cut you off. There's probably a reason they acted like they did, and it might be reasonable. Even if it's not, is there a role you could have played in the situation unfolding as it did? Did you set your expectations clearly enough? Are the processes you all put in place responsible? Are you about to drop a bomb over a mistake you allowed to happen by not being clear?

It always starts with you. Even if you end up being blameless, starting from a position of personal reflection gets your mind into solution-finding mode. Beginning with yourself as the root cause of problems allows your brain to start working instead of getting angry and attacking. And if you do find a way that you contributed to the problem, you will be able to come to your partner with more empathy and humility. A perfect way to start a tough conversation.

Speak Clearly and Privately

What are you trying to say? In complicated matters that arise in entrepreneurship, speaking off the cuff can be a bad move. Taking the time to consider your responses and clearly define your solutions is a very smart idea and can go a long way to lessen the chances that words and ideas can be misunderstood.

Be clear on the issue. What are we really talking about here? Give the problem measurable parameters. Avoid all-or-nothing statements like "Everything relies on this one piece, and you messed it up!" This turns molehills into mountains. Measure the problem so everyone is on the same page as to how severe it is.

Take a moment to share how important this issue is to you. "On this topic, I'm at an eight out of ten; what about you?" You may be surprised to learn that your partner is ignorant, not arrogant, about your level of concern and stress. Additionally, you may find common ground to start on when you discover that they are just as upset as you are.

Finally, as I've said in other chapters, always deal with issues privately. Your problems should stay between you and your partner. When you take the issue public, you should have a plan for the whole team, not a problem to drag them into.

Get Over It

Once the problem is resolved, let it die. Moping, biting responses, ignoring your partner, sarcasm, innuendos, and referencing past infractions and issues are all ways of passive-aggressively demonstrating you haven't moved on. If your cofounder is doing these things, you need to take a deep breath and recognize that they are still struggling. You need to ask yourself what you can do to help all of you get back on track.

Learn from Dayson

The brothers' fighting grew worse by the day. Communication continued to decline until finally Dayson turned to the best mediator he knew: their father. "It probably sounds immature to run to Daddy, but our father was a successful entrepreneur who had himself been part of a couple of partnerships." Dayson asked their father to hear out the situation the brothers found themselves in and to give them advice on what he saw. "Fortunately, my brother respects my dad and has a good relationship with him as well, so he was open to his honest feedback."

They laid out their challenges, and their father shared his insights and offered solutions. "First, he addressed the way that we interacted with one another. He told us that we needed to step up our professionalism within our company culture and demonstrate a more united front." He also called them out for not keeping the issues they were having private. "He shared that by arguing publicly and not watching how we spoke about one another in the presence of others, we were not instilling confidence in the management team."

Their father also helped them come up with a plan for what decisions could be made individually and what decisions needed to be made together. "Looking back, it seems obvious that these were the steps we needed to take. But when you are in the middle of emotion and handling the day-to-day operations of a growing business, the obvious can sometimes be disguised."

The repair process took months to complete and often got heated. But when it was over, the brothers both agreed that the air was cleared. And they were both optimistic about their ability to work together.

Today, Dayson and Logan use practical processes to keep communication open. "We meet for lunch on Mondays and discuss how things are going." They find that the frequent meetups ensure that nothing goes on too long that cannot be backpedaled without disruption. Additionally, the brothers work to always speak to one another with respect, not just in front of their team but also when they are alone together. "We decided to meet with a communication specialist to help us learn to have productive conversations, especially when we have differing opinions." Now they enjoy a thriving business and a rare partnership relationship that many should strive for.

Conflicts will come. How you handle them will define your cofounder relationship. Do the work in advance to manage your own issues, and make sure you approach your partner in a way that preserves the relationship. Your business is relying on you.

PART III

How to End the Partnership and Start Over

CHAPTER 15

Protect Yourself

S ometimes the best talent is too expensive.

My client Trevor hammered that point home when he wrote to me about the worst panic attack of his life. "It happened in 2013. I was driving on a well-lit highway on a warm summer night at one in the morning. The sunroof was open. I should have been relaxed. But the highway lights flashed by faster and faster, and the sound got louder and louder, until all the light and sound blurred into a single strained ear-piercing shriek as I struggled to breathe."

Trevor's business partnership had just ended earlier that day. "It was sudden. I honestly did not see it coming. My business partner called me into his office and, with a smirk, said 'I am leaving.'"

Trevor sat there in a moment of silence, stunned. When he asked why, his partner said, "I got a better offer." They spoke briefly about details of the partnership split and then, poof. The partnership was over.

What confused Trevor was the feeling of being punched in the gut. "We had a dissolution agreement already signed for such an event, so technically, the split should have been friendly and predictable." Instead, Trevor's partner met him with a strange tone of satisfaction mixed with a little animosity. "It felt like a knife twisting in my stomach."

Their partnership had shown such promise. Trevor started his IT consulting business in early 2000 and after a couple of years had built up a fairly impressive clientele that included one of the largest privately held social services organizations in the country. After a few years, he was running lean and mean, a one-man consultancy handling tech support for approximately 500 employees across his customer base. "To grow beyond this point meant it was time to start thinking about onboarding talent to help push the business to the next level." Instead of an employee, he decided he needed a business partner.

"My business partner, Anthony, was the best technician that I had seen in my entire career." Over the previous three years, he had become one of the main technology consultants that Trevor relied on. "Both of us loved technology, both of us were consumed by computers since we could remember, and we became fast friends." Where Trevor excelled at the administrative side with a heavy emphasis on technical skills, Anthony complemented his weaknesses in specific high-end technical areas. It seemed like a perfect fit. They set up a business partnership with a dissolution agreement and moved the company into new office space.

With the new office came an unexpected bonus: "Anthony seemed to know everyone. Every time I had a big technical issue to resolve beyond both of our abilities, he 'knew a guy' that could do the work. It seemed too good to be true."

At first, everything was great. But eventually, their demise began. When the pair needed an accountant, Anthony knew a guy who could do the work, so they brought him on board. When they needed a book-keeper, Anthony recommended his wife, and they brought her in. When they needed their first tech, he recommended his brother-in-law, and so on and so on.

Trever remembered his growing unease. "I was leery of nepotism, but it seemed like a small price to pay as a bridge for long-term gain. Besides, they were cheap." But the issues never stopped. Anthony started talking trash about clients when he returned from site visits. His wife insisted on listening to loud music in the office without asking if it was OK. Problems with the accounting system meant Anthony would resolve them with the accountant without including Trevor in the process. "The worst was when I asked his wife about her filing system so that I could look up documents. It was interpreted as a personal attack."

From nepotism to unjustified demands, the communication issues mounted until that fateful day when Trevor and Anthony terminated their relationship. Then came Trevor's high-speed panic attack.

What to Do If the Partnership Isn't Salvageable

Before we get into the details about how to handle a partnership dissolution, I want to discuss the concept of digging your well before you're thirsty. No matter what, every partnership will dissolve. It doesn't have to be in a dramatic crash-and-burn kind of way; it can happen following the joyous celebration of an epic acquisition or the quiet retirement of a pair of senior entrepreneurs. When we talk about the end of a partnership, we know it is inevitable, so we get ready for it, whatever "it" ends up looking like.

I would recommend, no matter what phase of partnership you are in, that you have in place plans for an exit. Ensuring through both your legal contracts and goal setting that space is made for a conclusion of the partnership will make navigating the process significantly simpler when it occurs. Working out a plan mitigates the heavy emotion that will likely come alongside the exit and takes away the need for knee-jerk reactions and last-minute decisions.

This chapter will cover what to do when you are in the moment, faced with the need to do something drastic like dissolve the partnership. Obviously, every business will have its own unique journey, but I will set out some suggestions and tools that you can use to navigate the uncharted waters.

Take a breath. Let's do this.

You've heard the saying "The best defense is a good offense." In this case, assessing the field before the situation reaches critical levels is key to landing on your feet. Follow these tips if your business relationship seems like it's headed for a breakup.

Know the Situation

So your partnership needs to end. What's actually happening? What are the circumstances that have brought you to this place? Lack of interest? Fraud? Illness? Financial difficulties? Life changes? Ineffectiveness? Taking the time to get a clear understanding of what you are dealing with will be valuable for determining your next steps.

What is the timeline? Do you absolutely need to act right now? Do you have time to find a replacement? Do you have the luxury of pursuing your options? Based on the severity of bad blood between the partners, your timeline may need to be moved up or made a priority.

Finally, who needs to know? Is this a decision that can remain between the partners for a time? I would recommend that you keep it on the DL until you are ready to pull the trigger, as rumors and insecurity can send even the most dedicated employees, customers, and investors running. This is what my partner and I did. We quietly undertook a proper search for my best replacement when I made the decision to leave. We didn't panic; we just calmly searched for and found the right person who could do the job, and I helped ease them in. The process was as painless as possible because we had time on our side. Even if this is just a decision in your own head right now, doing some preliminary work prior to discussing it with your partner and your team may have its advantages. Especially if fraud or a crime has been committed, doing some legwork on your own may assist you in finding a safe and beneficial solution.

Do you have a board of directors? Determine how the board needs to be involved. You may be required by law to inform them of your decision as soon as it is made. That said, they may also be able to provide great insight and possible solutions for you to consider prior to making your exit plan.

Consult a Mediator

A mediator hears both sides and offers a third opinion. This is a great course of action if you believe there is a chance for reconciliation or significant relationship damage. Should you decide to proceed with dissolving the partnership, a mediator can help you navigate those waters with as little friction as possible. The goal is to walk away with the friendship intact and everyone feeling positive about the experience.

Know Your Options

If your business partnership isn't working out and you genuinely feel that it is time to move toward a break up, you need to know what directions you can take. There may be more than one option available to you. You will need to identify them and begin the process of determining the priority level each path falls under.

Here are some ways you can exit a partnership:

Buyout:

This is an option in which one partner purchases the shares or stake of the other. In some circumstances, there may already be an equation in place for determining what the number would be through a legal contract drawn up in the early days of the partnership. In others, the partners may need to come up with it at the moment. Either way, you will need to determine the value of the business by taking into consideration assets, liabilities, key employees, scope of products or services, brand value, and so much more. To keep things simple, I would recommend hiring a firm that specializes in valuation so that no one can be accused of exaggerating or rigging the process for their personal benefit. Buying out a partner can be difficult, especially if the amount is significant. However, there are ways you can make it work. Banks are able to do loans to those partners who can demonstrate an ability to repay using future profits. Additionally, if the partnership is amicable, a long-term payout may be an option, even preferred, considering some countries' tax laws. Either way, a buyout is a great way to exit a partnership should one or more partners want to keep it going.

Sell:

There are obvious reasons why selling a business may be the preferred method to dissolve a partnership. If the business is valuable, the right buyer will likely be willing to pay what it is worth, allowing the partners to split the proceeds and go their separate ways. Having an eye on this option long before you decide to sell is a very smart move. Tailoring how your company functions and looks makes it easier for future buyers to see the potential in absorbing your business. If you have the luxury, tweaking your business to fit the needs of a buyer you have in mind can help move the process along much more swiftly.

Find a new partner:

There are reasons why bringing in a new partner might be the right move. Sometimes, as a company grows, a new skill set or someone with a certain type of experience is exactly the kind of fresh perspective that a leadership team needs. Without throwing the baby out with the bathwater, cofounders can redistribute equity to bring new life into the business.

Fire a founder:

A heavy-handed approach, this option will definitely need to be considered on a case-by-case basis. In the instance of theft or crime, termination may be the right move for not just the partnership but also for the company as a whole. Depending on the equity split, the choice to fire may or may not be possible, but it may be one to consider. This can be a very traumatic and potentially dangerous situation, so be sure that you have proper legal counsel and the right process in place for the day you do the deed.

Close the doors:

This one is tough but not unrealistic and sometimes the lesser of two evils. Depending on the situation, there may be times when it makes more sense to walk away and cut your losses than to drag things out and hope for a miracle. For some in this situation, it may be better to start over with a clean slate where the baggage from the old company isn't pulling you down.

Prepare Operations

You can't just snap your fingers and change the company's leadership. You need to contemplate everything that's going to change, from the top to the bottom. The more preparation time you give yourself, the better, and the more you can anticipate, the easier the work will be.

That means reassessing your systems. What roles and responsibilities does your partner handle? How is that going to change? Can you find a replacement, or are you going to have to recalibrate and reorganize your current workload to take on theirs?

Also reassess your mental and emotional systems. It's going to be a stressful time, and you need to build a community around you to get through it. You're used to working with someone. That means you had someone to talk to. Who will you talk to now? The board? A mentor? A trusted friend or colleague? Identifying who you can run ideas by or who can be your adviser is a crucial step in protecting your state of mind. Doing that means you'll have the mental energy to make better decisions as all these changes take place.

Talk to a Lawyer

It is likely that you will not be able to use your company's lawyer because of the conflict of interest and will need a new lawyer to represent you individually. So if there are legal considerations at play, and there usually are, your first call might be to a new lawyer.

Know what your legal obligations and options are according to the partnership agreement. Is there a buy-sell option? A shotgun clause stating that if one partner doesn't want to do a buyout, the other can? Get copies of your legal contracts and review them alone and with your lawyer.

Be honest about the state of the relationship. Do you need to end communication with the partner and speak exclusively through legal counsel? Sometimes it's better to prevent any further damage by letting the professionals handle the arrangements.

Discuss with an accountant what the financial hit might look like both for the company and for you personally. Look at all your options from a financial perspective and not just from a legal or lifestyle angle. What you most want to do may look very unattractive when compared to the tax advantages of another option.

How to End the Partnership without Losing Everything

The process of ending a partnership is difficult and guaranteed to be emotion filled and challenging. Once you navigate those waters, it's time to commence the next stage, the one that deals with those affected by the new situation. The question here becomes how to enter into this phase without losing your staff, your money, and your company.

Letting Staff Know

Pre-breakup, pay attention. Know where loyalties lie. It's common for employees to take sides. Don't take that personally; just accept that it happens. If you have a non compete or non solicitation agreement, be aware that you may need to remind employees of their contractual obligations. Identify who may leave, and consider having a one on one to discuss what staying with the company would look like. Those connected to the leaving cofounder may think their jobs are on the line; calming their concerns will go a long way toward maintaining a positive corporate culture.

Consider shoring up potential weaknesses in the flow of information to employees, investors, and clients. You need to maintain healthy and open communication with everyone. Do you know what the worst case scenario is? Rumors and blame. Mistruths that paint an even uglier picture than what is really happening and damage your team's morale. Stay ahead of the rumor mill by strengthening your communication flow.

Post-breakup, maintain positivity. Never, ever put down the leaving cofounder in public or in private with any employee. Even if you think they will keep your comments in confidence, don't do it. You could become your own worst enemy if you make it enticing for tongues to wag. Keep your complaints where they belong: in your lawyer's or therapist's office.

Be ready to provide a clear transition plan for your team: "As you know, this cofounder left, and here's how this will affect us and how it will not." Reassure employees that life will go on. Recast the company's vision, mission, and goals to give them confidence in the strength of leadership and the security of their jobs.

Talking to Customers and the Public

Once the shock of your cofounder declaring their intention to leave wears off, questions will start nagging at you. One question in particular always comes up: "How am I going to mitigate negative messaging? People are going to think my company is falling apart!"

Your pathway through the PR process depends on your situation and business. Before you make any statements, you need to have a perfectly clear understanding of what's going on and how it will be dealt with. Clarity instills confidence, so avoid ambiguity and always communicate with authority.

If you are a large business, hire a PR firm. They can help manage the messaging. If you're small, prepare a statement prior to the announcement. You do not need to get into the nitty-gritty details. Let the public and customers know the very basics and then share with them what will stay the same. Be honest about any changes, and provide additional methods for communication to field the uptick in questions and concerns that may come your way.

Don't Wait till It's Too Late

What happened to Trevor after his panic attack? Did his company survive the transition?

Yes. But it was tough, he told me. "With the benefit of hindsight, I thought that I acquired the best technician in the city and would be able to jumpstart our growth through an equity-sharing agreement. In reality, I brought on board a takeover of my business by proxy of a partnership." And when Anthony left, Trevor also lost key elements of his team. He didn't just have to replace a cofounder. He had to replace key roles within his company.

Trevor's failure to heed the warning signs and have the difficult conversations regarding Anthony's hiring and decision-making processes led to him losing control. That forced a costly detour on the way to his company's success. He had to make up for lost time and reassess his goals.

Learn from Trevor's story. Have challenging conversations while there's still time. Assess all your options yourself. Get counsel when you need it. All that will set you up in the best position when it's time to start over.

Once you've landed on your feet, the next chapter will show you how to start over without your cofounder.

CHAPTER 16

How to Start Over by Yourself

Kerry, a young and energetic entrepreneur, laughed as she told me her story. "I presumed that since I wanted to open a restaurant, the most obvious choice for a business partner would be a chef." After a short pause, she sighed. "Little did I know I needed so much more."

Kerry was raised by restaurateurs. Her parents had owned two restaurants when she was growing up, and at an early age, she knew that she would follow in their footsteps. "I loved everything about the hospitality industry. I loved the pace, the novelty, and the camaraderie. But I especially loved the culture." She spoke about listening to the daily drama that unfolded within her parent's businesses. The stories of torrid love affairs between staff, dine and dashers, the unfolding lives of their regulars, and the challenges of running a low-profit-margin business. "It felt like we lived in a real-life soap opera. I was caught up: hook, line, and sinker."

Kerry's parents were successful but always aware of the fragility of their businesses. "You had to manage the line between creating a great experience and conserving profits." She worked in every aspect of the business, from the dish pit to the office to the front of the house. "I became familiar with all the possible scenarios that happen in a restaurant and was eventually able to work out solutions on my own. That gave me valuable experience."

After university and with a degree in hospitality and business management under her belt, Kerry felt ready to carve her own way. "I wanted to start my type of restaurant, one that reflected the kind of dining experience I would enjoy." She knew that with her time managing restaurants, along with her newly developed academic background, she had a good chance of making a go of it. When her parents offered to give her a loan to get started, she jumped at the opportunity and began to plan her course.

"My parents were business partners, and I saw both the good and bad sides of this type of family dynamic." Stress in the workplace followed them home, which would often be a place of tension and stress. "They never left work at 'the office.' I'm not even sure they felt there should be a division." A rehashing of the workday and conversations about the inner workings of the company were often held at the dinner table. Arguments could very easily erupt as a result of having to hold private opinions and thoughts until they could be spoken away from the ears of staff and customers. "I often wondered what home life would have been like if one of my parents had a different career."

Kerry came to the decision that she would not mix business and family. She would seek an outside partner to mitigate what she felt would otherwise become an uninterrupted life of work.

Kerry was confident of her role in starting a restaurant and managing the business. "What I really felt I needed was someone who could handle the kitchen and all things that pertained to the menu." Kerry spoke to her parents and asked to approach one of their chefs to partner with her. "Carol was excellent in the kitchen and ran the back of the house with ease. She had great menu ideas, and her concepts for restaurants matched the direction that I wanted to go. It seemed like the perfect match: my expertise in running a restaurant and her expertise in running a kitchen."

She learned too late there were other factors she should have considered.

Kerry and Carol's partnership lingered in the honeymoon phase for the first six months before the tarnish started to break through. In her previous role at Kerry's parents' restaurant, Carol was head of the kitchen but ultimately didn't have the full weight of responsibility that came from being an owner. Once her capital investment was on the line, her need for security and control became apparent. "She became authoritarian and struggled with any suggestions I made that countered her established ideas."

Carol saw Kerry's penchant for out-of-the-box thinking as an unnecessary risk, and over time, she lost confidence in the direction that they had envisioned for the restaurant. Kerry mused, "In the beginning, we were something new and fresh, and it was reflected in not only our atmosphere but also our food. But two years in, we were like every other restaurant on the block." Carol's control issues also affected staff turnover. Carol began to micromanage everyone, and her standards were over the top. "No one wanted to work with her. She sounded like a scene from *Hell's Kitchen*. You could hear her yelling at staff in the kitchen all the way from the dining room."

To see if they could move past their issues, Kerry convinced Carol to hire a consultant to review their business and determine where they could improve. "I figured if a third party, without vested interest, could come in and see our business, any suggestions for improvement would be met with less skepticism." When the results of the review came back with some changes assigned to Carol, she found excuses why they were incorrect or unreasonable. "It was then I realized we were not going to be able to make it work."

Kerry's restaurant dream had turned into a nightmare. She had no choice but to sever the relationship. That meant starting over by herself, something she'd never done before.

Adapting to Solopreneur Life

Whether you have exited a partnership and are starting over in a new venture or find yourself alone in your current one because your partner left, you need to prepare to move forward.

First of all, figure out the narrative around your new situation. Determine how you will handle questions about the ended partnership. People will want to know what happened, so sit down and come up with a blanket response that you can use. Whatever you decide, make sure to keep it positive or at least neutral. Resist the urge to trash talk but instead simply say something like, "It was a great learning experience, but we both felt it was time to move on." You owe nobody more of an explanation than that.

Next, take some time to work on yourself and resolve any lingering hurt feelings and negative thoughts that are clinging to your experience. Understand that the cofounder relationship is an intimate one that has a big impact on your life. Don't underestimate how a failed or ended partnership can affect your plans and decisions going forward. If you feel that you need help in getting your perspective right, don't be afraid to speak with a professional. You do not want to taint the new venture you now lead solo.

I was fortunate to build four companies with the same cofounder. After we exited each business, we had yet to see the next one on the horizon, so we always felt that the previous was our last together. When a new opportunity came around, we usually started it gradually, researching its potential one day at a time, until the next thing we knew, we were back in business. I never set aside a period to reflect on our partnership, and while things worked out for us, I do see ways in which we could have mitigated some challenges if we each took time to reassess.

Every business is different, every stage is different, and depending on your situation, how you approach your new partnership should always be revisited. Capital injection, time commitment, life stages, time to market, and a new product or service are all factors that may change the way you structure your partnership. Be sure to look at each opportunity in a new light and come at it with a fresh perspective.

Ask the Tough Questions

Once you can reflect on what happened with your previous partner and be objective, recognize that you're sitting on a gold mine of truths. What lessons can you take away? And how, if your partnership had a negative ending, do you avoid bringing resentment and distrust with you? You've got a treasure trove of useful information from what you went through. Reflection gives you wisdom, and that wisdom can help you build again, stronger and more effective. Then, when you reach a place where you can sort through it all, you can use that data to become a better entrepreneur.

Ask questions like:

- What three words would describe me as a partner?
- How did I excel in my role in the business and as a partner?
- What could we have done differently together to improve our partnership?
- How could I have been better prepared for challenges within the partnership?
- What personality traits in my last partner will I look for in my next?
- What personality traits in my last partner will I try and avoid in my next?
- What processes did we have in place that strengthened our partnership?
- What conversations could I have to better understand whether a potential partner is right for me?
- What issues regularly come up in our partnership? How could we have avoided, mitigated, or solved them?
- Could I have built the business without a partner? Why or why not?
- Were there any gaps in the legal contracts that we drew up together?

Hindsight is the best teacher. Own your involvement in any issue. You may not have been able to do anything differently, but you can probably come up with an alternative path that will improve your experience in the future. Know clearly what you want to be different in the next partnership and what you will do specifically to enact those changes.

Take the Time to Start Again on the Right Foot

If you now find yourself running a business solo, take the time to let the dust settle before running out to find a new partner. There will be a transition time while you create processes to deal with the additional tasks that were once handled by your partner. Let your team settle into the idea that your partner is gone and give it some time to see if anyone leaves because of their allegiance. Wait until life has a feeling of normalcy so that you can think clearly and make good decisions in the right frame of mind.

When you feel ready to move forward, that's when it's time to determine what the future will look like. Are you bringing another cofounder into your existing business? Or are you in search of a new partner for a new venture? Either way, it's time to start the journey again. That's right. Go back to the beginning of the book and read it again as though it's your first time.

You are going to determine whether a partner is right for you. Take the self-assessment tests with a deeper understanding of how you work in a partnership environment. Vet new candidates. Keep your eyes and ears open for any warning signs that they are not the right fit. Determine roles, responsibilities, wants, and needs so that you can find someone who will align their goals with yours. Formally structure your partnership with strong legal documents, keeping in mind the need to plan for the many outcomes that can occur. Finally, move forward with excited optimism as this is a new beginning with so much potential!

A New Beginning

Kerry had to give up her dream of co-owning a restaurant. She knew that she and Carol just wouldn't be able to make it work.

Fortunately, Carol was of the same opinion. So they discussed the dissolution of the partnership. "We had a partnership agreement, but it didn't have a clause for separating." Neither Carol nor Kerry was in a strong financial position, but Kerry's parents were able to step in to help her buy Carol out. "I wasn't too excited to go back to my parents for help." But after seeing a taste of her earlier success, they knew their daughter would be able to bring the restaurant back to its former glory.

Once Carol exited, Kerry started her search to employ a new head chef. "I knew I could hire a good chef, that the skills were available in the marketplace, and I didn't necessarily need this person to be a partner." Kerry decided to hire for the role but is keeping an eye out for someone else to partner with who is more compatible with her personality. "I've left behind the notion that skill is first and foremost and instead am focusing on finding someone with the same ideals and comfort level in uncharted environments."

By attending restaurant conferences and other business owner events, Kerry is confident that she will be able to find that perfect person. "I'm searching for someone who has experience taking risks and building successful businesses. I'm not seeking a skill set I can hire anymore. I want someone with the same focus on winning."

Kerry got it right. She didn't let lingering resentment or fear cloud her perception of partnerships. She also didn't rush into another arrangement that might harm her business. She's playing it smart.

When it's your turn, I hope you play it smart too. Follow the steps above, and keep the long view in mind.

CHAPTER 17

Staying Close

Looking back on his childhood, Stephen is able to identify clues that entrepreneurship was his destiny. "The first sign was my penchant for cutting and opening things up, breaking them to find out how they worked so that I could then 'fix' them." It drove his parents nuts, he recalls with a laugh. However, it was this curiosity that Stephen figures played a huge role in his future success. "Eventually, I learned to hone this skill. My curiosity turned into ingenuity, and I became able to imagine ways to make things better without the need to break them first. It was an upgrade in thought and became how I approached opportunities."

Stephen credits curiosity and an early life lesson as the reasons he started his first venture, iQuiri. "At seventeen, I worked at a mall and managed to get a department store credit card, which I, like every seventeen-year-old, proceeded to max out and then forgot to pay." Cut to being nineteen years old when this mistake meant he was refused a cell phone because of a low credit score, a term he had never heard before. "I asked the guy at the counter what he was talking about, and he basically said, 'It's a financial report card for adults.'"

Ironically, this poor handling of his finances was the spark that ignited the path he would take in business over the next twenty-plus years.

The incident at the cell phone counter was embarrassing, but it also piqued his curiosity. "I wanted to know everything this report said about me." When Stephen turned to the web to find out, he realized that online delivery of the report was only available to US citizens. Being a Canadian meant he would have to head to an office in his hometown and apply for it in person. "The process was so antiquated." Knowing online access was possible in the US got Stephen thinking about how he could make a similar service available in Canada. "And I decided to pursue the idea."

Eager to take on this new venture, he thought about who he could invite to join him. When he began to consider the people in his social circle, he quickly realized the pool from which he could draw was quite small. "A large cohort of my friends had left for university and were busy pursuing their careers. Because that path never interested me, I realized that I would have to turn to the smaller group like me who were going in a different direction."

With all this in mind, one person stood out from the group. "Tanis and I had been friends since grade eight," Stephen states. "We had a lot of fun together over the years, and we got along well." Additionally, he recalled that throughout our time in junior and senior high, we had worked on many projects together, and because of this, he knew that, as a team, we could see things to completion. "Deep down, I knew that execution and perseverance would be two factors critical to our success. For Tanis and I, that was something we demonstrated from twelve years old when we first started our friendship." On top of everything, I had not chosen the university path either. But I was about to get married, "The added perk," Stephen points out, "Was that working together would ensure we would stay connected no matter where our other life decisions took us."

Over the next twenty-plus years, Stephen and I went on to start and build four successful tech companies together.

Stephen feels that the trust factor was the key to our success as partners. "Trust takes a long time to build. If you can get into business with someone you already know, that is a huge advantage." He explains that when trust isn't there, you end up questioning and analyzing everything your cofounder does, and it becomes impossible to have a thriving partnership. The opposite of this is being able to man your own lanes and work efficiently and effectively. Additionally, Stephen explains that having someone by your side whose gut you can rely on helps you weigh options and take the necessary leaps of faith. "This is critical because when you are all on your own, it's very easy to doubt yourself." Having a cofounder who can say, "I agree," or even "I disagree," makes you so much more effective in the decision-making process.

What if you don't have the luxury of knowing your cofounder in depth beforehand? Stephen says, "Trust but verify. . . . That means that when you get started, you let them do their job, handle money, make decisions, and so on but periodically do a check-in." Over time, Stephen says the verification process will build real trust, and you can carry on without the need to investigate. "Any other arrangement doesn't work. If you start a partnership with the impression that they have to earn your trust, you will micromanage, and the partnership will quickly sour."

Partners through It All

I want to end this book by returning to the greatest thing about a cofounder partnership: the opportunity to enjoy the one life we have on this planet with someone who shares your passion. As I've said so many times, the entrepreneurial journey can be incredibly rewarding, but it's not for the faint of heart. It's guaranteed to give you sleepless nights, headaches, and gray hairs, which is why I'm such an advocate for the cofounder partnership. I have experienced and seen others experience it as one of the most fulfilling relationships one can have. When done properly, it can be used as a tool to enhance all the things in this life that are wonderful. Taking the time to find ways to intentionally build a strong partnership will improve the chances of not only your company's success but also your personal success.

In the next pages, I will lay out ways in which I have seen cofounders take the business partnership from professional to invaluable. You don't need to do all the things I suggest, but I encourage you to pick at least four to integrate into your partnership and keep it exciting. After all, you are trading your time here on this planet for the opportunity to be an entrepreneur. There's no reason why it shouldn't be fun and fulfilling.

Family Time

Your partner is giving up time with their family and significant others to work alongside you. It is advantageous to have a good rapport with the people they head home to at the end of a long day. Finding ways to spend time together with your partner's family allows them to build trust with you and be at peace with your relationship.

I have seen many partnerships falter because those at home do not have any kind of connection with their loved one's business partner. This leads to a lack of loyalty and a sense of jealousy, perhaps even resentment. Setting aside time to connect, even once or twice a year, is well worth the investment. Even something as simple as a nice dinner out with their spouse or an afternoon at a park with their kids can go far in building bridges and bonds that will make the long workdays tolerable.

Fun in Travel

Ask someone who travels for work what it's like, and you will likely get a groan and a sigh. This is fine, and I get it; traveling for work has a totally different feel than traveling for pleasure. But I recommend you take a different approach. I've mentioned it before, but I am a big advocate of enjoying the journey. If you travel for work, this is your chance to use the journey in a way that is enviable. Memories are formed when novelty is experienced. Instead of pushing through travel focused purely on your work, take the time to experience your surroundings with your cofounder. Be tourists or, better yet, what I call "curious locals" who, whether it's their hometown or a vacation spot, explore the nooks and crannies for the interesting and exciting.

When you and your business partner take some time to visit somewhere unique or try something new, not only do you get a chance to expand your horizons but you also create a positive experience that will connect and bond you in a special way. Don't let the occasion for travel slip by when there's a major opportunity to bring fun and excitement to your partnership. Believe me, when all is said and done and you've long since exited your business, it won't be the meetings that you will remember. It'll likely be these types of experiences that leave a smile on your face.

Giving Space

In order to have connection, there needs to be a willingness for and an awareness of the other person's company. That said, connection also needs to be balanced with solitude, which means spending time apart so you mitigate the feeling of overexposure.

I've seen many cofounder partnerships in which the partners are constantly together or do not find a balance in their working relationship. Too much of a good thing can become a bad thing. If your partnership has been built on constant connection, take some time to find ways to pare it back a bit. Think of the adage "Absence makes the heart grow fonder." It's not just for personal relationships but also friendships and businesses.

There are plenty of ways you can give space. It's up to you to decide what works for you as a team. Some examples include:

- Don't share an office or have offices far apart.
- Choose a time of day to not interact.
- Take lunch and breaks separately.
- Travel alone or sit apart on planes.
- Have separate hotel rooms.
- Spend weekends away from each other.
- After work, limit time together.
- Conduct meetings separately when applicable.
- Do not live together. (The exception is for married couples, but that necessarily leads to other ways of creating boundaries, which is another book entirely.)
- No "partners with benefits."
- Interact with employees separately.
- Commute separately.
- Don't always pair up when teams are formed.

- Don't work out together.
- Take separate vacations.

I've spoken with partners who want time apart but are too afraid to tell the other for fear of bad feelings. It isn't that they don't like them; it's just that they are looking for a reprieve or less continuous contact. Think about it this way: most people don't even enjoy spending every moment with their family and loved ones! By setting up some parameters for solitude, you could be strengthening your partnership when you are together.

Goals and Rewards

Having your own reward system between partners is a great way to stay aligned and on track. Placing a carrot where an achievement or milestone needs to be met is a great method to stay motivated and build connections. Obviously, a successful business is the ultimate goal, but small rewards make the long trail much more exciting.

Identify an important goal in the near future and set a corresponding reward for when it is reached. Whether it is something as small as ordering in lunch or as grand as treating yourself to a pair of Rolex watches to mark an extra-special achievement, winning together is the best way to build a lasting partnership.

Anniversaries

I met two cofounders who celebrated the day they signed their partnership agreement. They decided that on that day, they would celebrate the official start of their business going forward as a team. With their staff, they celebrated the business, but between themselves, they exchanged little tokens of appreciation to commemorate their partnership. It allowed them, at least once a year, to stop and say, "Hey, thanks for doing this crazy thing with me. I'm glad to have you on my team." It was an invaluable tool for keeping them connected.

Take time to appreciate privately and publicly. Anniversary celebrations are a great place to start, but in reality, a more continuous show of appreciation needs to occur. We discussed this already, but it serves to reiterate that private and public words of affirmation are some of the most powerful ways of keeping negative emotions and damaging thoughts out of your partnership. Honest compliments and words of gratitude go a long way toward ensuring that your partner knows you're on their team and genuinely see them as a vital part of a whole.

Common Courtesy

Intentional compliments are great, but at a minimum (and believe me, I've seen that this is missing in a good portion of the teams I've spoken with), common courtesy and politeness are required. It's funny that we as humans can often be guilty of treating our loved ones worse than strangers. So it isn't a surprise that our cofounders can be recipients of contempt or even downright rudeness.

At a bare minimum:

- Greet each other with a smile and eye contact.
- Speak to one another in a respectful tone.
- Put your phone down and talk.
- Don't mock or make jokes about them.
- Offer to grab them something when you are getting something: "I'm getting a coffee; you want one?"

Laughter

Did you know that laughter bonds you? And it can pave the way for more bonding. People have also attributed healing from serious diseases and overcoming phobias to laughter. If your partnership is getting stale or starting to head down a path you feel could become damaging, inject a little laughter into your life, and watch it brighten up and improve. Share a meme or joke every morning, and be sure to let one another know when something funny happens or when a funny memory pops up. Laughter can ease the bumps in the road; use it generously.

Documentation

Carol and Melissa cofounded one business together, then sold it. They recognized in their second business that they needed to have better documentation of all the experiences they shared. So they started a journal that wasn't filled with the meetings they had or what they did that day but instead, the real-life lessons they learned as they built their business: musings about leadership, human relations, business, government, gender issues, money, entrepreneurship, and whatever else had an impact on them. It became a record of the experiences of two entrepreneurs as they went through the ups and downs of business ownership. And it provided a powerful way to gain perspective into their partner's life and built a connection in a way that was unique and simple.

Some couples keep a marriage journal. Do the same for your cofounder journey. Then, in a few years, look back and read the memories. This is a great way to inject laughter into the relationship; you can both say, "What were we thinking back then?"

Retreats

Business retreats can be an excellent way to grow together and connect in ways that would otherwise be difficult among your everyday distractions. Whether it's a leadership or self-growth retreat (the Cofounders Hub will be offering partnership-building retreats, by the way), being able to push yourselves to another level as a team is a brilliant way to stay connected. By doing weekends away, you can also share the responsibility for growth and ensure that one person doesn't progress while the other stagnates, which can cause resentment and frustration. Take time together to focus on your partnership and your roles as leaders within your company.

United

It's always us against them—with employees, investors, and customers.

The cofounder partnership is unique. There is not one other role that can be created in your company that will have the same type of makeup as being business partners. There is a deep level of intimacy, openness, transparency, vulnerability, and trust that happens when two or more people join together to lead a company. No matter what happens, there is a bond that is created, an impression made, that can never be replaced. Cofounders will always be the parts of a whole, and other people will be the accessories.

By seeing your partnership as the special and unique relationship that it is, you will be better able to hold it at a higher level of regard. By becoming and staying each other's comrades in battle, you create a foundation of courage and strength that will allow you to meet any challenge confidently. Partnerships that are running on all cylinders have an air of indestructibility, as each partner knows someone has their back, and they can go to them when they need a hand. Bask in this. Rest in it. This is what makes you invincible to the intrusions that would affect you were you a solo fighter. If you win, you win as a team, and if you fail, well, at least you fail together.

Learn from Stephen

When asked to share his overarching outlook on the cofounder partnership, Stephen says, "The experience is hard to describe. Until you do it, you don't realize how unique it is. What binds you and your cofounder is the journey of taking an idea and turning it into something tangible, and that experience you have together can never be replicated. It's like a fingerprint."

Having found success multiple times, Stephen adds a unique perspective. "One thing that fascinates me is that if you think about all the successful founders, to each other, no matter how big their companies have become, they are just the person they have worked a workload with over the years. If you watch how they interact, the successful ones have established a communication protocol that allows them to be honest with one another and never buy into the illusions of who they are dealing with. The world starts treating you differently when you reach a certain level of success and can presume you have all the answers. It's really refreshing to have cofounders that can call you out on your mistakes and failings.

It's actually very grounding and valuable. Because no matter how successful you become as founders, you crave that authentic relationship of people who actually know you and how you got where you are. There is comfort in that."

His final advice: "Whether the venture is successful or not, recognize from the outset the cofounder partnership and the experience you undertake together will become one you cherish as you look back on your life. Try your very, very best to protect it and make it a relationship to be proud of."

Which is exactly what this book is all about.

Acknowledgments

What a journey! Years in the making, but worth every minute of it when I see the final product. *The Cofounder's Handbook* is exactly what I hoped to achieve when I typed the first word on my laptop many moons ago. There are so many people who helped make this book possible. I will list a few here but know there are so many more who contributed in their own way. Thank you all for everything.

To my husband, Dave, and my boys, JJ and Nuno, who had to hear me talk about "my book" for years. Thank you for giving me the space to write it and for all your prodding and words of encouragement.

To my sister, Angela, who in many ways has been my "partner" since the day I was born. Thank you for journeying beside me down all my many roads and being my cheerleader, mentor, and guide through it all. I appreciate all that you have done for me, and I thank God that you are my sister.

To my parents, Ed and Eunice, for raising me to love entrepreneurship. For modeling what it means to set out and reach for your goals. For always encouraging me, reminding me that I can achieve anything I set my mind to.

To those who supported us in all our businesses: those who worked with us, invested in us, and partnered with us. Your willingness to support our dreams and goals means so much, and I am grateful for the trust and belief you put into our abilities.

To those I interviewed for the book. Thank you for sharing your story and trusting me with your unique partnership experience. Your willingness to be authentic, vulnerable, and transparent will go on to help countless entrepreneurs learn and grow from what you have achieved.

To Joshua Lisec, thank you for helping me get past the final hurdle writing this book. Your gift in articulating and putting on paper the thoughts and ideas of an author is truly an art form. Your optimism about the topic and excitement for assisting me in completing the book was the boost of positivity that helped bring this journey to completion. I hope we get to work together again in the future.

Finally, to you, the reader. I truly believe that entrepreneurship is the foundation of a strong economy and the ultimate method for helping people achieve their life goals. I believe that when people are able to take their destiny into their hands, the whole nation wins. I don't know what brought you to pick up this book, but I think it's because you are a dreamer, and you have a vision of achieving big things. Thank you for taking the risks and doing the work to bring innovation, new ideas, and new ways of doing things to the marketplace. I see you, I appreciate you, and I pray that this book will give you the knowledge you will need to find the right cofounder, build a partnership that will last, and succeed in whatever you put your hand to.

About the Author

Tanis Jorge is a serial tech entrepreneur and a leading adviser to start-up founders on entrepreneurship and building successful cofounder partnerships. Over the course of her career in start-ups, spanning the last twenty-plus years, Tanis has cofounded, scaled, and successfully exited multiple data-driven businesses. She is founder and CEO of The Cofounder's Hub, an online platform created to provide ongoing support, tools, and resources to cofounders looking to strengthen their partnerships.

Tanis cofounded her first start-up, iQuiri, in 1999. The company was one of the first to make consumer credit reports available online and was acquired by Experian in 2003. In 2004, she cofounded NCB Data Services, which was again acquired by Experian in 2006. In 2005, Tanis cofounded the identity management firm Pharos Global Strategies, which was also acquired four years later.

Her successes culminated with her most recent venture, Trulioo, which she cofounded in 2011 with her long-term business partner, Stephen Ufford. Between 2011 and 2015, Tanis served as chief operations officer of Trulioo, working to lay the groundwork and build the foundation for the trusted, innovative, and disruptive company it has become today. In 2021, Trulioo reached unicorn status (US$1.65 billion valuation), solidifying its place as the world's leading identity verification company and Jorge's track record for founding successful businesses. Following a record-breaking Series D, she stepped down from the board of Trulioo to focus on her cofounder advisory work.

Today, Tanis is one of the go-to voices and experts on the cofounder relationship, drawing on her experience cofounding multiple technology businesses. As an adviser for fast-growing start-ups and leading venture capitalists, she focuses on how cofounders can function in an open, productive, and symbiotic way to ensure continued and long-term business success.

Tanis also sits on the board of directors of Ally Global, a nonprofit that works to prevent human trafficking and supports survivors through safe homes, education, and work opportunities.

Tanis lives in Vancouver, BC, with her husband and two boys. When she isn't working she enjoys the "foodie" lifestyle with her husband David Jorge, *MasterChef Canada* winner. She loves water sports and is currently working toward turning her brown belt in kickboxing into black, a lifelong item on her bucket list. Tanis also takes time to mentor students at the private school she founded, Live Learn Launch Academy, which focuses on entrepreneurship, financial literacy, and life skills.